21世纪英语专业系列教材

Intelligent Reading of
CULTURE

文化智慧阅读

主　编 / 刘　琛
副主编 / 刘晓莉
编　者 / 苏　曼　高全孝　罗　雷　韩立钊

北京大学出版社
PEKING UNIVERSITY PRESS

图书在版编目（CIP）数据

文化智慧阅读 / 刘琛主编. — 北京：北京大学出版社，2022.10
21世纪英语专业系列教材
ISBN 978-7-301-31353-4

Ⅰ.①文⋯ Ⅱ.①刘⋯ Ⅲ.①英语－阅读教学－高等学校－教材
Ⅳ.①H319.37

中国版本图书馆CIP数据核字（2020）第103960号

书　　　名	文化智慧阅读 WENHUA ZHIHUI YUEDU
著作责任者	刘　琛　主编
责 任 编 辑	刘文静
标 准 书 号	ISBN 978-7-301-31353-4
出 版 发 行	北京大学出版社
地　　　址	北京市海淀区成府路205号　100871
网　　　址	http://www.pup.cn　新浪微博: @ 北京大学出版社
电 子 信 箱	liuwenjing008@163.com
电　　　话	邮购部010-62752015　发行部010-62750672 编辑部010-62754382
印　刷　者	河北滦县鑫华书刊印刷厂
经　销　者	新华书店
	880毫米×1230毫米　16开本　16.5印张　406千字 2022年10月第1版　2022年10月第1次印刷
定　　　价	68.00元

未经许可，不得以任何方式复制或抄袭本书之部分或全部内容。
版权所有，侵权必究
举报电话: 010-62752024　电子信箱: fd@pup.pku.edu.cn
图书如有印装质量问题，请与出版部联系，电话: 010-62756370

致谢 / I

Acknowledgements / II

前言《文化智慧阅读》：追索百年未有之大变局中的灵感 / III

Preface *Intelligent Reading of Culture*: An Inspiration to This Critical Time / VIII

Contents

1 **Globalization** / 1

2 **Career** / 39

3 **Love** / 75

4 **Lifestyle** / 107

5 **Mindset** / 135

6 **Cultivation** / 161

7 **Happiness** / 203

致 谢

本书得以完成要感谢国内外专家的大力支持。感谢英国伦敦政治经济学院前院长、社会学家安东尼·吉登斯教授（Anthony Giddens），感谢美国哈佛大学理查德·库珀教授（Richard Cooper），他们为本书贡献了自己的文章并悉心指导。感谢美国哈佛大学约瑟夫·奈教授（Joseph Nye）、安东尼·赛驰教授（Anthony Saich）、荷兰莱顿大学新丝路研究院负责人理查德·格里菲斯教授（Richard Griffiths）。

在此，要特别感谢经济合作与发展组织前总干事唐纳德·约翰逊爵士（Honorable Donald Johnston），他以宽广的国际视野和面向未来的国际发展观为本书提供了重要的指引。

感谢我的团队，本书副主编哈尔滨工业大学（威海）刘晓莉博士，四位编委——中国地质大学教师、北京外国语大学苏曼博士，西藏民族大学高全孝教授，中国地质大学罗雷副教授和西藏民族大学韩立钊副教授。

感谢北京大学出版社夏红卫书记、马建钧社长的支持，感谢刘文静编辑的辛苦付出。

感谢哈佛大学拉蒙特图书馆（Lamont Library）陪伴我完成本书，难忘在图书馆的日日夜夜。

本书献给我的父母、若琳和我的导师们。

刘 琛

2022 年 5 月于北京

Acknowledgements

Thanks to all the academics in and out China for their suggestions that we should write this book and for their beliefs that it might prove useful to students and teachers of reading class. I should like to thank the former president of the London School of Economics and Political Science (LSE), world-famous sociologist, Anthony Giddens, Harvard professor, talented economist, former provost of Yale, Richard Cooper for their heartfelt encouragement. I am very grateful to Harvard professor, founder of soft power theory, Joseph Nye, and renowned expert on China studies, director of Harvard Kennedy School of ASH Center, Professor Anthony Saich, economic historian Professor Richard Griffiths who now directs the New Silk Roads research project at the International Institute for Asian Studies, Leiden University. The book would have been impossible without their support.

I should like to thank in particular, the former Secretary-General of the Organization for Economic Co-operation and Development (OECD), the first non-European to head the OECD, Honorable Donald Johnston. His global outlook, especially his confidence of globalization that is truly for everyone, is always a great inspiration to this book.

I take pride in my team: the deputy editor-in-chief, Dr. Liu Xiaoli, and the four editors, Dr. Su Man, Professor Gao Quanxiao, Professor Luo Lei, and Professor Han Lizhao.

The editorial and production staff at Peking University Press deserve a vote of thanks for their support in bring this book to fruition. My very special thanks to Professor Xia Hongwei and Professor Ma Jianjun, and the editor of the book, Professor Liu Wenjing.

As always, I should like to thank Harvard Lamont Library who witnessed the completion of the book from the ground up. Miss the marvelous days and nights at Lamont.

Finally, For my parents, Ruolin and my supervisors!

Liu Chen

前言

《文化智慧阅读》：追索百年未有之大变局中的灵感

1970年，前美国国家安全顾问布热津斯基（Zbigniew Brzezinski）在他的著作《两个时代之间：美国在电子技术时代的角色》(*Between Two Ages: America's Role in the Technetronic Era*)中，首次使用了"全球化"（globalization）一词[1]。1992年10月24日，当时的联合国秘书长加利（Boutros Boutros-Ghali）在联合国日（United Nations Day）致辞中宣布，"真正的全球化的时代已经到来"[2]。

进入21世纪，迅速推进的全球化为世界经济增长提供了强劲动力，促进了国际交流与合作，带动了科技和文明的进步。与此同时，全球化进程中存在的不足也带来了一系列极其复杂的问题。如何在全球化达到更高水平的新历史阶段，妥善处理国际冲突与合作是国际社会共同面临的挑战。

2020年伊始，新型冠状病毒肺炎（COVID-19）引发全球关注。在共同抗击疫情的过程中，国际社会应当更加充分地意识到在全球化时代，当世界是平的，国际社会面临的不确定性更为复杂，也更为严峻。这些问题覆盖了从公共卫生到恐怖主义，到网络安全，到气候变化等人类社会可持续发展的几乎所有主要议题。在当前全球化处于曲折发展阶段，中国提出了人类命运共同体理念，倡导全球共担责任，共创未来。那么，在构建这一共同体的过程中，我们需要问作为教育工作者，我们能够做些什么？千头万绪的工作中，关键环节在哪里？

回答这一问题，美国著名人类学家鲁思·本尼迪克特（Ruth Benedict）的经典社会学研究可以给予我们灵感。在她的著名的《菊与刀：日本文化诸模式》(*The Chrysanthemum and the Sword: Patterns of Japanese Culture*)一书中，她对20世纪做出了总结，认为"20世纪面临的一个重大问题是我们对（文化）仍怀有最模糊，却也是最有偏见的解读，所以我们不理解日本何以为日本民族，美国何以为美利坚，法国何以为法兰西，俄国何以为俄罗斯。由于缺乏这方面的必要知识，国家间的误

---

[1] Zbigniew Brzezinski, *Between Two Ages: America's Role in the Technetronic Era*, New York: Viking Press, 1970.
[2] Boutros Boutros-Ghali, Maintaining International Peace and Security: The United Nations as Forum and Focal Point, https://digitalcommons.lmu.edu/cgi/viewcontent.cgi?referer=https://www.google.com.hk/&httpsredir=1&article=1313&context=ilr accessed November 1, 2021.

读难以避免"[1]。

通过历史回顾,鲁思·本尼迪克特阐释了文化在国际冲突与合作中的作用。那么,我们如何才能尽可能地避免源于文化,又以文化为载体而产生的偏见、误解以及刻板印象呢?

是智慧地阅读文化的意愿与责任感。文化阅读与文化智慧阅读的关键区别可以从2020年英国广播公司(British Broadcasting Corporation,BBC)播出的中国元素的纪录片《杜甫:中国最伟大的诗人》(*Du Fu: China's Greatest Poet*)中汲取灵感。

英国广播公司的《杜甫:中国最伟大的诗人》启发了中国学者重新思考文化智慧阅读对于理解他者的重要意义。

对此的讨论从反思为什么是杜甫被比作莎士比亚开始。在中国,通常会将明代著名戏剧家汤显祖比为中国的莎士比亚。主要原因有三个。第一,汤显祖与莎士比亚都对本国戏剧的复兴做出了突出贡献。在汤显祖的时代,经济相对繁荣,推动戏剧蓬勃发展。中国出现了类似16世纪上演莎剧的环球剧院的专门场所。第二,两位剧作家都留下了永恒的经典。莎士比亚有四大悲剧,即《哈姆雷特》(*Hamlet*)、《李尔王》(*King Lear*)、《奥赛罗》(*Othello*)和《麦克白》(*Macbeth*)。相应成章,汤显祖有"四梦",即《紫钗记》(*The Purple Hairpin*)、《南柯记》(*A Dream Under a Southern Bough*)、《邯郸记》(*Dream of Handan*)和他最著名的《牡丹亭》(*The Peony Pavilion*)。这些创作在两位剧作家的祖国都被视为本国戏剧的代表性成就。第三,汤显祖与莎士比亚都是语言大师。莎翁的戏剧犹如语言艺术的长河,并形成了鲜明的个人风格。汤显祖的作品也是巨制,充满想象。综上所述,两位戏剧家在中国经常被相互比较,更不必说两人都于1616年去世。

但是,英国广播公司的《杜甫:中国最伟大的诗人》启发中国学者从更为完整的视角去重新思考杜甫的经历、创作和时代及其作品对中国文化的影响。在这个过程中,文化阅读在走向文化智慧阅读。从这个角度看,英国剧作家本·琼生(Ben Johnson)对于莎剧的伟大性的著名总结可以带来灵感,即"他不只属于一个世纪,而是所有的时代"(He was not of an age, but for all time)[2]。是什么原因让莎士比亚自信自己的作品能够与"时光共存不老"(So long as men can breathe, or eyes can see, So long lives this, and this gives life to thee)?是真善美的力量。正如但丁在《神曲》(*The Divine Comedy*)

---

[1] Ruth Benedict, *The Chrysanthemum and the Sword: Patterns of Japanese Culture*, London: Secker & Warburg, 1947, p.13.

[2] Ben Johnson, To the Memory of My Beloved, the Author Mr. William Shakespeare, https://www.poetryfoundation.org/poems/44466/to-the-memory-of-my-beloved-the-author-mr-william-shakespeare, accessed November1, 2021.

前言

中所说,"想想你的出身,人不是为野蛮而生,而是为了美德与知识"(Consider your origin. You were not formed to live like brutes but to follow virtue and knowledge)[1]。

杜甫创作的伟大之处在于他一生都对国家和民众怀有深厚情感。这与擅长歌颂美好爱情的汤显祖多少有所不同。位卑未敢忘忧国的情怀是理解杜甫诗歌的关键之一。没有深刻的情感,难以写出"国破山河在,城春草木深"的传世佳句。

同样的,杜甫并不认为面对艰难只有忍受。相反的,他的创作给予苍生以勇气、力量与希望。所以他才能在困顿中写下,"安得广厦千万间,大庇天下寒士俱欢颜"的名句。

与杜甫一生坎坷有所不同,莎士比亚的时代是英国的高光时刻。因此,莎翁以激情诠释了与杜甫一样的爱与希望的情怀。例如:在《哈姆雷特》中,他写到"人是多么伟大的杰作,在行动上像天使,在智慧上像神"(What a piece of work is man. In action, how like an angel. In apprehension, how like a god.)[2]。

以上述的习惯与能力去阅读,我们或许能够理解正是在生活的艰难中看到希望,鼓励天下苍生在苦难中不是只有忍受,也可以战胜——是这种共通的力量让英国人将杜甫比作莎士比亚。这或许也是哈佛大学史蒂夫·欧文(Stephen Owen)教授将杜甫比作莎士比亚和但丁的原因,因为"这些诗人确立了诗歌创作的价值观,正是基于此,诗歌才得以评判"(poets who create values by which poetry is judged)[3]。

以上这种基于文化,依靠文化,服务文化的阅读就是文化智慧阅读。智慧地阅读英国广播公司的《杜甫:中国最伟大的诗人》所传递的文化思考是启发中国学者实现有质量的跨文化对话与交流的灵感所在。从这个意义上说,文化智慧阅读能够搭建世界交流与合作的桥梁。

当今我们所处的时代期待伟大的问题和伟大的答案。正是这种意识促使我带领团队,编写了本书《文化智慧阅读》,希望能够为向世界讲好中国故事贡献智慧和力量。

根据对中国和全球12个国家的调研,最终确定了当代青年职业规划中最关注的七大问题,即"全球化"(Globalization)、"事业"(Career)、"爱"(Love)、"生活方式"(Lifestyle)、"心态"(Mindset)、"提升"(Cultivation)和"幸福"(Happiness)。

紧密围绕这七个主题的内在逻辑,本书设计了四个部分。第一部分包括第一章"全球化",目的是介绍我们所处时代的背景。第二部分包括第二至五章,即"职

---

[1] Dante Alighieri, *The Divine Comedy*, New York: Thomas Y. Crowell & Co. Publishers, 1987, p.279.
[2] William Shakespeare, *Hamlet*, 2.2.303.
[3] Ian McKellen, Was Du Fu the Chinese Dante? BBC4 traces his footsteps, *Financial Times*, April 3, 2020, https://www.ft.com/content/534d6096-7291-11ea-ad98-044200cb277f accessed June.1, 2020.

业""爱""生活方式"和"心态"。目的是从不同角度比较各种解读方式,进而比较它们对生活态度的影响。在第二部分的讨论的基础上,第三部分是第六章"提升",旨在为读者分析和解决这些问题,提供建议和帮助。第四部分是第七章"幸福",意在与读者共同思考何为真正有意义的幸福人生。每个部分相辅相成,共同构成对文化智慧阅读关键点的阐释与训练(见图1)。

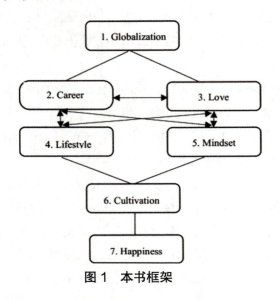

图1 本书框架

本书的主要目的是帮助读者了解和掌握文化智慧阅读的重要观点与技能。通过七个选题,能够锻炼如何智慧地解读所传递的文化信息。为完成这一培养目标,本书在每章设计了八个部分——"本章导读""独立阅读""即时提问"(While-reading questions)"背景知识""文化注释""语言技能练习""思辨问题"和"本章小结任务"。

为了突出多元化的特点,智慧阅读培养主要围绕两个重点。一是文体多元化。选篇来自政府工作报告、演讲、报纸、期刊、文学名著、诗歌、研究报告等,帮助学生了解不同文体的特点,掌握相应方法,培养学生跨体裁阅读、提炼观点的能力。二是国别多元化。选篇既来自美英等主要英语国家,也选取了中国、印度等东方国家,并且有针对性地补充了加拿大、澳大利亚、法国、芬兰等国家的英语文献,帮助学生从更为广阔的全球视野观察和分析社会文化问题。

综上所述,这本书是针对当前所处的百年未有之大变局,对如何智慧地阅读文化做出的首次尝试。诚然,仅凭智慧阅读的习惯与能力并不能实现有效阅读,但没有智慧的阅读是一定不会有效果的。

按照英国路透社的结论,我们正在应对自第二次世界大战以来最大的危机。在危机中，更加需要真善美的文化力量带给人们以希望。正如著名国际关系学者、哈佛大学教授约瑟夫·奈在其 2019 年的最新著作《道德有力量吗？：美国总统的外交政策从罗斯福到特朗普》(*Do Morals Matter?: Presidents and Foreign Policy from FDR to Trump*)中所总结的，有伦理的公共政策才是有力量的[1]。

"全球化改变了世界的样貌，也改变了我们看待世界的方式。透过一个全球化的视角，我们更加意识到我们的问题会影响到世界，而世界的问题会影响到我们"——这是英国著名社会学家安东尼·吉登斯（Anthony Giddens）在其《社会学》（第三版）(*Sociology*（3rd Edition））中对全球化带给人的影响的表述[2]。从这个意义上说，我们今天所处的时代是一个相互依赖的时代，这也是未来的大趋势。如何从各美其美迈上美美与共的历史性高度，让我们从文化智慧阅读起步。

刘琛

2021 年 5 月于北京

---

[1] Joseph Nye, *Do Morals Matter?: Presidents and Foreign Policy from FDR to Trump*, London: Oxford University Press, 2019.
[2] Anthony Giddens, *Sociology* (6th Edition), London: Polity Press, 2009, p.56.

Preface

Intelligent Reading of Culture: An Inspiration to This Critical Time

Globalization, the term which now is well-known on every continent was coined by Mr. Zbigniew Brzezinski, the former U.S. national security adviser. He created the term in his *Between Two Ages: America's Role in the Technetronic Era*[1], which was published in 1970 to refer to a new era that the world was proceeding. On the United Nations Day of 1992, Mr. Boutros Boutros-Ghali, then the secretary general of the United Nations addressed, "We now are in an age of Globalization"[2].

At the start of the twenty-first century, with the rapid growth of a deepening global society, we can sense a series of new challenges and opportunities as diverse as economy, politics, health, education, technology, and arts and the humanities. Accordingly, the imperatives of international conflicts and cooperation have increasingly been home to global concerns.

Coronavirus outbreak (COVID-19), the global health crisis verifies over again, although in a different context, the matter of fact that as borders become porous to everything from infectious diseases to terrorism to cyber criminals, to climate change, the uncertainty, more urgent and more complicated, confronting the whole world has reached new serious and difficult milestone. Then, we have to ask what we can do to step up to the challenges at the critical time?

In answer to this question, Ruth Benedict, one of the most compelling intellectual figures in the twentieth-century American life was an inspiration. She wrote in her famous *The Chrysanthemum and the Sword*, "One of the handicaps of the twentieth century is that we still have the vaguest and most biased notions, not only of what makes Japan a nation of Japanese, but of what makes the U.S. a nation of Americans,

---

1 Zbigniew Brzezinski, *Between Two Ages: America's Role in the Technetronic Era*, New York: Viking Pres, 1970.
2 Boutros Boutros-Ghali, Maintaining International Peace and Security: The United Nations as Forum and Focal Point, https://digitalcommons.lmu.edu/cgi/viewcontent.cgi?referer=https://www.google.com.hk/&https redir=1&article=1313&context=ilr accessed November1, 2021.

Preface

France a nation of Frenchmen, and Russia a nation of Russians. Lacking this knowledge, each country misunderstands the other"[1].

Looking closely back at history, Ruth Benedict identified the role of understanding of culture in international conflicts and cooperation. Then, what can we do to avoid as much as possible bias, misunderstanding, and stereotype rooted in culture and presented through culture?

It is willingness and commitment to intelligent reading of culture that holds the key. What distinguishes intelligent reading of culture from reading of culture? "Du Fu: China's Greatest Poet", a documentary aired on BBC in the April of 2020 is a useful example.

BBC's "Du Fu: China's Greatest Poet" inspired the Chinese scholars to rethink why intelligent reading of culture is significant to understanding the otherness.

Question to the Chinese scholars started in the reflection upon why it is Du Fu (712-770 AD) who was compared by the West to Shakespeare? For them, Tang Xianzu (1550-1616), China's greatest dramatist in Ming Dynasty should have got involved. China's comparative analyses normally emphasize three major points: First, they both played a leading role in their own country's Renaissance, a revolution either in terms of social development or in light of theater reform. In Tang Xianzu's time, the court of Ming Dynasty had conducted a series of new policies in favour of liberalism, and managed to put them together to great acclaim. Thriving on the economic growth, and humanistic revival, the popular operas like Shakespeare's works in the Globe Theatre in the 16th century appeared in China. Tang Xianzu took a lead in the movement; Second, both of them reached the pinnacle of drama, and contributed enduring global legacy. With regard to their masterpieces, Shakespeare is well-known for his four greatest tragedies, *Hamlet*, *King Lear*, *Othello*, and *Macbeth*. Coincidently, Tang's Four Dreams, *Zi Chaiji* (*The Purple Hairpin*), *Nan Keji* (*A Dream under a Southern Bough*), *Handan Meng* (*Dream of Handan*), and his most famous *Mu Danting* (*The Peony Pavilion*) are widely considered one of the highest points of traditional Chinese opera; And third, the two are master of rhetoric. Shakespeare's work is like a long, big river of words perfectly in tune with his style. Tang's *Mu Danting* would feature a large cast and many scenes

---

1 Ruth Benedict, *The Chrysanthemum and the Sword: Patterns of Japanese Culture*, London: Secker & Warburg, 1947, p.13.

playing over several days in his time. Thus, there is no going around it: Tang Xianzu is China's Shakespeare not to mention that the two great dramatists departed in the same year of 1616.

Yet, BBC's "Du Fu: China's Greatest Poet" inspired the Chinese scholars to rethink Du Fu's life, works and times, and explore his profound influence on the Chinese culture from a more complete perspective. In doing so, Ben Johnson's famous statement on the greatness of Shakespeare that "He was not of an age, but for all time"[1] is inspiring. What the greatness will be eternal that "So long as men can breathe, or eyes can see, So long lives this, and this gives life to thee" (Shakespeare, Sonnet 18)? Only the true, the good, and the beautiful in sheer purity and merciful serenity. As Dante wrote in his *The Divine Comedy* that "Consider your origin. You were not formed to live like brutes but to follow virtue and knowledge"[2].

The spirit of the true, the good, and the beautiful in Du Fu's works rests upon his lifelong love of his Tang Dynasty, and his common people, which differs dramatically from that of Tang Xianzu whose works are focused primarily on love between young men and women. Like most of his contemporaries, Confucianism was essential to Du Fu's values. Many priorities—focusing on your role assigned when Tang Dynasty is in prosperity, while asking what you can do when Tang Dynasty is in adversity, —were important to his poetry. "Spring Scene", for instance, described Du Fu's pain in face of the collapse of his beloved Tang Dynasty. Without pure and vehement love, it was not possible for any writer to write such stanzas which gave people hope when fears were rising, "In fallen states, hills and streams are still there. The city is in Spring, grass and leaves abound".

Just as importantly, Du Fu refused to accept that man in hardships or sufferings merely had to endure. Instead, his poems worked as the pillars to uplift people from fear and despair. Actually, Du Fu lived in the shadow of poverty, setbacks and turmoil throughout his life. However, the agony and sweat did nothing but to remind him of the power of courage, compassion, and hope. When his small thatched cottage was destroyed by storm, he wrote his most recognized stanzas, "Could I get mansions

---

[1] Ben Johnson, To the Memory of My Beloved, the Author Mr. William Shakespeare, https://www.poetryfoundation.org/poems/44466/to-the-memory-of-my-beloved-the-author-mr-william-shakespeare accessed November1, 2021.
[2] Dante Alighieri, *The Divine Comedy*, New York: Thomas Y. Crowell & Co. Publishers, 1987, p.279.

covering ten thousand miles, I'd house all people poor and make them beam with smiles. Alas! Should these houses appear before my eye, Frozen in my unroofed cot, content I'd die".

Unlike Du Fu, Shakespeare's time was a time of glory of the Great Britain. Thus, Shakespeare's works were full of enthusiasm in spite of the same pity, sacrifice and love as that of Du Fu. In his globally well-known *Hamlet*, Shakespeare wrote, "What a piece of work is man. In action, how like an angel. In apprehension, how like a god"[1].

In reading so, we might understand that a life's work in the agony and sweat of the spirit of the true, the good, and the beautiful; a life's confidence in writing to help people endure and prevail—that somehow identifies why Du Fu is compared to Shakespeare, and why Professor Stephen Owen of Harvard included Du Fu in the very select company of Shakespeare, and Dante as "poets who create values by which poetry is judged"[2].

The reading of culture, by culture, and for culture and more, it's intelligent reading of culture. Through intelligent reading of culture, BBC's "Du Fu" became an inspiration to the Chinese scholars in pursuit of fruitful intercultural communication with the world. In answer to the question that why we compare Tang Xianzu to China's Shakespeare, while it is Du Fu who is seen more comparable in Shakespeare's home, it helps we Chinese to think from a more complete perspective. In this sense, we need more works like "Du Fu: China's Greatest Poet" to bridge the large divides the world faces.

The awareness of the significance of intelligent reading of culture to this world in pursuit of great questions, and great answers, I lead this team and contribute the textbook to reading-compacity building, in particular, for the youth in China and the world.

According to the surveys we conducted in China, and twelve other countries around the world, seven topics that represent the most important concerns on the youth career planning agenda are selected, namely "Globalization" "Career" "Love" "Lifestyle" "Mindset" "Cultivation" and "Happiness".

In light of the plan of the textbook, the first part of the textbook, Chapter 1

---

1 William Shakespeare, *Hamlet*, 2.2.303.
2 Ian McKellen, Was Du Fu the Chinese Dante? BBC4 traces his footsteps. *Financial Times*, April 3, 2020, https://www.ft.com/content/534d6096-7291-11ea-ad98-044200cb277f accessed June 1, 2021.

"Globalization" illustrates the context of the world in which we are living. Chapters 2-5, "Career" "Love" "Lifestyle" "Mindset" open the second part of the textbook by examining how the patterns in life and existence vary and the impacts on attitude to the most important issues of general concern. Based on the discussion of Part II, Chapter 6 in Part III, "Cultivation" makes suggestions for readers to deal better with the problems. Part IV, Chapter 7 "Happiness" provides every reader an opportunity to discuss what is really meaningful to life (see Figure 1).

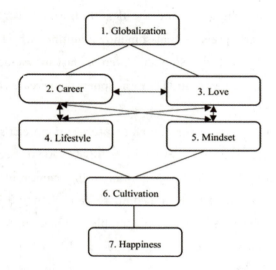

Figure 1　The Plan of the Textbook

The primary goal of the textbook is to prepare students to learn the most important ideas and analytical tools in reading of culture, and be able to intelligently read publications exploring the seven topics through an intelligent interpretation of culture. To that end, eight major parts are designed.

Part 1, "Introduction": illustrates the topic of the chapter, introduces the aim of the readings in the chapter, and identifies the underlying logic that connects the readings selected. Readers may better understand the goal of this chapter, and how better use the reading materials.

Part 2, "Reading": provides readers opportunities to be open to different viewpoints, and different experiences on the seven topics. The readings selected are based on two

Preface

major determinants. First, diversity of forms as diverse as classic literature, poetry, newspaper articles, speeches, book chapters, and journal papers, and research reports and so on. Second, diversity of regions encompassing countries in the East, and the West.

Part 3, "While-reading questions": is focused on exercising the abilities to read intelligently. Readers are asked to discuss the questions throughout their reading. The questions are designed to help readers to diagnose the "bad habits" which lead to reading culture "badly", and help them to overcome them.

Part 4, "Background Information": provides the information useful for the readers who are not familiar with the writers, publishers, organizations, and events, and so on.

Part 5, "Notes": provides supports necessary for the readers.

Part 6, "Exercise": goes further to examine whether readers grasp the knowledge delivered in the chapter.

Part 7, "Questions for Further Thought": encourage readers to think from a more complete perspective, and to embrace the culture of curiosity that the textbook wishes to create.

Part 8, "Mini-task": provides teamwork-centric exercises so as to foster reader's greater confidence and conviction in working as a team.

In all, the textbook is a first-ever attempt to explore how we can read culture intelligently at the critical time to-date. Intelligent reading is not the only thing that matter in reading effectively, but no reading can survive without it.

Our world is battling the "biggest crisis" since World War Two in line with Reuters' report. In fears, the belief in the true, the good, and the beautiful holds the key. As a piece of evidence, Joseph Nye, Harvard professor, a world's leading scholar of international relations, in his most recent book, *Do Morals Matter?: Presidents and Foreign Policy from FDR to Trump*[1] scores the role of ethics through a penetrating historical analysis of the US foreign policy.

"Globalization is changing the way the world looks, and the way we look at the world. By adopting a global outlook, we become more aware of our connections to people in other societies. We also become more conscious of that many problems the world faces

---

1 Joseph Nye, *Do Morals Matter?: Presidents and Foreign Policy from FDR to Trump*, London: Oxford University Press, 2019.

at the start of the twenty-first century" stated by Anthony Giddens, an eminent British sociologist in his *Sociology* (3rd Edition) [1]. To build upon a house of difference in the age of interdependence, let's begin with exercising intelligent reading of culture.

Liu Chen
Beijing Foreign Studies University
Harvard Mason Fellow

---

[1] Anthony Giddens, *Sociology* (6th Edition), London: Polity Press, 2009, p.56.

1 Globalization

Passage 1 The Impact of Globalization on Our Lives / 4
Passage 2 The Rise of Asia's Universities / 12
Passage 3 Female Political Leaders / 20
Passage 4 Mutual Understanding Between China and the World / 24

[本章导读]

1992年，时任联合国秘书长（United Nations Secretary-General）加利（Boutros-Ghali）在联合国日致词中指出，"第一个真正的全球化时代已经到来"。时至近日，全球化进程极大地改变了世界的面貌，让国家与地区间的联系变得更为密切。在2015年"亚非领导人会议"上，习近平主席发表了《弘扬万隆精神推进合作共赢》（"Carry Forward the Bandung Spirit for Win-win Cooperation"）的讲话，其中指出，"和平、发展、合作、共赢的时代潮流更加强劲，各国越来越成为你中有我、我中有你的命运共同体"。

毋庸置疑，全球化正在改变着人类的生存与交往方式，为青年学子提供了更为广阔的世界舞台。同时，全球化也赋予青年一代新的历史使命，对其能力、视野、心态等提出了更为全面的要求。那么，全球化时代的青年人该如何把握历史机遇，更好地锻炼自己，以迎接未来的挑战呢？本章的四篇文章将与大家共同探讨这一问题。第一篇选自英国著名社会学家安东尼·吉登斯教授（Anthony Giddens）的《社会学》（*Sociology*）第三版第三章，旨在帮助读者了解"全球化"的基本概念、突出特点以及"全球化"对于人们日常生活和工作的深远影响，以此为背景，本章探讨全球化背景下的教育意义。第二篇《亚洲大学的崛起》（"The Rise of Asia's Universities"）选自耶鲁大学（Yale University）校长理查德·雷文博士（Richard C. Levin）2010年2月1日在英国伦敦皇家学会（The Royal Society, London, England）的演讲。他以中国等亚洲国家为例，剖析了全球化态势下高等教育的新使命。那么，时代的变化以及由此带来的具有全球性意义的教育改革对个体的影响与进步意义如何体现？第三篇文章《女性政治领袖》（"Female Political Leaders"）的作者是著名经济学家、美国前经济事务副国务卿、耶鲁大学前副教务长、哈佛大学教授理查德·库珀（Richard Cooper）。该选篇视角独特，分析透彻，指出全球化时代每个人都拥有了更加广阔的舞台，问题在于你是否已经做好了准备。第四篇是习近平主席于2012年11月15日在中共中央新一届政治局常委与中外记者见面会上的讲话。让我们了解中国如何讲述、并理解全球化，如何才能"让中国更了解世界，让世界更了解中国"。

总之，通过本章学习，青年学子们可以了解我们所生活的时代有着怎样的规律，从而进一步思考，我们如何才能更为准确地把握时代脉搏，顺时代潮流而动。

[Passage 1]

The Impact of Globalization on Our Lives[1]

Although globalization is often associated with changes within "big" systems, such as the world financial markets, production and trade, and telecommunications, the effects of globalization are felt equally strongly in the private realm. <u>Globalization is not something that is simply "out there", operating on a distant plane and not intersecting with individual affairs. Globalization is an "in here" phenomenon that is affecting our intimate and personal lives in many diverse ways.</u> Inevitably, our personal lives have been altered as globalizing forces enter into our local contexts, our homes and our communities through impersonal sources—such as the media, the internet and popular culture—as well as through personal contact with individuals from other countries and cultures.

Globalization is fundamentally changing the nature of our everyday experiences. As the societies in which we live undergo profound transformations the established institutions which used to **underpin** them have **become out of place**. This is forcing a redefinition of intimate and personal aspects of our lives, such as the family, gender roles, sexuality, personal identity, our interactions with others and our relationships to work. <u>The way we think of ourselves and our connections with other people is being profoundly altered through globalization.</u>

The Rise of Individualism

In our current age, individuals have much more opportunity to shape their own lives than once was the case. At one time, tradition and custom exercised a very strong influence on the path of people's lives. Factors such as social class, gender, ethnicity and

---

1 Anthony Giddens, *Sociology* (3rd Edition), London: Polity Press, 1997, pp. 80–89.

Margin notes:
- Explain "out there" and "in here" with examples.
- Discuss how globalization changes our ways of communication.

even religious **affiliation** could close off certain avenues for individuals, or open up others. Being born the eldest son of a tailor, for example, would probably ensure that a young man would learn his father's craft and carry on practicing that craft throughout his lifetime. <u>Tradition held that a woman's natural sphere was in the home; her life and identity were largely defined by those of her husband or father.</u> In times past, individuals' personal identities were formed in the context of the community into which they were born. The values, lifestyles and ethics **prevailing** in that community provided relatively fixed guidelines according to which people lived their lives.

Under conditions of globalization, however, we are faced with a move towards a new individualism in which people have actively to constitute themselves and construct their own identities. The weight of tradition and established values is retreating as local communities interact with a new global order. The "<u>social codes</u>" which formerly guided people's choices and activities have significantly loosened. Today, for example, the eldest son of a tailor could choose any number of paths in constructing his future, women are no longer restricted to the domestic realm, and many of the other **signposts** which shaped people's lives have disappeared. Traditional frameworks of identity are dissolving and new patterns of identity are emerging. Globalization is forcing people to live in a more open, reflexive way. This means that we are constantly responding and adjusting to the changing environment around us; as individuals, we evolve with and within the larger context in which we live. Even the small choices we make in our daily lives—what we wear, how we spend our leisure time, how we take care of our health and our bodies—are part of an ongoing process of creating and recreating our self-identities.

Work Patterns

Work is at the center of many people's lives—both on a day-to-day basis, and in terms of larger life goals. Although we may regard work as a "chore" or a "necessary evil", it is undeniable that work is a crucial element in our personal lives. We spend great amounts of time "working" or "at work", and find that <u>many aspects of our existence—from our friends to our leisure pursuits—are shaped by our work patterns.</u>

Globalization has **unleashed** profound transformations within the world of work. New patterns of international trade and the move to a knowledge economy have had a significant impact on long-standing employment patterns. Many traditional industries have been made **obsolete** by new technological advances, or are losing their share of the market to competitors abroad whose labor costs are lower than in industrialized countries. Global trade and new forms of technology have had a strong effect on traditional manufacturing communities, where industrial workers have been left unemployed and without the types of skills needed to enter the new knowledge-based economy. The industrial Midlands of England and the coal communities of Wales, for example, are facing a new set of social problems, including long-term unemployment and rising crime rates, as a result of economic globalization.

If at one time people's working lives were dominated by employment with one employer over the course of several decades—the so-called "job for life" framework—today many more individuals create their own career paths, pursuing individual goals and exercising choice in attaining them. Often this involves changing jobs several times over the course of a career, **building up** new skills and abilities, and transferring them to diverse work contexts. Standard patterns of full-time work are being dissolved into more flexible arrangements: working from home with the help of information technology, job sharing, short-term consulting projects, "flexitime", and so forth (Beck 1992).

Women have entered the labor force in large numbers, a fact which has strongly affected the personal lives of people of both sexes. Expanded professional and educational opportunities have led many women to put off marriage and children until after they have begun a career. These changes have also meant that many working women return to work shortly after having children, instead of remaining at home with young children as was once the case. These shifts have required important adjustments within families, in the nature of the domestic division of labor, in the role of men in child-rearing, and with the emergence of more "family friendly" working policies to accommodate the needs of "dual earner couples".

I. Background Information

Anthony Giddens (born 18 January, 1938) is a British sociologist famous for his theory of structuration and his holistic view of modern societies. Considered one of the most prominent modern socialists, he not only outlined what sociology is, presenting a theoretical and methodological understanding of that field, but also developed the theory of structuration with works such as *Central Problems in Social Theory* (1979) and *The Constitution of Society* (1984) earning him international fame in the field of sociology. More recently, along with critique of post-modernity, he has focused more on modernity, globalization and politics, especially the impact of modernity on social and personal life.

This passage is an excerpt of Chapter 3 in Giddens' *Sociology* (3rd Edition) (2003), in which the profound influence of globalization upon people's lives are vividly analyzed from two aspects of individualism and work patterns. It also pointed out that such shifts require important adjustment outside and within families.

II. Notes

1. **Underpin:** *v.* support; make ...more firm
2. **Affiliation:** *n.* social or business relationship
3. **Prevailing:** *adj.* most frequent or common at present
4. **Signpost:** *n.* a post bearing a sign that gives directions or shows the way
5. **Unleash:** *vt.* release; *vi.* turn loose or free from restraint
6. **Obsolete:** *adj.* no longer in use or valid or fashionable
7. **Become out of place:** become inappropriate
8. **Build up:** enlarge / develop / or increase by degrees; form or accumulate steadily

III. Reading Comprehension

Read the book excerpt, and choose the best answer to each question.

Globalization and Risk[1]

The consequences of globalization are far-reaching, affecting virtually all aspects of the social world. Yet because globalization is an open-ended and internally contradictory process, it produces outcomes that are difficult to predict and control. Another way of thinking of this dynamic is in terms of risk. Many of the changes wrought by globalization are presenting us with new forms of risk which differ greatly from those which existed in previous eras. Unlike risks from the past which had established causes and known effects, today's risks are incalculable in origin and indeterminate in their

---

[1] Anthony Giddens, *Sociology* (3rd Edition), London: Polity Press, 1997.

consequences.

Humans have always had to face risks of one kind or another, but today's risks are qualitatively different than those that came in earlier times. Until quite recently, human societies were threatened by external risk—dangers such as drought, earthquakes, famines and storms that spring from the natural world and are unrelated to the actions of humans. Today, however, we are increasingly confronted with various types of manufactured risk—risks that are created by the impact of our own knowledge and technology on the natural world. As we shall see, many environmental and health risks facing contemporary societies are instances of manufactured risk—they are the outcomes of our own interventions into nature.

Environmental Risks

One of the clearest illustrations of manufactured risk can be found in threats currently posed by the natural environment. One of the consequences of accelerating industrial and technological development has been the steady spread of human intervention into nature. There are few aspects of the natural world that remain untouched by man—urbanization, industrial production and pollution, large-scale agricultural projects, the construction of dams and hydroelectric plants, and nuclear power programs are just some of the ways in which human beings have had an impact on their natural surroundings. The collective outcome of such processes has been the creation of widespread environmental destruction whose precise cause is indeterminate and whose consequences are similarly difficult to calculate.

In our globalizing world, ecological risk confronts us in many guises. Concern over global warming has been mounting in the scientific community for some years; it is now generally accepted that the earth's temperature has been increasing from the build-up of harmful gases within the atmosphere. The potential consequences of global warming are devastating: if polar ice caps continue to melt as they currently are, sea levels will rise and may threaten low-lying land masses and their human populations. Changes in climate patterns have been cited as possible causes of the severe floods that afflicted parts of China in 1998 and Mozambique in 2000.

Because environmental risks are diffuse in origin, it is unclear how they should be addressed, or who bears responsibility for taking action to remedy them. A simple example demonstrates why this is so. Scientists have found that chemical pollution levels have had a harmful effect on certain of the Antarctic penguin colonies. But it is impossible to identify accurately either the exact origins of the pollution or its possible consequences for the penguins in the future. In such an instance—and in hundreds of similar cases—it is likely that effective action will not be taken to address the risk because the extent of both the cause and the outcome is unknown and unfixed.

Health Risks

In the past decade, the dangers posed to human health by manufactured risks have attracted great attention. In the media and public health campaigns, for example, people have been urged to limit their exposure to the harmful ultraviolet rays of the sun and to apply sun-screen lotion to prevent burning. In recent years, sun exposure has been linked to a heightened risk of skin cancer in many parts of the world. This is thought to be related to the depletion of the ozone layer—the layer of the earth's atmosphere which normally filters out ultraviolet light. Due to the high volume of chemical emissions that are produced by human activities and industry, the concentration of ozone in the atmosphere has been diminishing and, in some cases, ozone "holes" have opened up.

There are many examples of manufactured risk that are linked to food. Modern farming and food production techniques have been heavily influenced by advances in science and technology. For example, chemical pesticides and herbicides are widely used in commercial agriculture and many animals (such as chickens and pigs) are pumped full of hormones and antibiotics. Some people have suggested that farming techniques such as these compromise food safety and could have an adverse effect on humans. In recent years, two particular controversies have raised widespread public concern over food safety and manufactured risk: the debate over Genetically Modified foods (GM foods) and "mad cow disease".

Bovine Spongiform Encephalopathy (BSE), known popularly as "mad cow disease", was first detected in British cattle in 1986. Scientists have linked BSE infection to the practice of raising cattle—normally herbivores—on feed containing traces of the parts of other animals. After the outbreak, the government took steps to control the disease among cattle, but it claimed that eating beef was safe and posed no danger to humans. Only in the mid-1990s was it admitted that several human deaths from Creutzfeldt-Jakob disease, a degenerative brain condition, had been linked to the consumption of beef from infected cattle. Thousands of British cattle were killed and strict legislation was passed to regulate cattle farming and the sale of beef products.

Although extensive scientific research has been launched to determine the risks to humans from BSE, the findings remain inconclusive. There is a risk that individuals who consumed British beef in the years preceding the discovery of BSE may have been exposed to infection. Yet as recently as December 1999 the European Union's Scientific Steering Committee declared that "the infectious dose to humans is currently not known". Calculating the risks humans run from BSE is an example of the complexity of risk assessment in the contemporary world. It is necessary to know if and when infected cattle were part of a certain food chain, the level and distribution of the infection that was present in the cattle, the way in which the beef was processed, and many other details. The sheer quantity of unknown factors has complicated the task and made any precise analysis of risk challenging.

1. The following belong to external risk EXCEPT_____.

(A) drought   (B) earthquakes   (C) floods   (D) snowstorms

2. What is the widely accepted cause of global warming?

(A) The construction of dams and hydroelectric plants.

(B) The build-up of harmful gases within the atmosphere.

(C) Chemical pollution.

(D) The melting polar ice caps.

3. The following statements are true EXCEPT_____.

(A) Skin cancer has something to do with exposure to the harmful ultraviolet rays of the sun.

(B) The increasing chemical emissions have resulted in the diminishing concentration of ozone in the atmosphere.

(C) There are possibly no effective actions to address the widespread environmental destruction due to incalculable origin and indeterminate consequences.

(D) Immediately after the outbreak of BSE in Britain, thousands of British cattle were killed and strict legislation was passed to regulate cattle farming and the sale of beef products.

IV. Questions for Further Thought

1. How does globalization change your daily life? (illustrate with at least THREE examples)

2. Discuss the different impacts of globalization on developed and developing countries.

[Passage 2]

The Rise of Asia's Universities[1]

It is a great pleasure to be with you this evening, and an especially great honor to have been asked to deliver the Seventh Annual Lecture of the Higher Education Policy Institute.

I stand before you this evening as a representative of the third oldest university in the United States, little more than 50 miles from the two oldest universities in the English-speaking world. Today, the strongest British and American universities—such as Oxford, Cambridge and Yale, not to mention Harvard, Stanford, Berkeley, MIT, University College London and Imperial College London—call forth worldwide admiration and respect for their leadership in research and education. Sitting atop the global league tables, these institutions set the standard that others at home and abroad seek to **emulate**; they define the concept of "world-class university". They excel in the advancement of human knowledge of nature and culture; they provide the finest training to the next generation of scholars; and they provide outstanding undergraduate and professional education for those who will emerge as leaders **in all walks of life**.

But, as we all know at this, the beginning of the 21st century, the East is rising. The rapid economic development of Asia since the Second World War—starting with Japan, South Korea, extending to Singapore, and finally **taking hold** powerfully in China and India—has altered the balance of power in the global economy and hence in geopolitics. The rising nations of the East all recognize the importance of an educated workforce as a means to economic growth and they understand the impact of research in driving innovation and competitiveness. In the 1960s, 1970s, and 1980s, the higher education

---

1 Richard C. Levin, A Speech in the Seventh Annual Lecture of the Higher Education Policy Institute, *The Royal Society,* London, February 1, 2010.

agenda in Asia's early developers—Japan, South Korea—was first and foremost to increase the fraction of their populations provided with postsecondary education. Their initial focus was on expanding the number of institutions and their enrollments, and impressive results were achieved.

Today, the later and much larger developing nations of Asia—China and India—have an even more ambitious agenda. Both these emerging powers seek to expand the capacity of their systems of higher education, and China has done so dramatically since 1998. But they also **aspire** simultaneously to create a limited number of "world class" universities to take their places among the best. This is an **audacious** agenda, but China, in particular, has the will and resources that make it feasible. This aspiration is shared not only by other nations in Asia but also by certain resource-rich nations in the Middle East.

Consider the following recent developments:

In the Gulf States, hundreds of millions of dollars are being spent to open branches of top U.S. and European universities such as Cornell in Qatar and the Sorbonne in Abu Dhabi.

This past autumn, the new King Abdullah University of Science and Technology opened in Saudi Arabia. Its $10 billion **endowment** exceeds that of all but five American universities.

In Singapore, planning is underway to build a new public university of Technology and Design, and a new American-style liberal arts college **affiliated** with the National University.

In China, the nine universities that receive the most supplemental government funding to enhance their global competitiveness recently self-identified as the C9—China's Ivy League.

In India, the Education Ministry recently announced its intention to build 14 new comprehensive universities of "world-class" stature.

This evening I want to discuss the motivations for attempting to build world-class universities, the practical obstacles that must be overcome, and the potential consequences of success. Because the circumstances in the Middle East are very different, I will **confine** my attention to Asia.

There are other important trends that are changing the global landscape of higher

---

1 Globalization

Passage 2

Discuss President Levin's statement.

What are the impacts of university ranking on students' choice of universities?

Comment on the strategies adopted by Asian countries to propel higher education.

13

education: the rapidly increasing flow of students across borders, the expanding number of satellite campuses being established by U.S. and European universities, the emergence of for-profit providers of both on-site and distance education, and the urgent need to strengthen higher education in the world's poorest nations, most notably in sub-Saharan Africa. I lack the time this evening to cover this entire **terrain**, so I shall confine myself to analyzing the prospects for and the potential consequences of developing world-class universities in Asia. The broader topic—the globalization of higher education—is the subject of an excellent new book by **Ben Wildavsky**, entitled *The Great Brain Race*, to be published this spring by the Princeton University Press.

Asian Ambitions: Expanding Access to Higher Education

In the early stages of postwar Asian development, it was well understood that expanded access to higher education was a **requisite** for sustained economic growth. A literate, well-trained labor force was a key ingredient in transforming Japan and South Korea over the course of the past half century, first from agricultural to manufacturing economies and subsequently from low-to high-skill manufacturing. With substantial government investment, the capacity of the **tertiary educational** systems in both countries expanded rapidly. The gross enrollment rate, the ratio of students enrolled in tertiary education to the size of the age cohort, rose from 9 percent in Japan in 1960 to 42 percent by the mid-1990s. In South Korea, the increase was even more dramatic, from 5 percent in 1960 to just over 50 percent in the mid-1990s.

In this earlier period, China and India **lagged** far behind. By the mid-1990s, only 5 percent of college-age Chinese attended college, putting China **on par with** Bangladesh, Botswana, and Swaziland. In India, despite a postwar effort to create first a set of national comprehensive universities and later the elite and very small Indian Institutes of Technology, the gross enrollment rate stood at 7 percent in the 1990s.

Speaking at the 100th anniversary celebration of Peking University in 1998, China's former president, Jiang Zemin, publicly set his country's sights on greatly expanding its system of higher education, and his administration made it happen—<u>faster than ever before in human history</u>. By 2006, China was spending 1.5 percent of its GDP on higher education, nearly triple the share of GDP it was spending a decade earlier.

The results of this investment have been staggering. Over the decade following Jiang

Zemin's declaration, the number of institutions of higher education in China more than doubled, from 1,022 to 2,263. Meanwhile, the number of Chinese who enroll in college each year has **quintupled**—rising from 1 million students in 1997 to more than 5.5 million students in 2007. This expansion in capacity is without precedent. China has built the largest higher education sector in the world in merely a decade's time. In fact, the increase in China's postsecondary enrollment since the turn of the millennium exceeds the total postsecondary enrollment in the United States.

China still has a long way to go to achieve its aspirations concerning access to higher education. Despite the enormous surge, China's gross enrollment rate for tertiary education stands at 23 percent, compared to 58 percent in Japan, 59 percent in the UK, and 82 percent in the United States. Expansion has slowed since 2006, owing to concerns that enrollments have outstripped the capacity of faculty to maintain quality in some institutions. The student-teacher ratio has roughly doubled over the past decade. But enrollment will continue to rise as more teachers are prepared, because <u>the Chinese leaders are keenly aware of the importance of a well-educated labor force for economic development.</u>

India's achievement to date has not been nearly so impressive, but its aspirations are no less ambitious. In two decades, it will be the most populated country in the planet, and by 2050, if growth can be sustained, it could become the second largest economy in the world. To sustain that growth, India's Education Minister, Kapil Sibal, aims to increase his country's gross enrollment ratio in postsecondary education from 12 to 30 percent by 2020. Sibal's goal translates to an increase of 40 million students in Indian universities over the next decade—perhaps more than can feasibly be achieved, but even getting half way there would be a remarkable accomplishment.

I. Background Information

Richard Charles Levin (born April 7, 1947), a professor of economics, has been serving as tenured president of Yale University from 1993 to 2013. Under his presidency, Yale's endowment has increased from USD3.2 billion to more than USD20 billion. Levin has made a special effort in expanding Yale's engagement with China and a program for undergraduates in Beijing was established in 2006. He was elected to the board of the National Committee on United States-China Relations.

This passage is an excerpt from his speech in the Seventh Annual Lecture of the **Higher Education Policy Institute** in The Royal Society, London, on Feb 1, 2010, which focuses on the development of higher education in Asia, especially in China and India.

II. Notes

1. **Emulate:** *v.* strive to equal or match, especially by imitating
2. **Aspire:** *v.* have an ambitious plan or a lofty goal
3. **Audacious:** *adj.* invulnerable to fear or intimidation
4. **Endowment:** *n.* money or the act of endowing with a permanent source of income
5. **Affiliate:** *v.* join in an affiliation
6. **Confine:** *v.* restrict or limit
7. **Terrain:** *n.* field, domain or realm
8. **Requisite:** *n.* anything indispensable
9. **Lag:** *v.* fall behind
10. **Quintuple:** *v.* become five times as much as or four times more than
11. **In all walks of life:** in every profession and trade
12. **Take hold:** be larger in quantity, power, status or importance; occupy a commanding position
13. **Ben Wildavsky:** a guest scholar at the Brookings Institution, a senior scholar in Research and Policy at the Ewing Marion Kauffman Foundation and the author of *The Great Brain Race* (published by Princeton University Press on April 5th, 2010)
14. **Tertiary education:** higher education / postsecondary education
15. **On par with:** at the same level with
16. **Higher Education Policy Institute (founded in 2002):** the UK's only independent think tank devoted exclusively to higher education with the mission of researching and reforming higher education policy

III. Writing

Read the book excerpt, and write an approximately 300-word essay, discussing the factors that are key to positive, and active cultural dialogue for the world's greater good.

Silk Road as a Metaphor[1]

Many of the transport developments described in the preceding paragraphs are unknown outside a small circle of experts and policy-makers. UNESCAP publications and pronouncements rarely attract banner newspaper headlines, or much academic attention for that matter. Yet scarcely had President Xi's announcements in September and October 2013 had been made than they began to attract the attention of the international press. Of course, this was partly because the initiative was seen as a major departure in China's foreign policy. However part of the reason was that the initiative had been framed in a powerful metaphor. The new Silk Road promised the revival of a legendary trade route, whose past had been studded with exotic locations. Now it was mixed in with that boyhood fantasy of a railway stretching into the distance to unknown destinations. Well, it certainly got me hooked!

However, the Silk Road has been employed before as a foreign policy metaphor. In 1997 the Japanese government employed the term "Silk Road Diplomacy" to describe its intensified development efforts in Central Asia and the adoption of a more active policy towards both Russia and China. The Ministry of Foreign Affairs formulated "three principles" which underpinned Japan's relations in the area, and these were promulgated in a speech by the prime minister, Hashimoto Ryutaro, to a group of businessmen in July 2007. Towards Russia, he formulated the principles in terms of trust, mutual benefit and long-term perspective. Towards Central Asia he described them as political dialogue, economic cooperation and efforts to promote democratization and security.[2] In the wake of the speech, Japan increased its diplomatic representation in the area, and with the space of a few years it had become the largest provider of overseas development assistance (ODA) to Kazakhstan, Kyrgyzstan and Uzbekistan. Most of the aid was in the form of loans, because the Japanese believed that the recipient government would be more careful in the selection and implementation of projects if the sums involved had to be repaid. The loan projects tended to focus on connectivity—improvements in roads, rail, air and telephone infrastructure.[3]

---

1 Richard T. Griffiths, *Revitalizing the Silk Road*, The Netherlands: HIPE Publications, 2017, pp. 19–21.
2 Ryutaro Hashimoto, Address by Prime Minister Ryutaro Hashimoto to the Japan Association of Corporate Executives (provisional translation).
3 Kawato Aldo, What is Japan up to in Central Asia?, in C. Len, U. Tomohiko and H. Tetsuya (eds.), *Japan's Silk Road Diplomacy: Paving the Road Ahead*, Washington, 2008, pp. 15–29.

The idea of a "new Silk Road" was also employed by the USA. It was conceived as a metaphor and a proposal for action by S. Frederick Starr, in a series of articles published between 2000 and 2007 as part of a policy pre-scription for the region after the American withdrawal from Afghanistan.[1] The idea was taken up in September 2011 by the then Secretary-of-State, Hillary Clinton, who suggested that an Afghanistan at peace would have to re-establish its normal economic relations with its neighbors. Then, in a burst of lyricism, she continued:

> For centuries, the nations of South and Central Asia were connected to each other and the rest of the continent by a sprawling trading network called the Silk Road. Afghanistan's bustling markets sat at the heart of this net work. Afghan merchants traded their goods from the court of the Pharaohs to the Great Wall of China. As we look to the future of this region, let's take this precedent as inspiration for a long-term vision for Afghanistan and its neighbors. Let's set our sights on a new Silk Road—a web of economic and transit connections that will bind together a region too long torn apart by conflict and division.[2]

Subsequent details that emerged indicated that the plan would involve both the construction of new infrastructure such as highways, railways, electricity networks and pipelines (the so-called "hardware" portion) and the reduction of legal barriers to trade (the "software"). In addition to aiding Afghanistan the plan seemed intent on orienting Central Asia away from the North (and its historical orientation on Russia) and towards India and Pakistan. However, India and Pakistan were never symbols for cross-border cooperation, and with potential investors likely to baulk at the risks, and without substantial external government financial backing, the scheme seemed doomed from the start.[3] When hostilities in Afghanistan did not die out, the project

---

[1] S. Frederick Starr (ed.), *The New Silk Roads: Transport and Trade in Greater Central Asia.* Washington, 2007.
He was the founding chairman of the Central Asia-Caucasus Institute and Silk Road Studies Program of Johns Hopkins University
[2] US Department of State, *Remarks at the New Silk Road Ministerial Meeting,* September 22, 2011.
[3] J. Kucera, The New Silk Road?, *The Diplomat,* November 11, 2011.

perished, though it still gets a page on the State Department's website.

The Silk Road, of course, was never a single road, but a series of paths and tracks along which people and goods travelled at a pace dictated by geography and season. Boundaries and borders are strangely absent, though there were always tolls and taxes—how else did the magnificent cities of the ancient Silk Road get built? The metaphor goes deeper. It was not only goods that passed along its routes, but languages and cultures, technology and knowledge, food, spices and cuisines. The Silk Road evokes thoughts of an open and welcoming spirit a mutually beneficial meeting and exchange of peoples and ideas. It is also a very Asian story, representing epochs when their civilizations equalled or surpassed the levels attained in Europe. It was from Asia to Europe that the treasures and knowledge largely flowed. It was an epoch in which space was not primarily defined by "states", though it was often anchored by looser "empires", and it evokes a largely borderless world in which all places along its route could benefit from the advantages that exchanges could offer. Moreover, although the entire route was often convulsed by warfare and savagery, the highest flowering of trade and the peaks of its prosperity coincided with periods of peace.

IV. Questions for Further Thought

1. How can a globalizing world promote international cooperation and coordination?
2. Make suggestions on the reform of China's Gaokao.

[Passage 3]

Female Political Leaders[1]

    I write from Yonsei University in Seoul, capital of South Korea. South Korea is a remarkable country. It was one of the world's poorest countries in 1960, poorer than Ghana, Senegal, and a number of other African countries. Moreover, its future economic prospects were thought at that time to be **dismal**: it had no consequential natural resources, a high population relative to the **arable** land available, and above all the Confucian ethic, with its **reverence** for the past and its resistance to change. Koreans demonstrated just how wrong such assessments can be. For 25 years, from 1965 to 1990, Korean economic output (GDP) grew at 9.7 percent a year, highest in the world. Korea showed that a stable social structure, right incentives for effort, saving, and risk taking, and engagement with the world economy can produce dramatic growth even in an economy with seemingly limited prospects. To be sure, the Koreans occasionally made mistakes, such as the attempt in the early 1970s to launch a program of support for heavy and chemical industries. Only steel and its derivative ship-building succeeded. But unlike many other countries, South Korea's leaders recognized and corrected their mistakes relatively early, rather than continuing to **pour good money after bad**.

    South Korea's president during the first 14 years of this period of rapid growth was Park Chung-Hee, a former general who had led a **coup** against the corrupt government in 1961. Park's daughter, Park Geun-hye, was recently elected Korea's president in a free and democratic election—the first female political leader in this country. She joins ten other female heads of government around the world—some presidents, some prime ministers, depending on the exact form of government. Angela Merkel of Germany is perhaps the best known, but the list includes Cristina Kirshner of Argentina, Julia Gillard of Australia, Sheikh Hasina of Bangladesh, Dilma Rousseff of Brazil, Helle

---

1 Richard N. Cooper, Female Political Leaders, *Century Weekly*, May, 2013.

Thorning-Schmidt of Denmark, Ellen Johnson Sirleaf of Liberia, Dalia Grybauskaite of Lithuania, Yingluck Shinawatra of Thailand, and Kalma Persad-Bissette of Trinidad—in all about 5 percent of the national heads of government of today.

If we look back over the past half century, there have been an additional 18 female heads of government, starting with Sirimavo Bandaranaike in Sri Lanka in 1960, the first female prime minister. The best known are probably Margaret Thatcher (who just passed away in 2013), prime minister of the United Kingdom (1979—1986), and Indira Gandhi, prime minister of India (1966—1977; 1980—1984). Sri Lanka, Bangladesh, the Philippines, and Argentina have each had two female heads of government. And there has been one each in Canada, Chile, Guyana, Iceland (just stepped down before an election last month), Norway, Israel, Pakistan, Indonesia, and New Zealand.

All the habitable continents have had at least one female leader—only one, in the cases of Africa and North America. By region, South Asian countries have been the most receptive, followed by Western Europe and South America. Ukraine has had a female prime minister, as has France, but both served under strong presidencies, thus were not heads of government. Some leaders slid into office as widows or daughters of preceding male leaders, but most made it on their own. Almost all have been selected in democratic elections. And many subsequently lost elections.

Of course, throughout history there have been female leaders, most prominent among them probably Cleopatra of Egypt, Queen Isabella, co-monarch of Spain, Queen Elizabeth I of England, Maria Theresa of Austria, and Catherine the Great of Russia. But they were selected by inheritance or marriage, not by a wider electorate. And there have been many women behind the throne, such as the Dowager Empress Cixi of China.

Feminists in America and Europe—and perhaps elsewhere—believe there should be more female political leaders, and have even suggested minimum female **quotas** for legislatures, often a stepping stone to being head of government. The underlying thought is that females would bring different qualities to leadership, and implicitly better qualities, than do males. With a **cumulative** experience of 29 female political leaders around the world, we perhaps have enough evidence to put those claims to a test. But that is a topic for a different—and more **contentious**—article.

1 Globalization
Passage 3

Introduce Queen Dowager and her role in Nanyue and Han Dynasty.

I. Background Information

Richard Newell Cooper (1934—2020) was an American economist, policy adviser, academic and professor of International Economics at Harvard University used to serve as Deputy Assistant Secretary of State for International Monetary Affairs in the United States Department of State between 1965 and 1966.

This excerpt is an article written by Richard Newell Cooper for the *Century Weekly* in May 2013, in which he claimed that females would bring different qualities to leadership, and implicitly better qualities than males, based on recalling and commenting on the experiences of the 29 famous female political leaders around the world.

II. Notes

1. **Dismal:** *adj.* gloomy and depressing
2. **Arable:** *adj.* (of farmland) capable of being farmed productively
3. **Reverence:** *n.* feeling of respect and worship
4. **Coup:** *n.* a sudden and decisive change of government by force
5. **Quota:** *n.* prescribed number
6. **Cumulative:** *adj.* increasing by successive addition
7. **Contentious:** *adj.* likely to cause controversy
8. **Pour good money after bad:** throw good money after bad

III. Translation

1. Translate the following paragraph into English with hints given in brackets.

近年来，随着中国经济实力（economic strength）的增强，中国人的钱包越来越鼓，出境旅游（outbound tourism）的人数大幅提升，中国游客在境外旅游时的不文明行为（uncivil behaviors）屡遭曝光，为中国形象带来很大的负面影响，严重损害（tarnish）了中国的国家形象。2013年中国成为世界第一大出境旅游国，中国游客是国际旅游业的最大消费群体，世界旅游组织（UNWTO: the United Nations World Tourism Organization）报道称，2012年中国游客在境外花费达1020亿美元。因此，提升中国游客的形象、规范文明旅游的行为（polite tourist behaviors）已经到了刻不容缓（urgent）的时候。

2. Translate the following paragraph into Chinese with hints given in brackets.

The process of globalization is often portrayed solely as an economic phenomenon.

Much is made of the role of transnational corporations (跨国公司), whose massive operations now stretch across national borders, influencing global production processes and the international distribution of labor. Others point to the electronic integration (电子一体化) of global financial markets and the enormous volume of global capital flows (资本流动). Still others focus on the unprecedented scope (史无前例的规模) of world trade, involving a much broader range of goods and services than ever before.

IV. Questions for Further Thought

1. What are the most important qualities in exercising leadership?

2. What are the causes of the glass ceiling of gender as political leaders and how best can it be tackled?

文化智慧阅读

[Passage 4]

Mutual Understanding Between China and the World[1]

Xi Jinping, general secretary of the Central Committee of the Communist Party of China (CPC), led the other newly-elected members of the Standing Committee of the 18th CPC Central Committee Political Bureau to meet the press Thursday morning at the Great Hall of the People.

"I am very glad to meet friends from the news media here today", Xi said, citing that the 18th CPC National Congress "came to a successful conclusion".

"During the past several days, you have extensively covered the congress and <u>let the world hear China's voice.</u> On behalf of the secretariat of the congress, I wish to express our sincere thanks to you for your professionalism, dedication and hard work", Xi said.

"We have just held the first plenary session of the 18th Central Committee of the Communist Party of China and elected a new central leadership", Xi said.

"I was elected general secretary of the Party Central Committee by the plenary session. I wish to introduce to you the other six newly elected members of the Standing Committee of the Political Bureau", he said.

"They are: Comrade Li Keqiang, Comrade Zhang Dejiang, Comrade Yu Zhengsheng, Comrade Liu Yunshan, Comrade Wang Qishan, and Comrade Zhang Gaoli. Comrade Li Keqiang was a member of the Standing Committee of the Political Bureau of the 17th Party Central Committee, and all the others were members of the Political Bureau of the 17th Party Central Committee. I believe their names are familiar to you", Xi said.

"On behalf of the members of the newly elected central leadership, I wish to express our heartfelt thanks to all other members of the Party for the great trust they have

> Discuss how China can invite the world to listen.

---

[1] Xi Jinping, Edited By Chen Zhi, *Xi Leads Top Leadership*, Meeting Press, November 15, 2012, https://www.fmprc.gov.cn/ce/ceindo/eng/ztbd/25879/t989375.htm accessed November 1, 2021.

placed in us. We will **strive** to be worthy of their trust and fulfill our mission", Xi said.

"We are greatly encouraged by both the trust all the comrades of the Party have placed in us and the great expectation the people of all ethnic groups in China have of us, and we are keenly aware that this is also an important responsibility for us", he said.

"We have taken on this important responsibility for our nation. Ours is a great nation. Throughout more than five thousand years of evolution as a civilization, the Chinese nation has made **indelible** contribution to the progress of human civilization", he said.

"In modern times, however, China endured untold hardships and sufferings, and its very survival hung in the balance. Countless Chinese patriots rose up one after another and fought for the renewal of the Chinese nation, but all ended in failure", Xi said.

"Since its founding, the Communist Party of China has made great sacrifices and forged ahead against all odds. It has rallied and led the Chinese people in transforming the poor and backward old China into an increasingly prosperous and powerful new China, thus opening a completely new horizon for the great renewal of the Chinese nation", he said.

"Our responsibility now is to **rally** and lead the entire Party and the people of all ethnic groups in China in taking over the relay baton passed on to us by history, and in making continued efforts to achieve the great renewal of the Chinese nation, make the Chinese nation stand **rock-firm** in the family of nations, and make even greater contribution to **mankind**", Xi said.

"We have taken on this important responsibility for the people. Our people are a great people. During the long course of history, the Chinese people have, working with diligence, bravery and wisdom, created a beautiful homeland where all ethnic groups live in harmony, and developed a great and dynamic culture", he said.

"Our people have an **ardent** love for life. They wish to have better education, more stable jobs, more income, greater social security, better medical and health care, improved housing conditions, and a better environment", Xi said.

"They want their children to have sound growth, have good jobs and lead a more enjoyable life. To meet their desire for a happy life is our mission. It is only hard work that creates all happiness in the world", he said.

"To fulfill our responsibility, we will rally and lead the whole Party and the people of all ethnic groups in China in making continued efforts to free up our minds, carry out

文化智慧阅读

What qualities should Chinese students cultivate in university to meet the demands of globalization?

reform and opening up, further release and develop the productive forces, work hard to resolve the difficulties the people face in both work and life, and **unwaveringly** pursue common **prosperity**", Xi said.

"We have taken on this important responsibility for the Party. Our Party is dedicated to serving the people. It has led the people in making **world-renowned** achievements, and we have every reason to take pride in these achievements", Xi said.

"But we are not complacent, and we will never rest on our **laurels**. Under the new conditions, our Party faces many severe challenges, and there are also many pressing problems within the Party that need to be resolved, particularly corruption, being divorced from the people, going through formalities and bureaucratism caused by some Party officials", Xi said.

"We must make every effort to solve these problems. The whole Party must stay on full alert", Xi said.

"To address these problems, we must first of all conduct ourselves honorably. Our responsibility is to work with all the comrades in the Party to uphold the principle that the Party should supervise its own conduct and run itself with strict discipline, effectively solve major problems in the Party, improve our conduct, and maintain close ties with the people", he said.

Paraphrase the sentence.

"By doing so, we will ensure that our Party will remain at the core of leadership in advancing the cause of socialism with Chinese characteristics", Xi said. "It is the people who have created history, and it is the people who are true heroes. The people are the source of our strength", Xi said.

"We are well aware that the capability of one individual is limited. But when we are united as one, we will create an awesome power and we can certainly overcome all difficulties", Xi said.

Paraphrase the sentence.

"One can only work for a limited period of time, but there is no limit to serving the people with dedication. Our responsibility is weightier than Mount Tai, and our road ahead is a long one", he said.

How can the Chinese youth make contributions to connecting China and the World?

"We must always be of the same mind with the people and share the same destiny with them, and we must work together with them and diligently for the public good so as to live up to the expectations of both history and the people", Xi said.

"Just as China needs to learn more about the world, so does the world need to learn more about China", Xi said, hoping that the press continues efforts to deepen mutual understanding between China and the world.

I. Background Information

Xi Jinping is the General Secretary of the Communist Party of China (CPC), the President of the People's Republic of China (PRC), and the Chairman of the Central Military Commission.

The speech at the press conference on November 15, 2012 is regarded as the premiere of the 18th Central Committee of the Communist Party of China, which consists of rich information about the new vision for the new administration. Xi's proclamation that "Just as China needs to learn more about the world, so does the world need to learn more about China" has been interpreted as China's willingness and commitment to develop understanding with World.

II. Notes

1. **Strive:** *v.* to attempt by employing effort; to exert much effort or energy
2. **Indelible:** *adj.* cannot be removed, washed away or erased
3. **Rally:** *v.* gather or bring together; return to a former condition
4. **Rock-firm:** *adj.* unshakable and securely fixed
5. **Ardent:** *adj.* characterized by strong enthusiasm or intense emotion
6. **Unwaveringly:** *adv.* with resolute determination
7. **World-renowned:** *adj.* world-famous
8. **Rest on our laurels:** stop working hard because of former victory

III. Discussion

Read the book excerpt, and discuss which factors are key to China's economic growth.

China's Economic Growth[1]

One way of explaining economic performance is by "growth accounting". This involves estimating the contribution of different factors of production and the efficiency in their use. In the case of China, this exercise would reveal that its growth was fuelled by a high savings/ investment rate and an ability to transfer labour from low-productivity sectors

---

1 Richard T. Griffiths, *Revitalizing the Silk Road*, The Netherlands: HIPE Publications, 2017, pp. 52–54.

(agriculture) to industry and services or, differently put, from the countryside to the cities. Beyond these sources of growth, there was an exogenous contribution to growth from the renewal of industrial capital and from reaping the benefits of economies of scale. Basically, this was the result of the optimal use of inward FDI, the market reforms that had been introduced and the access to export markets.[1]

The huge increase in manufacturing that accompanied China's growth required an enormous increase in the volume of fuel and raw materials that needed to be brought to the factories, and a large volume of finished goods to be transported to domestic (urban) markets and abroad. This demanded a vast investment in infrastructure.[2] Between 1990 and 2013, the length of China's railway network almost doubled to reach 103,000 km (60% electrified) by 2013. Although China possessed the world's third largest railway network, 25% of the world's traffic was carried on just 6% of the total track. This impression of an overstretched network is confirmed when it is realized that 59% of passengers and 35% of freight traffic were carried on only 13% of the tracks. A symbol of China's modernization is its high-speed rail network, which grew from nothing in 2006 to 19,000 km by 2016. This total was more than the rest of the world combined. Moreover, since 1990 the size of the highway network had quadrupled, not only to carry the increased volume of goods, but also to accommodate the growing number of passenger vehicles as consumer incomes rose.[3]

The insatiable demand for raw materials and the massive export drive also contributed to the development of China's ports and harbors. Seven of the world's largest ports by cargo volume today are located in China. The country's port development was largely driven by local state authorities, which provided much of the investment and oversaw the administration of portcities, often combining port investment with various development zone incentives. Although this had the advantage of creating synergies, it also led to an over-concentration of manufacturing activities within a relatively restricted area, with all the environmental damage that that incurred. The port itself was

---

1 B. Bosworth and S.M Collins, Accounting for Growth: Comparing China and India, *Journal of Economic Perspectives*, 2008, pp. 45—66.
2 P. Sahoo, R.K. Dash and G. Nataraj, Infrastructure Development and Economic Growth in China, *IDE Discussion Paper*, 2010, p. 261; Idem., China's Growth Story: The Role of Physical and Social Infrastructure, *Journal of Economic Development*, 2012, pp. 53—75.
3 China Statistical Yearbook, 2014; KPMG, *Infrastructure in China. Foundation for Growth*, 2009. H. Chan Hing Lee, Prospects of Chinese Rail Export under "One Belt, One Road", in T. W. Lin, H. Chan Hing Leee, K. Tseng Hui-Yi and W. X. Lim (eds.) *China's One Belt One Road Initiative*, London, 2016, pp. 197—235.

often seen as a medium to ensure the profitability or sustainability of local enterprise rather than a venture in its own terms.[1] In terms of efficiency China's container ports can also compete with the world's best, with the country boasting five of the top ten and eight of the top twenty. However, in other areas there is room for improvement. In coal it has three in the top ten and four in the top twenty. For oil it has none in the top ten but three in the top twenty. For iron ore it has one in the top ten and two in the top sixteen, and for bulk grain harbors it has one in the top twenty.[2]

IV. Questions for Further Thought

1. What are the major challenges confronting the renewal of China?

2. How can university students prepare themselves to get ready for the country's development?

[Mini-task for Chapter 1]

Executive Summary

The following is President of China, Xi Jinping's keynote speech for Boao Forum for Asia Annual Conference 2015. Write an approximately 200-word executive summary of his speech.

President Xi's Speech at Boao Forum[3]

Your Excellencies, Heads of State and Government, Ministers, Heads of International and Regional Organizations, Members of the Board of Directors of the Boao Forum for Asia, Ladies and Gentlemen, Dear Friends,

Boao today greets us with vast ocean, high sky and warm breeze. In this beautiful season of spring, it is of great significance that so many distinguished guests gather here to discuss the development strategies for Asia and the world.

At the outset, let me extend, on behalf of the Chinese government and people and in my own name, heartfelt welcome to all the distinguished guests attending the Boao Forum for Asia Annual Conference 2015, and my warm congratulations on the opening

---

1 J. J. Wang, *Port-City Interplays in China* (2nd ed.), Abingdon: New York, 2014.
2 O. Merk and T. Dang, Efficiency of World Ports in Container and Bulk Cargo (Oil, Coal, Ores and Grain), *OECD Regional Development Working Papers*, 2012.
3 Xi Jinping, *Towards a Community of Common Destiny and A New Future for Asia*, Speech at Boao Forum, March 28, 2015, http://www.china.org.cn/world/2015-03/29/content_50812317.htm accessed February 20, 2017.

of the conference.

The theme of this year's conference is "Asia's New Future: Towards a Community of Common Destiny". The timing could not be better in that the theme has not only great immediate relevance but also long-term historical significance. And I am looking to all of you to express yourselves fully and contribute your insightful views to the cause of peace and development of Asia and beyond.

Ladies and Gentlemen, Dear Friends,

There are certain historic occasions that are likely to remind people of what happened in the past and set people reflecting on them. This year marks the 70th anniversary of the end of the World Anti-Fascist War, the victory of the Chinese People's War of Resistance against Japanese Aggression and the founding of the United Nations. This year is also the 60th anniversary of the Bandung Conference and will witness the completion of the ASEAN Community. As such, it is an important year to be commemorated as well as a historic juncture to reflect on the past and look to the future.

Over the past 70 years, the world has experienced profound changes as never before, making a difference to the destiny of mankind. With the days of global colonialism and the Cold War long gone, countries are now increasingly interconnected and interdependent. Peace, development and win-win cooperation have become the prevailing trend of our times. The international forces are shifting in a way that is more favorable to maintaining world peace. Countries are now in a better position to uphold general stability in the world and seek common development.

Over the past 70 years, Asia has also gone through unprecedented changes. After gaining national independence, Asian countries took their destiny in their own hands and strengthened the force for regional and world peace. Asian countries were the first to advocate the Five Principles of Peaceful Co-existence and, together with African countries, put forward the Ten Principles on handling state-to-state relations at the Bandung Conference. Since the end of the Cold War, Asian countries have gradually come up with an Asian way of cooperation in the course of advancing regional cooperation, which features mutual respect, consensus-building and accommodation of each other's comfort levels. All this has contributed to a proper approach to state-to-state relations and to progress in building a new type of international relations.

Over the past 70 years, more and more Asian countries have found development paths that suit their own national conditions and embarked on a fast-track of economic growth. Having emerged from poverty and backwardness, they are on course to achieve development and prosperity. Regional and inter-regional cooperation is flourishing. Connectivity is pursued at a faster pace. As a result, there is a strong momentum in Asia with countries striving to outperform each other. Accounting for one third of the world economy, Asia is one of the most dynamic regions with the most potential and its global strategic importance has been rising.

Over the past 70 years, Asian countries have gradually transcended their differences in ideology and social system. No longer cut off from each other, they are now open and inclusive, with suspicion and estrangement giving way to growing trust and appreciation. The interests of Asian countries have become intertwined, and a community of common destiny has increasingly taken shape. Be it the arduous struggle for national independence, or the difficult periods of the Asian financial crisis and the international financial crisis, or the hard time in the wake of devastating disasters including the Indian Ocean tsunami and earthquake in Wenchuan, China, the people of Asian countries have always come to those in need with a helping hand and worked together to overcome one challenge after another, demonstrating the power of unity in face of difficulties and the spirit of sharing weal and woe. This said, Asia still faces numerous challenges. Some are the old issues left over from history and others are new ones associated with current disputes. Asia is also confronted with various traditional and non-traditional security threats. Hence it remains an uphill battle for Asian countries to grow the economy, improve people's livelihood and eliminate poverty.

A review of the path traversed over the past 70 years shows that what has been accomplished in Asia today is attributable to the persistent efforts of several generations of people in Asian countries and to the hard work of many statesmen and people of great vision. Tomorrow, Singapore will hold a state funeral for Mr. Lee Kuan Yew. Mr. Lee was a strategist and statesman respected across the world for his outstanding contribution to the peace and development of Asia and the exchanges and cooperation between Asia and the world. I want to take this opportunity to pay high tribute to Mr. Lee Kuan Yew and all those who made contribution to Asia's peace and development.

Ladies and Gentlemen, Dear Friends,

文化智慧阅读

Asia belongs to the world. For Asia to move towards a community of common destiny and embrace a new future, it has to follow the world trend and seek progress and development in tandem with that of the world.

The international situation continues to experience profound and complex changes, with significant development in multi-polarization and economic globalization. Cultural diversity and IT application are making constant progress while readjustment is accelerating in international landscape and order. Countries around the world are losing no time in adjusting their development strategies, pursuing transformation and innovation, changing their economic development models, improving economic structures and opening up new horizons for further development. At the same time, however, the world economy is still in a period of profound adjustment, with risks of low growth, low inflation and low demand interwoven with risks of high unemployment, high debt and high level of bubbles. The performance and policies of major economies continue to diverge, and uncertainties in the economic climate remain prominent. Geopolitical factors are more at play and local turmoil keep cropping up. Non-traditional security threats and global challenges including terrorism, cyber security, energy security, food security, climate change and major infectious diseases are on the rise, and the North-South gap is still wide. The noble cause of peace and development remains a long and arduous journey for mankind.

We have only one planet, and countries share one world. To do well, Asia and the world could not do without each other. Facing the fast changing international and regional landscapes, we must see the whole picture, follow the trend of our times and jointly build a regional order that is more favorable to Asia and the world. We should, through efforts towards such a community for Asia, promote a community of common interest for all mankind. I wish to take this opportunity to share with you my thoughts on this vision.

To build a community of common destiny, we need to make sure that all countries respect one another and treat each other as equals. Countries may differ in size, strength or level of development, but they are all equal members of the international community with equal rights to participate in regional and international affairs. On matters that involve us all, we should discuss and look for a solution together. Being a big country means shouldering greater responsibilities for regional and world peace and development, as opposed to seeking greater monopoly over regional and world affairs.

To respect one another and treat each other as equals, countries need to, first and foremost, respect other countries' social systems and development paths of their own choice, respect each other's core interests and major concerns and have objective and rational perception of other countries' growing strength, policies and visions. Efforts should be made to seek common ground while shelving differences, and better still to increase common interests and dissolve differences. The hard-won peace and stability in Asia and the sound momentum for development should be upheld by all. All of us must oppose interference in other countries' internal affairs and reject attempts to destablize the region out of selfish motives.

To build a community of common destiny, we need to seek win-win cooperation and common development. Our friends in Southeast Asia say that the lotus flowers grow taller as the water rises. Our friends in Africa say that if you want to go fast, walk alone; and if you want to go far, walk together. Our friends in Europe say that a single tree cannot block the chilly wind. And Chinese people say that when big rivers have water, the small ones are filled; and when small rivers have water, the big ones are filled. All these sayings speak to one same truth, that is, only through win-win cooperation can we make big and sustainable achievements that are beneficial to all. The old mindset of zero-sum game should give way to a new approach of win-win and all-win cooperation. The interests of others must be accommodated while pursuing one's own interests, and common development must be promoted while seeking one's own development. The vision of win-win cooperation not only applies to the economic field, but also to the political, security, cultural and many other fields. It not only applies to countries within the region, but also to cooperation with countries from outside the region. We should enhance coordination of macroeconomic policies to prevent negative spill-over effects that may arise from economic policy changes in individual economies. We should actively promote reform of global economic governance, uphold an open world economy, and jointly respond to risks and challenges in the world economy.

China and ASEAN countries will join hands in building an even closer China-ASEAN community of common destiny. The building of an East Asia economic community for ASEAN, China, Japan and ROK will be completed in 2020. We should actively build a free trade cooperation network in Asia and strive to conclude negotiations on an upgraded China-ASEAN FTA and on Regional Comprehensive Economic Partnership (RCEP) in 2015. In advancing economic integration in Asia, we need to stay committed to open regionalism and move forward trans-regional cooperation, including APEC, in a coordinated manner.

We will vigorously promote a system of regional financial cooperation, explore a platform for exchanges and cooperation among Asian financial institutions, and advance complementary and coordinated development between the Asian Infrastructure Investment Bank (AIIB) and such multilateral financial institutions as the Asian Development Bank and the World Bank. We will strengthen practical cooperation in currency stability, investment and financing, and credit rating, make progress in institution building for the Chiang Mai Initiative Multilateralization and build a regional financial security network. We will work towards an energy and resources cooperation mechanism in Asia to ensure energy and resources security.

China proposes that plans be formulated regarding connectivity building in East Asia and Asia at large to advance full integration in infrastructure, policies and institutions and personnel flow. We may increase maritime connectivity, speed up institution building for marine cooperation in Asia, and step up cooperation in marine economy, environmental protection, disaster management and fishery. This way, we could turn the seas of Asia into seas of peace, friendship and cooperation for Asian countries.

To build a community of common destiny, we need to pursue common, comprehensive, cooperative and sustainable security. In today's world, security means much more than before and its implications go well beyond a single region or time frame. All sorts of factors could have a bearing on a country's security. As people of all countries share common destiny and become increasingly interdependent, no country could have its own security ensured without the security of other countries or of the wider world. The Cold War mentality should truly be discarded and new security concepts be nurtured as we explore a path for Asia that ensures security for all, by all and of all.

We believe that countries are all entitled to take an equal part in regional security affairs and all are obliged to work to ensure security for the region. The legitimate security concerns of each country need to be respected and addressed. At the same time, in handling security issues in Asia, it is important to bear in mind both the history and reality of Asia, take a multi-pronged and holistic approach, improve coordinated regional security governance, and safeguard security in both the traditional and non-traditional realms. It is important to conduct dialogue and cooperation to enhance security at national and regional levels, and to increase cooperation as the way to safeguard peace and security. It is important to resolve disputes through peaceful means, and oppose the willful use or threat of force. Security should be given equal emphasis as development, and sustainable development surely provides a way to sustainable security. Countries in Asia need to step up cooperation with countries and organizations outside the region and all parties are welcome to play a positive and constructive role in upholding development and security in Asia.

To build a community of common destiny, we need to ensure inclusiveness and mutual learning among civilizations. History, over the past millennia, has witnessed ancient civilizations appear and thrive along the Yellow and Yangtze Rivers, the Indus, the Ganges, the Euphrates, and the Tigris River as well as in Southeast Asia, each adding its own splendor to the progress of human civilization. Today, Asia has proudly maintained its distinct diversity and still nurtures all the civilizations, ethnic groups and religions in this big Asian family.

Mencius, the great philosopher in ancient China, said, "Things are born to be different". Civilizations are only unique, and no one is superior to the other. There need to be more exchange and dialogue among civilizations and development models, so that each could draw on the strength of the other and all could thrive and prosper by way of mutual learning and common development. Let us promote inter-civilization exchanges to build bridges of friendship for our people, drive human development and safeguard peace of the world.

China proposes that a conference of dialogue among Asian civilizations be held to provide a platform upon which to enhance interactions among the youth, people's groups, local communities and the media and to form a network of think-tank cooperation, so as to add to Asian people's rich cultural life and contribute to more vibrant regional cooperation and development.

Ladies and Gentlemen, Dear Friends,

Right now, the Chinese people are working in unison under the strategic plans to complete the building of a moderately prosperous society in all respects, and to comprehensively deepen reform, advance law-based governance, and enforce strict

Party conduct. Our objective is to realize the "two centenary" goals for China's development and for realizing the Chinese dream of great national rejuvenation. I wish to use this opportunity to reaffirm China's commitment to the path of peaceful development, and to promoting cooperation and common development in the Asia-Pacific. China will be firm in its determination and resolve and all its policies will be designed to achieve such a purpose.

Now, the Chinese economy has entered a state of new normal. It is shifting gear from high speed to medium-to-high speed growth, from an extensive model that emphasized scale and speed to a more intensive one emphasizing quality and efficiency, and from being driven by investment in production factors to being driven by innovation. China's economy grew by 7.4% in 2014, with 7% increase in labor productivity and 4.8% decrease in energy intensity. The share of domestic consumption in GDP rose, the services sector expanded at a faster pace, and the economy's efficiency and quality continued to improve. When looking at China's economy, one should not focus on growth rate only. As the economy continues to grow in size, around 7% growth would be quite impressive, and the momentum it generates would be larger than growth at double digits in previous years. It is fair to say that the Chinese economy is highly resilient and has much potential, which gives us enough room to leverage a host of policy tools. Having said that, China will continue to be responsive to the new trend and take initiatives to shape the new normal in our favor. We will focus on improving quality and efficiency, and give even greater priority to shifting the growth model and adjusting the structure of development. We will make more solid efforts to boost economic development and deepen reform and opening-up. We will take more initiatives to unleash the creativity and ingenuity of the people, be more effective in safeguarding equity and social justice, raise people's living standards and make sure that China's economic and social development are both sound and stable.

This new normal of the Chinese economy will continue to bring more opportunities of trade, growth, investment and cooperation for other countries in Asia and beyond. In the coming five years, China will import more than US$10 trillion of goods, Chinese investment abroad will exceed US$500 billion, and more than 500 million outbound visits will be made by Chinese tourists. China will stick to its basic state policy of opening up, improve its investment climate, and protect the lawful rights and interests of investors. I believe that together, the people of Asian countries could drive this train of Asia's development to take Asia to an even brighter future.

What China needs most is a harmonious and stable domestic environment and a peaceful and tranquil international environment. Turbulence or war runs against the fundamental interests of the Chinese people. The Chinese nation loves peace and has, since ancient times, held high such philosophies that "harmony is the most valuable", "peace and harmony should prevail" and "all men under heaven are brothers". China has suffered from turbulence and war for more than a century since modern times, and the Chinese people would never want to inflict the same tragedy on other countries or peoples. History has taught us that no country who tried to achieve its goal with force ever succeeded. China will be steadfast in pursuing the independent foreign policy of peace, the path of peaceful development, the win-win strategy of opening-up, and the approach of upholding justice while pursuing shared interests. China will work to promote a new type of international relations of win-win cooperation and will always remain a staunch force for world peace and common development.

Close neighbors are better than distant relatives. This is a simple truth that the Chinese people got to know in ancient times. That explains China's firm commitment to building friendship and partnership with its neighbors to foster an amicable, secure and prosperous neighborhood. Under the principle of amity, sincerity, mutual benefit and inclusiveness, China is working actively to deepen win-win cooperation and connectivity with its neighbors to bring them even more benefit with its own development. China has signed treaties of good-neighborliness, friendship and cooperation with eight of its neighbors and is holding discussion to sign a same treaty with ASEAN. China stands ready to sigh such a treaty with all its neighbors to provide strong support for the development of bilateral relations as well as prosperity and stability in the region.

In 2013, during my visit to Kazakhstan and Indonesia, I put forward the initiatives of building a Silk Road economic belt and a 21st century maritime Silk Road. The "Belt and Road" initiative, meeting the development needs of China, countries along the routes and the region at large, will serve the common interests of relevant parties and answer the call of our time for regional and global cooperation.

In promoting this initiative, China will follow the principle of wide consultation, joint contribution and shared benefits. The programs of development will be open and inclusive, not exclusive. They will be a real chorus comprising all countries along the routes, not a solo for China itself. To develop the "Belt and Road" is not to replace existing mechanisms or initiatives for regional cooperation. Much to the contrary, we will build on the existing basis to help countries align their development strategies and form complementarity. Currently, more than 60 countries along the routes and international organizations have shown interest in taking part in the development of the "Belt and Road". The "Belt and Road" and the AIIB are both open initiatives. We welcome all countries along the routes and in Asia, as well as our friends and partners around the world, to take an active part in these endeavors.

The "Belt and Road" initiative is not meant as rhetoric. It represents real work that could be seen and felt to bring real benefits to countries in the region. Thanks to the concerted efforts of relevant parties, the vision and action paper of the initiative has been developed. Substantive progress has been made in the establishment of the AIIB. The Silk Road Fund has been launched, and constructions of a number of infrastructure connectivity projects are moving forward. These early harvests have truly pointed to the broad prospects the "Belt and Road" initiative will bring.

Ladies and Gentlemen, Dear Friends,

The cause of peace and development of mankind is as lofty as it is challenging. The journey ahead will not be smooth sailing, and success may not come easily. No matter how long and difficult the journey may be, those who work together and never give up will eventually prevail. I believe that as long as we keep to our goals and make hard efforts, we will together bring about a community of common destiny and usher in a new future for Asia.

I wish the Annual Conference a complete success.

Thank you very much.

[Further Reading]

1. Anthony Giddens, *Sociology* (12th Edition), New York: W. W. Norton & Company, 2021.
2. Thomas L. Friedman, *The World Is Flat*, UK: Penguin Books Ltd., 2007.
3. Liu Chen, *The Chinese Story in Global Order*, Germany: Springer, 2022.

2 Career

- **Passage 1**　Global Development　/ 43
- **Passage 2**　Three Days to See　/ 48
- **Passage 3**　Sources of Soft Power　/ 61
- **Passage 4**　Speech at University of Warwick　/ 68

[本章导读]

"工作将会占据你生活中很大的一部分,而唯一能让你真正获得满足感的就是从事伟大的事业"(Your work is going to fill a large part of your life, and the only way to be truly satisfied is to do what you believe is great work.)。史蒂夫·乔布斯(Steve Jobs)这样形容事业对人生的影响。事业是一个人生命中不可或缺的组成部分,可以奉献一生的事业,无疑是令人向往的。那么,对于青年人来说,怎样才能培养科学的择业观和事业观呢?

本章选篇的主题将与大家共同探讨这一问题。个人事业的发展需要与时代紧密联系。为此,本章第一篇选自英国著名社会学家安东尼·吉登斯(Anthony Giddens)教授的《社会学》(Sociology)第五版第二章,旨在让读者了解在当前的全球化时代背景下世界各国社会发展的基本特点,全面认识"发展中国家"(the developing world)和"新型工业化国家"(the newly industrialized countries)的发展任务与愿景,帮助读者从发展的角度思考个人的事业追求与所处时代的内在关系。理解事业的社会意义与价值需要榜样的引导。第二篇选自美国作家、教育家海伦·凯勒(Helen Keller)1933年发表于《大西洋月刊》(Atlantic Monthly)的散文,文中想象了假如给她三天光明,她将如何度过。海伦·凯勒堪称传奇的人生以及她为盲人、聋人的公益事业做出的努力和贡献,希望能够为青年学子培养未来事业所需的意志品格,提供一个学习的注脚。对于事业的理解需要以积极、正向的价值判断为基础。第三篇文章的作者是美国著名政治学家、哈佛大学教授约瑟夫·奈(Joseph S. Nye)。选篇来自他的《软实力:世界政治中的成功之道》(Soft Power: The Means to Success in World Politics)一书的第一章。本文从三个方面阐述了形成文化软实力的主要着力点,希望为读者思考如何树立正确的事业价值观提供一个思路。在全球化的时代背景下,每个人的事业追求都需要具备宽广的国际视野。因此,第四篇选自经济合作与发展组织前总干事、加拿大自由党前党主席唐纳德·约翰逊(Donald Johnston)2020年1月31日在英国华威大学(The University of Warwick)的公共演讲。本次演讲从全球可持续发展的视角,凝练了全球化挑战,尤

文化智慧阅读

其是气候变化和全球减贫,呼吁年轻人为解决世界发展的共同挑战贡献智慧和力量。

毫无疑问,事业是每个人都必须审慎对待的人生课题。然而,事业的成功需要以正确事业观为基础。在此,阿尔伯特·爱因斯坦(Albert Einstein)的感悟或许会对我们有所启示,"不要只想着成为一个成功的人,而要努力成为一个有价值的人"(Try not to become a man of success but rather try to become a man of values.)。

2 Career

Passage 1

[Passage 1]

Global Development[1]

From the seventeenth to the early twentieth century, the Western countries established colonies in numerous areas that were previously occupied by traditional societies, using their superior military strength where necessary. Although virtually all these colonies have now attained their independence, the process of colonialism was central to shaping the social map of the globe as we know it today. In some regions, such as North America, Australia and New Zealand, which were only thinly populated by hunting and gathering communities, Europeans became the majority population. In other areas, including much of Asia, Africa and South America, the local populations remained in the majority.

Societies of the first of these types, including the United States, have become industrialized and are often referred to as developed societies. Those in the second category are mostly at a much lower level of industrial development and are often referred to as developing societies, or the developing world. Such societies include China, India, most of the African countries (such as Nigeria, Ghana and Algeria) and those in South America (for example, Brazil, Peru and Venezuela). Since many of these societies are situated south of the United States and Europe, they are sometimes referred to collectively as the South and contrasted to the wealthier, industrialized North. This is a generalization, though, and as countries of the global south become industrialized, this simple division of the world becomes less and less accurate.

You may often hear developing countries referred to as part of the Third World. The term Third World was originally part of a contrast drawn between three main types

How did the local population become the minority in these regions?

Give some exceptions to the generalization.

---

1 Anthony Giddens, *Sociology* (5th Edition), London: Polity Press, 2006, pp. 41—43.

文化智慧阅读

of society found in the early twentieth century. First World countries were (and are) the industrialized states of Europe, the United States, Canada, Greenland, Australasia (Australia and New Zealand), South Africa and Japan. Nearly all First World societies have multiparty, parliamentary systems of government. Second World societies meant the communist countries of what was then the Soviet Union (USSR) and Eastern Europe, including, for example, **Czechoslovakia**, Poland, East Germany and Hungary. Second World societies had centrally planned economies, which allowed little room for private property or competitive economic enterprise. They were also one-party states: the Communist Party dominated both the political and economic systems. For some 75 years, world history was affected by a global rivalry known as the Cold War, between the Soviet Union and Eastern European countries on the one hand and the capitalistic societies of the West and Japan on the other. Today that rivalry is over. With the ending of the Cold War and the **disintegration** of communism in the former USSR and Eastern Europe, the Second World has effectively disappeared.

Share your understanding of the global impacts of the Cold War.

Should the Three Worlds model be adjusted in the age of globalization? Why or why not?

Even though the Three Worlds model is still sometimes used in sociology textbooks, today it has **outlived** whatever usefulness it might once have had as a way of describing the countries of the world. It can be argued that the ranking of First, Second and Third Worlds always reflected a value judgement, in which "first" means "best" and "third" means "worst". It is therefore best avoided.

The Developing World

Many developing societies are in areas that underwent colonial rule in Asia, Africa and South America. A few colonized areas gained independence early, like Haiti, which became the first **autonomous** black republic in January 1804. The Spanish colonies in South America acquired their freedom in 1810, while Brazil broke away from Portuguese rule in 1822. However, most nations in the developing world have become independent states only since the Second World War, often following bloody anti-colonial struggles. Examples include India, a range of other Asian countries (like Burma, Malaysia and Singapore) and countries in Africa (including, for example, Kenya, Nigeria, Zaire, Tanzania and Algeria).

While they may include people living in traditional fashion, developing countries are very different from earlier forms of traditional societies. Their political systems are modelled on systems that were first established in the societies of the West — that is to say, they are nation-states. While most of the population still live in rural areas, many of these societies are experiencing a rapid process of urban development.

Although agriculture remains the main economic activity, crops are now often produced for sale in world markets rather than for local consumption. Developing countries are not merely societies that have "lagged behind" the more industrialized areas. They have been in large part created by contact with Western **industrialism**, which has undermined earlier, more traditional systems.

Conditions in some of the most **impoverished** of these societies have **deteriorated** rather than improved over more recent years. There are still around one billion people living on the equivalent of less than one US dollar a day.

The world's poor are concentrated particularly in South and East Asia and in Africa and Latin America, although there are some important differences between these regions. For example, poverty levels in East Asia and the Pacific have declined over the past decade, while they have risen in the nations of sub-Saharan Africa. During the 1990s, the number of people living on less than one dollar per day in this region has grown from 241 million to 315 million (World Bank 2004). There have also been significant increases in poverty in parts of South Asia, Latin America and the Caribbean. Many of the world's poorest countries also suffer from a serious debt crisis. Payments of interest on loans from foreign lenders can often amount to more than governments' investments in health, welfare and education.

Newly Industrializing Countries

While the majority of developing countries are not as economically developed as the societies of the West, some have successfully embarked on a process of industrialization. These countries or regions are sometimes referred to as newly industrializing societies (NICs) including Brazil and Mexico in Latin America, South Korea and Singapore in East Asia. The rates of economic growth of the most successful NICs, such as those in East Asia, are several times those of the Western industrial economies. No developing country figured among the top 30 exporters in the world in 1968, but 25 years later

文化智慧阅读

South Korea was in the top 15.

The East Asian NICs have shown the most sustained levels of economic prosperity. They are investing abroad as well as promoting growth at home. South Korea's production of steel has doubled in the last decade and its shipbuilding and electronics industries are among the world's leaders. Singapore is becoming the major financial and commercial centre of Southeast Asia. Taiwan of China is an important presence in the manufacturing and electronics industries. <u>All these changes in the NICs have directly affected countries such as the United States, whose share of global steel production, for example, has dropped significantly over the past 30 years.</u>

How did the NICs affect the developed countries?

I. Background Information

In industrialized societies, industrial production is the main basis of the economy. Industrialized countries include the nations of the West and Japan, Australia, and New Zealand. The developing world, in which a majority of the world's population live, is almost all formerly colonized areas. The majority of the population works in agricultural production, some of which is geared to world markets.

II. Notes

1. **Czechoslovakia:** *n.* a former country in central Europe, now divided between the Czech Republic and Slovakia

2. **Disintegration:** *n.* the process of becoming much less strong or united and being gradually destroyed

3. **Outlive:** *v.* to continue to exist after sth. else has ended or disappeared

4. **Autonomous:** *adj.* (of a country, a region or an organization) able to govern itself or control its own affairs

5. **Industrialism:** *n.* an economic and social system based on industry

6. **Impoverished:** *adj.* very poor; without money

7. **Deteriorate:** *v.* to become worse

III. Reading Comprehension

Complete the following table according to Passage 1.

Societies in the modern world		
Type	Period of existence	Characteristics
First World societies	Eighteenth century to the present.	Based on 1._____. Majority of people live in 2._____; a few work in rural agricultural pursuits. Major class inequalities, though less pronounced than in traditional states. Distinct political communities or nation-states, including the nations of West, Japan, Australia and New Zealand.
Second World societies	Early twentieth century (Russian Revolution of 1917 to early 1990s).	Based on 3._____. Small proportion of the population work in agriculture; most live in towns and cities. Major class inequalities 4._____. Distinct political communities or nation-states. Until 1989, composed of the 5._____, but social and political changes began to transform them into free enterprise economic systems, according to the model of First World societies.
Developing societies ("Third World societies")	Eighteenth century (mostly as colonized areas) to the present.	Majority of the population work in 6._____, using traditional methods of production. Some agricultural produce sold on 7._____. Some have free enterprise systems, while others are 8._____. Distinct political communities or nation-states, including China, India and most African and South American nations.
Newly industrializing societies (NICs)	1970s to the present.	Former developing societies now based on 9._____. Majority of people live in towns and cities, a few work in agricultural pursuits. Major class inequalities, more pronounced than First World societies. Average per capita income considerably 10.____ than First World societies. Include South Korea, Singapore, Brazil and Mexico, etc.

IV. Questions for Further Thought

1. In July 2021, the United Nations Conference on Trade and Development (UNCTAD) upgraded South Korea's status from a developing country to a developed country. It is the first time the UN body upgraded a country's classification from developing to developed since its establishment in 1964. What are the elements that make a developed country?

2. What changes have happened in China during the transition of industrialization? How will these changes affect your future career?

[Passage 2]

Three Days to See[1]

I

All of us have read thrilling stories in which the hero had only a limited and specified time to live. Sometimes it was as long as a year; sometimes as short as twenty-four hours. But always we were interested in discovering just how the doomed man chose to spend his last days or his last hours. I speak, of course, of free men who have a choice, not condemned criminals whose sphere of activities is strictly delimited.

Such stories set us thinking, wondering what we should do under similar circumstances. What events, what experiences, what associations, should we crowd into those last hours as mortal beings? What happiness should we find in reviewing the past, what regrets?

What does it refer to?

Sometimes I have thought it would be <u>an excellent rule</u> to live each day as if we should die tomorrow. Such an attitude would emphasize sharply the values of life. We should live each day with a gentleness, a vigor, and a keenness of appreciation which are often lost when time stretches before us in the constant panorama of more days and months and years to come. There are those, of course, who would adopt the **epicurean** motto of "<u>Eat, drink, and be merry</u>", but most people would be **chastened** by the certainty of impending death.

Would you like to adopt this motto? Why or why not?

In stories, the doomed hero is usually saved at the last minute by some stroke of fortune, but almost always his sense of values is changed. He becomes more appreciative of the meaning of life and its permanent spiritual values. It has often been noted that those who live, or have lived, in the shadow of death bring a mellow sweetness to

---

1 Helen Keller, *Three Days to See*, January 1933, Volume 151, No. 1, pp. 35—42.

everything they do.

Most of us, however, take life for granted. We know that one day we must die, but usually we picture that day as far in the future. <u>When we are in buoyant health, death is all but unimaginable.</u> We seldom think of it. The days stretch out in an endless **vista**. So we go about our petty tasks, hardly aware of our listless attitude toward life.

The same **lethargy**, I am afraid, characterizes the use of all our faculties and senses. Only the deaf appreciate hearing, only the blind realize the manifold blessings that lie in sight. Particularly does this observation apply to those who have lost sight and hearing in adult life. But those who have never suffered impairment of sight or hearing seldom make the fullest use of these blessed faculties. Their eyes and ears take in all sights and sounds hazily, without concentration and with little appreciation. It is the same old story of not being grateful for what we have until we lose it, of not being conscious of health until we are ill.

<u>I have often thought it would be a blessing if each human being were stricken blind and deaf for a few days at some time during his early adult life.</u> Darkness would make him more appreciative of sight; silence would teach him the joys of sound.

Now and then I have tested my seeing friends to discover what they see. Recently I was visited by a very good friend who had just returned from a long walk in the woods, and I asked her what she had observed. "Nothing in particular," she replied. I might have been **incredulous** had I not been accustomed to such responses, for long ago I became convinced that <u>the seeing see little.</u>

How was it possible, I asked myself, to walk for an hour through the woods and see nothing worthy of note? I who cannot see find <u>hundreds of things to interest me through mere touch.</u> I feel the delicate symmetry of a leaf. I pass my hands lovingly about the smooth skin of a **silver birch**, or the rough, **shaggy** bark of a pine. In spring I touch the branches of trees hopefully in search of a bud, the first sign of awakening Nature after her winter's sleep. I feel the delightful, velvety texture of a flower, and discover its remarkable **convolutions**; and something of the miracle of Nature is revealed to me. Occasionally, if I am very fortunate, I place my hand gently on a small tree and feel the happy quiver of a bird in full song. I am delighted to have the cool waters of a brook rush through my open fingers. To me a lush carpet of pine needles or spongy grass is more welcome than the most luxurious Persian rug. To me the **pageant** of seasons is a thrilling and unending drama, the action of which streams through my finger tips.

At times my heart cries out with longing to see all these things. If I can get so much pleasure from mere touch, how much more beauty must be revealed by sight. Yet, those who have eyes apparently see little. The panorama of color and action which fills the world is taken for granted. It is human, perhaps, to appreciate little that which we have and to long for that which we have not, but it is a great pity that in the world of light the gift of sight is used only as a mere convenience rather than as a means of adding fullness to life.

If I were the president of a university <u>I should establish a compulsory course in "How to Use Your Eyes."</u> The professor would try to show his pupils how they could add joy to their lives by really seeing what passes unnoticed before them. He would try to awake their **dormant** and **sluggish** faculties.

> *Why did Helen want to establish such a course?*

II

Perhaps I can best illustrate by imagining what I should most like to see if I were given the use of my eyes, say, for just three days. And while I am imagining, suppose you, too, set your mind to work on the problem of how you would use your own eyes if you had only three more days to see. If with the oncoming darkness of the third night you knew that the sun would never rise for you again, how would you spend those three precious intervening days? What would you most want to let your gaze rest upon?

I, naturally, should want most to see the things which have become dear to me through my years of darkness. You, too, would want to let your eyes rest long on the things that have become dear to you so that you could take the memory of them with you into the night that loomed before you.

<u>If, by some miracle, I were granted three seeing days, to be followed by a</u> **relapse** <u>into darkness, I should divide the period into three parts.</u>

On the first day, I should want to see the people whose kindness and gentleness and companionship have made my life worth living. First I should like to <u>gaze long upon the face of my dear teacher, Mrs. Anne Sullivan Macy</u>, who came to me when I was a child and opened the outer world to me. I should want not merely to see the outline of her face, so that I could cherish it in my memory, but to study that face and find in it the living evidence of the sympathetic tenderness and patience with which she accomplished the difficult task of my education. I should like to see in her eyes that

> *Summarize Helen's plan for the three days.*
>
> *What would Helen like to see in her teacher?*

strength of character which has enabled her to stand firm in the face of difficulties, and that compassion for all humanity which she has revealed to me so often.

I do not know what it is to see into the heart of a friend through that "window of the soul," the eye. I can only "see" through my finger tips the outline of a face. I can detect laughter, sorrow, and many other obvious emotions. I know my friends from the feel of their faces. But I cannot really picture their personalities by touch. I know their personalities, of course, through other means, through the thoughts they express to me, through whatever of their actions are revealed to me. But I am denied that deeper understanding of them which I am sure would come through sight of them, through watching their reactions to various expressed thoughts and circumstances, through noting the immediate and fleeting reactions of their eyes and **countenance**.

Friends who are near to me I know well, because through the months and years they reveal themselves to me in all their phases; but of casual friends I have only an incomplete impression, an impression gained from a handclasp, from spoken words which I take from their lips with my finger tips, or which they tap into the palm of my hand.

How much easier, how much more satisfying it is for you who can see to grasp quickly the essential qualities of another person by watching the subtleties of expression, the quiver of a muscle, the flutter of a hand. <u>But does it ever occur to you to use your sight to see into the inner nature of a friend or acquaintance?</u> Do not most of you seeing people grasp casually the outward features of a face and let it go at that?

For instance, can you describe accurately the faces of five good friends? Some of you can, but many cannot. As an experiment, I have questioned husbands of long standing about the color of their wives' eyes, and often they express embarrassed confusion and admit that they do not know. And, incidentally, it is a chronic complaint of wives that their husbands do not notice new dresses, new hats, and changes in household arrangements.

The eyes of seeing persons soon become accustomed to the routine of their surroundings, and they actually see only the startling and spectacular. But even in viewing the most spectacular sights the eyes are lazy. Court records reveal every day how inaccurately "eyewitnesses" see. A given event will be "seen" in several different ways by as many witnesses. Some see more than others, but few see everything that is within the range of their vision.

How will you answer Helen's questions here?

文化智慧阅读

Oh, the things that I should see if I had the power of sight for just three days!

The first day would be a busy one. I should call to me all my dear friends and look long into their faces, imprinting upon my mind the outward evidences of the beauty that is within them. I should let my eyes rest, too, <u>on the face of a baby</u>, so that I could catch a vision of the eager, innocent beauty which precedes the individual's consciousness of the conflicts which life develops.

Why would Helen like to let her eyes rest on the face of a baby?

And I should like to look into the loyal, trusting eyes of my dogs—the grave, canny little Scottie, Darkie, and the **stalwart**, understanding Great Dane, Helga, whose warm, tender, and playful friendships are so comforting to me.

On that busy first day I should also view <u>the small simple things</u> of my home. I want to see the warm colors in the rugs under my feet, the pictures on the walls, the intimate trifles that transform a house into home. My eyes would rest respectfully on the books in raised type which I have read, but they would be more eagerly interested in the printed books which seeing people can read, for during the long night of my life the books I have read and those which have been read to me have built themselves into a great shining lighthouse, revealing to me the deepest channels of human life and the human spirit.

How could "the small, simple things" transform a house into a home?

In the afternoon of that first seeing day, I should take a long walk in the woods and intoxicate my eyes on the beauties of the world of Nature, trying desperately to absorb in a few hours the vast splendor which is constantly unfolding itself to those who can see. On the way home from my woodland jaunt my path would lie near a farm so that I might see the patient horses ploughing in the field (perhaps I should see only a tractor!) and the serene content of men living close to the soil. And I should pray for the glory of a colorful sunset.

When dusk had fallen, I should experience the double delight of being able to see by artificial light, which the genius of man has created to extend the power of his sight when Nature decrees darkness.

<u>In the night of that first day of sight, I should not be able to sleep, so full would be my mind of the memories of the day.</u>

How could you make changes to Helen's plan for the first day to make it more efficient? Summarize the activities Helen would undertake on the second day.

III

The next day—<u>the second day of sight</u>—I should arise with the dawn and see the thrilling miracle by which night is transformed into day. I should behold with awe the magnificent **panorama** of light with which the sun awakens the sleeping earth.

This day I should devote to a hasty glimpse of the world, past and present. I should want to see the pageant of man's progress, the **kaleidoscope** of the ages. How can so much be compressed into one day? Through the museums, of course. Often I have visited the New York Museum of Natural History to touch with my hands many of the objects there exhibited, but I have longed to see with my eyes the condensed history of the earth and its inhabitants displayed there—animals and the races of men pictured in their native environment; gigantic **carcasses** of dinosaurs and **mastodons** which roamed the earth long before man appeared, with his tiny stature and powerful brain, to conquer the animal kingdom; realistic presentations of the processes of evolution in animals, in man, and in the implements which man has used to fashion for himself a secure home on this planet; and a thousand and one other aspects of natural history.

I wonder how many readers of this article have viewed this panorama of the face of living things as pictured in that inspiring museum. Many, of course, have not had the opportunity, but I am sure that many who have had the opportunity have not made use of it. There, indeed, is a place to use your eyes. You who see can spend many fruitful days there, but I, with my imaginary three days of sight, could only take a hasty glimpse, and pass on.

My next stop would be the Metropolitan Museum of Art, for just as the Museum of Natural History reveals the material aspects of the world, so does the Metropolitan show the myriad facets of the human spirit. Throughout the history of humanity the urge to artistic expression has been almost as powerful as the urge for food, shelter, and procreation. And here, in the vast chambers of the Metropolitan Museum, is unfolded before me the spirit of Egypt, Greece, and Rome, as expressed in their art. I know well through my hands the sculptured gods and goddesses of the ancient Nile land. I have felt copies of **Parthenon friezes**, and I have sensed the rhythmic beauty of charging Athenian warriors. Apollos and Venuses and the Winged Victory of Samothrace are friends of my fingertips. The **gnarled**, bearded features of Homer are dear to me, for he, too, knew blindness.

My hands have lingered upon the living marble of Roman sculpture as well as that of later generations. I have passed my hands over a plaster cast of Michelangelo's inspiring

---

2 Career

Passage 2

Why did Helen wish to understand the present in light of the past?

Introduce the Metropolitan Museum of Art.

and heroic Moses; I have sensed the power of Rodin; I have been awed by the devoted spirit of Gothic wood carving. These arts which can be touched have meaning for me, but even they were meant to be seen rather than felt, and I can only guess at the beauty which remains hidden from me. I can admire the simple lines of a Greek vase, but its figured decorations are lost to me.

So on this, my second day of sight, I should try to probe into the soul of man through his art. The things I knew through touch I should now see. More splendid still, the whole magnificent world of painting would be opened to me, from the Italian Primitives, with their serene religious devotion, to the Moderns, with their feverish visions. I should look deep into the canvases of Raphael, Leonardo da Vinci, Titian, Rembrandt. I should want to feast my eyes upon the warm colors of Veronese, study the mysteries of El Greco, catch a new vision of Nature from Corot. Oh, there is so much rich meaning and beauty in the art of the ages for you who have eyes to see!

Upon my short visit to this temple of art I should not be able to review a fraction of that great world of art which is open to you. I should be able to get only a superficial impression. Artists tell me that for a deep and true appreciation of art one must educate the eye. One must learn through experience to weigh the merits of line, of composition, of form and color. If I had eyes, how happily would I embark upon so fascinating a study! Yet I am told that, to many of you who have eyes to see, the world of art is a dark night, unexplored and unilluminated.

It would be with extreme reluctance that I should leave the Metropolitan Museum, which contains the key to beauty—a beauty so neglected. Seeing persons, however, do not need a Metropolitan to find this key to beauty. The same key lies waiting in smaller museums, and in books on the shelves of even small libraries. But naturally, in my limited time of imaginary sight, I should choose the place where the key unlocks the greatest treasures in the shortest time.

The evening of my second day of sight I should spend at a theatre or at the movies. Even now I often attend theatrical performances of all sorts, but the action of the play must be spelled into my hand by a companion. But how I should like to see with my own eyes the fascinating figure of Hamlet, or the gusty Falstaff amid colorful Elizabethan trappings! How I should like to follow each movement of the graceful Hamlet, each strut of the hearty Falstaff! And since I could see only one play, I should be confronted by a many-horned dilemma, for there are scores of plays I should want to see. You who have eyes can see any you like. How many of you, I wonder, when you gaze at a play, a movie, or any spectacle, realize and give thanks for the miracle of sight which enables you to enjoy its color, grace, and movement?

I cannot enjoy the beauty of rhythmic movement except in a sphere restricted to the touch of my hands. I can vision only dimly the grace of a Pavlowa, although I know something of the delight of rhythm, for often I can sense the beat of music as it vibrates through the floor. I can well imagine that cadenced motion must be one of the most pleasing sights in the world. I have been able to gather something of this by tracing with my fingers the lines in sculptured marble; if this static grace can be so lovely, how much more acute must be the thrill of seeing grace in motion.

One of my dearest memories is of the time when Joseph Jefferson allowed me to touch his face and hands as he went through some of the gestures and speeches of his beloved Rip Van Winkle. I was able to catch thus a **meagre** glimpse of the world of drama, and I shall never forget the delight of that moment. But, oh, how much I must miss, and how much pleasure you seeing ones can derive from watching and hearing the interplay of speech and movement in the unfolding of a dramatic performance! If I could see only one play, I should know how to picture in my mind the action of a hundred plays which I have read or had transferred to me through the medium of the manual alphabet.

So, through the evening of my second imaginary day of sight, the great figures of dramatic literature would crowd sleep from my <u>eyes</u>.

How would you rearrange Helen's plan for the second day? Why?

IV

The following morning, I should again greet the dawn, anxious to discover new delights, for I am sure that, for those who have eyes which really see, the dawn of each day must be a perpetually new revelation of beauty.

This, according to the terms of my imagined miracle, is to be my third and last day of sight. I shall have no time to waste in regrets or longings; there is too much to see. The first day I devoted to my friends, animate and inanimate. The second revealed to me the history of man and nature. Today I shall spend in the workaday world of the present, amid the haunts of men going about the business of life. <u>And where can one</u>

What was Helen eager to see in New York? Why?

find so many activities and conditions of men as in New York? So the city becomes my destination.

I start from my home in the quiet little suburb of Forest Hills, Long Island. Here, surrounded by green lawns, trees, and flowers, are neat little houses, happy with the voices and movements of wives and children, havens of peaceful rest for men who toil in the city. I drive across the lacy structure of steel which spans the East River, and I get a new and startling vision of the power and ingenuity of the mind of man. Busy boats chug and **scurry** about the river—racy speed boats, **stolid**, snorting tugs. If I had long days of sight ahead, I should spend many of them watching the delightful activity upon the river.

I look ahead, and before me rise the fantastic towers of New York, a city that seems to have stepped from the pages of a fairy story. What an awe-inspiring sight, these glittering spires, these vast banks of stone and steel—structures such as the gods might build for themselves! This animated picture is a part of the lives of millions of people every day. How many, I wonder, give it so much as a second glance? Very few, I fear. Their eyes are blind to this magnificent sight because it is so familiar to them.

I hurry to the top of one of those gigantic structures, the Empire State Building, for there, a short time ago, I "saw" the city below through the eyes of my secretary. I am anxious to compare my fancy with reality. I am sure I should not be disappointed in the panorama spread out before me, for to me it would be a vision of another world.

Now I begin my rounds of the city. First, I stand at a busy corner, merely looking at people, trying by sight of them to understand something of their lives. I see smiles, and I am happy. I see serious determination, and I am proud. I see suffering, and I am compassionate.

I stroll down Fifth Avenue. I throw my eyes out of focus, so that I see no particular object but only a seething kaleidoscope of color. I am certain that the colors of women's dresses moving in a throng must be a gorgeous spectacle of which I should never tire. But perhaps if I had sight I should be like most other women—too interested in styles and the cut of individual dresses to give much attention to the splendor of color in the mass. And I am convinced, too, that I should become an **inveterate** window shopper, for it must be a delight to the eye to view the myriad articles of beauty on display.

From Fifth Avenue I make a tour of the city—to Park Avenue, to the slums, to factories, to parks where children play. I take a stay-at-home trip abroad by visiting the foreign quarters. Always my eyes are open wide to all the sights of both happiness and misery so that I may probe deep and add to my understanding of how people work and live. My heart is full of the images of people and things. My eye passes lightly over no single trifle; it strives to touch and hold closely each thing its gaze rests upon. Some sights are pleasant, filling the heart with happiness; but some are miserably pathetic. To these latter I do not shut my eyes, for they, too, are part of life. To close the eye on them is to close the heart and mind.

My third day of sight is drawing to an <u>end</u>. Perhaps there are many serious pursuits to which I should devote the few remaining hours, but I am afraid that on the evening of that last day I should again run away to the theatre, to a hilariously funny play, so that I might appreciate the overtones of comedy in the human spirit.

At midnight my temporary **respite** from blindness would cease, and permanent night would close in on me again. Naturally in those three short days I should not have seen all I wanted to see. Only when darkness had again descended upon me should I realize how much I had left unseen. But my mind would be so crowded with glorious memories that I should have little time for regrets. Thereafter the touch of every object would bring a glowing memory of how that object looked.

Perhaps this short outline of how I should spend three days of sight does not agree with the programme you would set for yourself if you knew that you were about to be stricken blind. I am, however, sure that if you actually faced that fate your eyes would open to things you had never seen before, storing up memories for the long night ahead. You would use your eyes as never before. Everything you saw would become dear to you. Your eyes would touch and embrace every object that came within your range of vision. Then, at last, you would really see, and a new world of beauty would open itself before you.

I who am blind can give one hint to those who see—one **admonition** to those who would make full use of the gift of sight: Use your eyes as if tomorrow you would be stricken blind. And the same method can be applied to the other senses. Hear the music of voices, the song of a bird, the mighty strains of an orchestra, as if you would be stricken deaf tomorrow. Touch each object you want to touch as if tomorrow your **tactile** sense would fail. Smell the perfume of flowers, taste with relish each **morsel**, as if tomorrow you could never smell and taste again. Make the most of every sense;

文化智慧阅读

Why did Helen say that sight must be the most delightful?

glory in all the facets of pleasure and beauty which the world reveals to you through the several means of contact which Nature provides. <u>But of all the senses, I am sure that sight must be the most delightful.</u>

I. Background Information

Helen Adams Keller (1880—1968) was an American author, disability rights advocate, political activist and lecturer. Born in West Tuscumbia, Alabama, she lost her sight and hearing after a bout of illness at the age of nineteen months. She then communicated primarily using home signs until the age of seven, when she met her first teacher and life-long companion Anne Sullivan, who taught her language, including reading and writing. She also learned how to speak and to understand other people's speech using the Tadoma method. After an education at both specialist and mainstream schools, she attended Radcliffe College of Harvard University and became the first deafblind person to earn a Bachelor of Arts degree. She worked for the American Foundation for the Blind (AFB) from 1924 until 1968, during which time she toured the United States and traveled to 35 countries around the globe advocating for those with vision loss.

II. Notes

1. **Epicurean:** *adj.* devoted to pleasure and enjoying yourself

2. **Chasten:** *v.* to make sb feel sorry for sth they have done

3. **Vista:** *n.* a range of things that might happen in the future

4. **Lethargy:** *n.* the state of not having any energy or enthusiasm for doing things

5. **Incredulous:** *adj.* not willing or unable to believe sth.; showing an inability to believe sth.

6. **Shaggy:** *adj.* long and untidy

7. **Convolutions:** *n.* a twist or curve, especially one of many

8. **Pageant:** *n.* ~ (of sth.) something that is considered as a series of interesting and different events

9. **Dormant:** *adj.* not active or growing now but able to become active or to grow in the future

10. **Sluggish:** *adj.* moving, reacting or working more slowly than normal and in a way that seems lazy

11. **Relapse:** *v.* ~ (into sth) to go back into a previous condition or into a worse state after making an improvement

12. **Countenance:** *n.* a person's face or expression

13. **Stalwart:** *adj.* loyal and able to be relied on, even in a difficult situation

14. **Panorama:** *n.* a view of a wide area of land

15. **Kaleidoscope:** *n.* a situation, pattern, etc. containing a lot of different parts that are always changing

16. **Carcass:** *n.* the dead body of an animal

17. **Mastodon:** *n.* a large extinct elephant-like proboscidean mammal of the genus Miocene, common in Pliocene times

18. **Parthenon:** *n.* the temple on the Acropolis in Athens built in the 5th-century B.C. and regarded as the finest example of the Greek Doric order

19. **Frieze:** *n.* a border that goes around the top of a room or building with pictures or carvings on it

20. **Gnarled:** *adj.* (of a person or part of the body) bent and twisted because of age or illness

21. **Trappings:** *n.* the possessions, clothes, etc. that are connected with a particular situation, job or social position

22. **Strut:** *n.* an act of walking in a proud and confident way

23. **Meagre:** *adj.* small in quantity and poor in quality

24. **Scurry:** *v.* to move there quickly and hurriedly

25. **Stolid:** *adj.* always remaining the same and not reacting or changing

26. **Inveterate:** *adj.* done or felt for a long time and unlikely to change

27. **Respite:** *v.* ~ (from sth) a short break or escape from sth difficult or unpleasant

28. **Admonition:** *n.* a warning to sb about their behavior

29. **Tactile:** *adj.* connected with the sense of touch; using your sense of touch

30. **Morsel:** *n.* a small amount or a piece of sth, especially food

31. **Silver birch:** a tree with smooth, very pale grey or white bark and thin branches, that grows in northern countries

III. Translation

Translate the following excerpts from Passage 2 into Chinese.

1. In stories, the doomed hero is usually saved at the last minute by some stroke of fortune, but almost always his sense of values is changed. He becomes more appreciative of the meaning of life and its permanent spiritual values. It has often been noted that those who live, or have lived, in the shadow of death bring a mellow sweetness to everything they do.

2. Now and then I have tested my seeing friends to discover what they see. Recently I was visited by a very good friend who had just returned from a long walk in the woods, and I asked her what she had observed. "Nothing in particular," she replied. I might have been incredulous had I not been accustomed to such responses, for long ago I became convinced that the seeing see little.

3. This day I should devote to a hasty glimpse of the world, past and present. I should want to see the pageant of man's progress, the kaleidoscope of the ages. How can so much be compressed into one day? Through the museums, of course.

4. Use your eyes as if tomorrow you would be stricken blind. And the same method can be applied to the other senses. Hear the music of voices, the song of a bird, the mighty strains of an orchestra, as if you would be stricken deaf tomorrow. Touch each object you want to touch as if tomorrow your tactile sense would fail. Smell the perfume of flowers, taste with relish each morsel, as if tomorrow you could never smell and taste again. Make the most of every sense; glory in all the facets of pleasure and beauty which the world reveals to you through the several means of contact which Nature provides. But of all the senses, I am sure that sight must be the most delightful.

IV. Questions for Further Thought

1. Comment on Helen Keller's contributions to advocating disability rights.

2. What do you know about the difficulties of a child with special needs? Discuss facilities needed in our society for special children.

3. Critics argue that life is a long journey full of ups and downs. Supposing you are in a difficult situation, what will be your coping strategies?

[Passage 3]

Sources of Soft Power[1]

The soft power of a country rests primarily on three resources: its culture (in places where it is attractive to others), its political values (when it lives up to them at home and abroad), and its foreign policies (when they are seen as legitimate and having moral authority.)

Let's start with culture. Culture is the set of values and practices that create meaning for a society. It has many manifestations. It is common to distinguish between high culture such as literature, art, and education, which appeals to elites, and popular culture, which focuses on mass entertainment.

When a country's culture includes universal values and its policies promote values and interests that others share, it increases the probability of obtaining its desired outcomes because of the relationships of attraction and duty that it creates. Narrow values and **parochial** cultures are less likely to produce soft power. The United States benefits from a universalistic culture. The German editor Josef Joffe once argued that America's soft power was even larger than its economic and military assets. "US culture, low-brow or high, radiates outward with an intensity last seen in the days of the Roman Empire—but with a novel twist. Rome's and Soviet Russia's cultural sway stopped exactly at their military borders. America's soft power, though, rules over an empire on which the sun never sets."

Some analysts treat soft power simply as popular cultural power. They make the mistake of equating soft power behavior with the cultural resources that sometimes help produce it. They confuse the cultural resources with the behavior of attraction.

> Comment on the statement.

> According to Nye, why cannot we simply treat soft power as popular culture power?

---

1 Joseph S. Nye, *Soft Power: the Means to Success in World Politics*, New York: Public Affairs, 2004, pp. 11—15.

文化智慧阅读

For example, the historian Niall Ferguson describes soft power as "nontraditional forces such as cultural and commercial goods" and then dismisses it on the grounds "that it's, well, soft." Of course, Coke and Big Macs do not necessarily attract people in the Islamic world to love the United States. The North Korean dictator Kim Jong Il is alleged to like pizza and American videos, but that does not affect his nuclear programs. Excellent wines and cheeses do not guarantee attraction to France, nor does the popularity of Pokémon games assure that Japan will get the policy outcomes it wishes.

How does this statement inspire cross-cultural communication?

This is not to deny that popular culture is often a resource that produces soft power, but as we saw earlier, the effectiveness of any power resource depends on the context. Tanks are not a great military power resource in swamps or jungles. Coal and steel are not major power resources if a country lacks an industrial base. **Serbs** eating at McDonald's supported Milosevic, and Rwandans committed **atrocities** while wearing T-shirts with American logos. American films that make the United States attractive in China or Latin America may have the opposite effect and actually reduce American soft power in Saudi Arabia or Pakistan. But in general, polls show that our popular culture has made the United States seem to others "exciting, exotic, rich, powerful, trend-setting—the cutting edge of modernity and innovation." And such images have appeal "in an age when people want to partake of the good life American-style, even if as political citizens, they are aware of the downside for ecology, community, and equality." For example, in explaining a new movement toward using lawsuits to assert rights in China, a young Chinese activist explained, "We've seen a lot of Hollywood movies—they feature weddings, funerals and going to court. So now we think it's only natural to go to court a few times in your life." If American objectives include the strengthening of the legal system in China, such films may be more effective than speeches by the American ambassador about the importance of the rule of law.

Discuss how Hollywood movies convey American culture to the world with examples.

The background attraction (and repulsion) of American popular culture in different regions and among different groups may make it easier or more difficult for American officials to promote their policies. In some cases, such as Iran, the same Hollywood images that repel the ruling **mullahs** may be attractive to the younger generation. In China, the attraction and rejection of American culture among different groups may cancel each other out.

What similarities do these contexts (commerce, personal contact, visit, and exchange) share?

Commerce is only one of the ways in which culture is transmitted. It also occurs through personal contacts, visits, and exchanges. The ideas and values that America exports in the minds of more than half a million foreign students who study every year in American universities and then return to their home countries, or in the minds of the Asian entrepreneurs who return home after succeeding in Silicon Valley, tend to reach elites with power. When the United States was trying to persuade President Musharraf of Pakistan to change his policies and be more supportive of American measures in Afghanistan, it probably helped that he could hear from a son working in the Boston area.

Government policies at home and abroad are another potential source of soft power. For example, in the 1950s racial segregation at home undercut American soft power in Africa, and today the practice of capital punishment and weak gun control laws undercut American soft power in Europe. Similarly, foreign policies strongly affect soft power. **Jimmy Carter's** human rights policies are a case in point, as were government efforts to promote democracy in the Reagan and Clinton administrations. In Argentina, American human rights policies that were rejected by the military government of the 1970s produced considerable soft power for the United States two decades later, when the Peronists who were earlier imprisoned subsequently came to power. Policies can have long-term as well as short-term effects that vary as the context changes. The popularity of the United States in Argentina in the early 1990s reflected Carter's policies of the 1970s, and it led the Argentine government to support American policies in the UN and in the Balkans. Nonetheless, American soft power eroded significantly after the context changed again later in the decade when the United States failed to rescue the Argentine economy from its collapse.

Government policies can reinforce or **squander** a country's soft power. Domestic or foreign policies that appear to be hypocritical, arrogant, indifferent to the opinion of others, or based on a narrow approach to national interests can undermine soft power. For example, in the steep decline in the attractiveness of the United States as measured by polls taken after the Iraq War in 2003, people with unfavorable views for the most part said they were reacting to the Bush administration and its policies rather than the United States generally. So far, they distinguish American people and culture from American policies. The publics in most nations continued to admire the United States for its technology, music, movies, and television. But large majorities in most countries said they disliked the growing influence of America in their country.

The 2003 Iraq War is not the first policy action that has made the United States unpopular. Three decades ago, many people around the world objected to America's war in Vietnam, and the standing of the United States reflected the unpopularity of that policy. When the policy changed and the memories of the war receded, the United States recovered much of its lost soft power. Whether the same thing will happen in the aftermath of the Iraq War will depend on the success of policies in Iraq, developments in the Israel-Palestine conflict, and many other factors.

The values a government champions in its behavior at home, in international institutions (working with others), and in foreign policy (promoting peace and human rights) strongly affect the preferences of others. Governments can attract or repel others by the influence of their example. But soft power does not belong to the government in the same degree that hard power does. Some hard-power assets such as armed forces are strictly governmental; others are inherently national, such as oil and mineral reserves, and many can be transferred to collective control, such as the civilian air fleet that can be mobilized in an emergency. In contrast, many soft-power resources are separate from the American government and are only partly responsive to its purposes. In the Vietnam era, for example, American popular culture often worked at cross-purposes to official government policy. Today, Hollywood movies that show **scantily clad** women with **libertine** attitudes or fundamentalist Christian groups that **castigate** Islam as an evil religion are both (properly) outside the control of government in a liberal society, but they undercut government efforts to improve relations with Islamic nations.

I. Background Information

Joseph S. Nye JR. (born January 19, 1937), former dean of the Kennedy School of Government at Harvard University, was Chairman of the National Intelligence Council and an Assistant Secretary of Defense in the Clinton administration. He is the author of several works of nonfiction, including *The Paradox of American Power and Bound to Lead* as well as one novel, *The Power Game*. His most recent books include *The Power to Lead*; *The Future of Power*; *Presidential Leadership and the Creation of the American Era*; and *Is the American Century Over*. He is a fellow of the American Academy of Arts and Sciences, the British Academy, and the American Academy of

Diplomacy. In a recent survey of international relations scholars, he was ranked as the most influential scholar on American foreign policy, and in 2011, *Foreign Policy* named him one of the top 100 Global Thinkers.

II. Notes

1. **Parochial:** *adj.* only concerned with small issues that happen in your local area and not interested in more important things

2. **Serb:** *n.* a native or inhabitant of Serbia, also Serbian

3. **Atrocity:** *n.* a cruel and violent act, especially in a war

4. **Mullah:** *n.* a Muslim teacher of religion and holy law

5. **Squander:** *v.* ~ sth (on sb./sth.) to waste money, time, etc.

6. **Scantily clad:** wearing clothes that do not cover much of your body

7. **Libertine:** *n.* a person, usually a man, who leads an immoral life and is interested in pleasure, especially sexual pleasure

8. **Castigate:** *v.* to criticize sb/sth severely

9. **Jimmy Carter:** 39th President of the United States (1924—   ).

III. Writing

Read the following opinions on soft power, and write an approximately 200-word summary of the main critiques of Nye's three sources.

Soft Power: Power of Attraction or Confusion?[1]

In ancient China, soft power was perceived stronger and more powerful than hard power, as suggested by proverbial wisdoms: to use soft and gentle means to overcome the hard and strong (以柔克刚); and drips of water can penetrate a stone (滴水穿石). Sun Tze (544—496BC), a military strategist of 2500 years ago, advocates winning a battle without a fight. The Chinese philosopher, Confucius (551—479BC) believes that the ruler should win the allegiance of people with virtue (soft power) not by force (hard power). Similarly, Mencius (372—289BC) advocates rule in kingly way (王道) rather than the tyrant way (霸道). The kingly way refers to governing by moral example whereas the tyrant way involves governing by brutal force. Lao Tze, a contemporary

---

1 Ying Fan, Soft power: Power of attraction or confusion?. *Place Branding and Public Diplomacy*, 4(2), 2008, pp. 147—158.

of Confucius, says in *Tao Te Ching*, "I know the benefit of doing nothing (无为); the softest can win the hardest. Invisible force can pass through the intangible."

Coupled with the problems in definition, it is equally confusing on what exactly constitutes soft power. Nye identifies three sources as: American culture, international laws and institutions, and American multinational corporations. But the list has changed to culture, political values and foreign policy: "the attractiveness of its culture, the appeal of its domestic political and social values, and the style and substance of its foreign policies". Nye did not offer any explanation why such changes were made. A close examination of these three key components of soft power shows some confusion. Firstly, policy, by definition, is the course or general plan of action adopted by state. A country's foreign policy itself is not a separate form of soft power but the mere manifestation of its hard power (political power in the case of military intervention; economic power in the case of aid or sanction). No matter how attractive the style of a country's foreign policies, it cannot be separated from its substance which is an integral part of hard power. The US policies of the war on terror are good examples. Secondly, core values and domestic institutions are an essential part of any society's culture, not a separate source. Thus, with only one component left, this makes the concept simpler and much clearer: soft power is cultural power.

Devoting a large proportion of his new book to the description of the sources of soft power in the US as well as in other countries, Nye lists a wide range of various examples as the proxy measures of soft power:

foreign immigrants	Nobel prize winners
asylum applications	life expectancy
international students	overseas aids
tourists	number of Internet hosts
book sales and music sales popular sports	spending on public diplomacy

With more examples added Nye seems to miss the point as to what soft power exactly is as the concept has been so stretched that the term comes to mean almost everything and therefore almost nothing. In all these examples given by Nye resources, sources (cause) and impact (effect) are mixed up. It is important to note sources and resources are not power per se but potential for power. The owners of these resources have to convert them into power. Four key factors must be in place for power conversion: capital, political structure, social capital and social structure.

A key question still remains unanswered: whether the sources of soft power are universal or vary from one culture to another? Both China and India have rich cultural resources, but do they have the same type of soft power? If cultural power is soft power, why does a country like Egypt with a history of seven thousand years seem weaker compared with the US, founded only two hundred years ago? Clearly, culture per se is not soft power but sources of potential soft power. Whether a cultural asset can be converted into soft power depends on other factors.

IV. Questions for Further Thought

1. Comment on the source of soft power, respectively from the perspectives of China and the US.

2. Discern the relations between "soft power" and "hard power" of a country.

[Passage 4]

Speech at University of Warwick[1]

Two years ago, I wrote a book entitled *Missing the Tide: Global Governments in Retreat*. David Ignatius, a well-known journalist with *the Washington Post* wrote a **blurb** for the cover which began "Read it and weep". Why did he write that? I will tell you. Had I written that book in the mid-1990s when you students were children and some perhaps not yet born, part of the narrative of the book which I touch upon today would have been quite different. I explain why in a moment.

It would have spoken to a rapidly changing world holding areas of great promise for your generation in almost every area of human endeavor. Over the years I have listened to multiple speeches telling graduating students and others of what a wondrous, exciting peaceful and prosperous world they look forward to. I have been **guilty** to some such speeches myself. That is not my message today.

My friends John and Marcy McCall MacBain, created the McCall McBain Foundation (MMF) (which I chaired for many years,) and being extraordinary **philanthropists**, they have recently committed over 100 million dollars to the Rhodes Trust and 200 million for McCall MacBain graduate scholarships at McGill University. The scholarships focus on leadership potential which I will return to in conclusion. John is also the founder and first chair of the European Climate Foundation (ECF) said to me on my 80th birthday "... Donald... as things are going perhaps it is not bad to be in your 80s." I hope not, but I do worry about the future more than I ever have as an adult.

The title *Missing the Tide*, which I took from your local **Bard**, would have been quite different in 1995. It comes from Shakespeare's *Julius Caesar* in which as many of you here will recall Brutus says:

---

1 Donald Johnston, *Speech at University of Warwick*, January 31, 2020.

> "There is a tide in the affairs of men,
>
> Which, taken at the flood, leads on to fortune;
>
> Omitted, all the voyage of their life
>
> Is bound in shallows and in miseries.
>
> On such a full sea are we now afloat,
>
> And we must take the current when it serves,
>
> Or lose our ventures."
>
> (William Shakespeare, *Julius Caesar*, Act 4, scene 3, pp. 218—224)

When I arrived at the OECD as Secretary General in 1996, we seemed to be at the flood...On such a full sea we were then afloat and ready to take that current. Sadly, my generation did not take the current and it now falls to your generation to attempt to recover <u>lost opportunities</u>, if it is not too late.

Interpret the "lost opportunities".

I elaborate. There were a number of major challenges 25 years ago, but it seemed that leaders could turn them into wonderful opportunities for rapid and sustainable economic and social progress. The exciting prospect of global free trade and investment under the newly established World Trade Organization (WTO) was seen as bringing economic growth and rising prosperity everywhere, but especially to the developing world. <u>Trade not aid became the new **mantra**.</u>

Paraphrase the sentence.

Those challenges and opportunities included geopolitical restructuring in the wake of the fall of the Berlin Wall and the evolution of the European Union; the expansion of the proven Marshall Plan formula to other regions fractured by division and conflict; a long-overdue international commitment to protecting the biosphere and its natural capital; and improvements to the stunning success of healthy capitalism through good governance and appropriate regulatory frameworks across the globe, accompanied by the gradual spread of democracy and transparent, honest government for the benefit of billions of people.

Yes, we saw the biosphere deteriorating at a rapid pace, especially through global warming and climate change, but we knew how to fix it and repeatedly said so. In July 1997 we faced the Asian financial crisis and with the increasing global interdependence of financial markets, we feared a global crisis through contagion. But the fear was short lived, and it was thought that the successful containment and resolution of that crisis

augured well for the future.

We were witnessing improved and massive transportation networks complemented by the awesome power of information and communication technologies, together making Marshall McLuhan's global village concept a reality. We witnessed the creation of the UN Millennium Development Goals, which, when achieved by 2015, together with liberalized trade and investment would lift billions out of poverty and bring them closer to the standards of living of developed countries.

We also saw the cancer of corruption continuing to limit the growth of emerging market economies and diverting precious foreign aid into the pockets of dishonest public officials in both the developing and developed world. But we were well on our way to securing an international agreement through a binding convention (often referred to as the OECD Anti-Bribery Convention) to cure that disease.

With the end of the Cold War, we foresaw new and promising relations with Russia and China, and the Damocles Sword of massive international armed conflict seemed destined for the dustbin of history. Hostilities in the Balkans had ceased with the Dayton Accords, and the IRA had laid down its weapons in Northern Ireland. Terrorism seemed confined to isolated incidents from traditional sources.

Perhaps even more importantly, we saw what we thought was the emergence of new democratic governments in Russia itself, as well in other former members of the Soviet Union and in countries of Europe that had lived under the Soviet **yoke** since the end of the Second World War. The democratic revolution seemed planet-wide with countries in South America, Asia, and Africa providing many good examples.

Sadly, it was to be short lived. How, in less than two decades, did our story turn from one of bright hope to one of pessimism and despair?

That is the question I put to you today because you represent the global leadership of tomorrow. My generation has failed and failed badly. Think of the following issues measured against the prevailing optimism of that period.

The environment continues to deteriorate. The outcome of the December 2015 Paris conference, while received with enthusiasm in many quarters, did not produce enforceable solutions, only aspirational hopes that had virtually no possibility of arresting greenhouse gas emissions and then putting them into decline. And we are now picking through the **debris** of COP 25 at Madrid which can only be considered a dismal failure with key issues being deferred to the next COP gathering in 2020.

Indeed only a few of the opportunities outlined above have been realized and, in some cases, they have been completely lost. Much of the wonderful story we told ourselves only 25 years ago is now in a state of **shambolic** self-destruction.

Why have we failed, and failed so badly? Of the opportunities I described above, the mechanisms which have facilitated globalization, namely transportation and the extraordinary transformational power of information and communication technology (ICT) have been real game changers. Unfortunately, ICT has also been exploited to facilitate the undermining of values liberal democracies cherish, even to the point of interfering in democratic electoral processes.

How did ICT change the game?

When we compare human and societal evolution to a relay race one generation must pass the baton on to the next. In a small way that is what I am saying to you today.

I am persuaded that the latter may be our fate in the absence of conviction, hard work and sacrifice for a better world. What should you do? What can you do?

I have described the state of the world today as analogous to my fireplace at my country home. It is usually fully loaded with tinder, kindling and dry wood. All it awaits is a match. Unfortunately, there are many matches out there waiting to be lit and spread their deadly destruction to regions, if not the planet as a whole.

What does a "match" represent?

Finally, a comment on the two most dangerous threats of those cited above.

The first is to the market economies which far sighted academics, politicians, statesmen and women have fought for and built over generations. The second dangerous issue, of the many described above, is the challenge of obvious and perhaps irreversible climate change. It is the most important global threat today, which like a number of others, demands concerted action and cooperation amongst approximately 200 countries. How will the world act to counter global warming and climate change which it has been unable to do for almost 5 decades since 1972? In assessing the way ahead, I often refer to the wisdom of Maynard Keynes who advocated "Examine the present in light of the past for the purposes of the future". Let us indulge in that exercise for a moment.

What might be the challenges of cooperating with 200 countries?

As early as 1896, a Swedish scientist, Svante Arrhenius (Nobel Prize for Chemistry, 1903) identified the warming effects of the CO_2 emitted by burning coal. Alarm bells rang at the Stockholm UN environmental conference in 1972. Concern was expressed about greenhouse gas emissions (GHGs), but their measurement and impact were

Why was the account of issues concerning climate change traced back to the earliest literature?

not broadly understood until the UN creation of the International Panel on Climate Change (IPCC) in 1988. The alarm bells rang louder after the UN's Brundtland report ("Our Common Future") was released in 1987, and especially after the UN's Earth Summit in Rio in 1992, where the United Nations Framework Convention on Climate Change (UNFCC) was adopted by 197 countries.

The UN General Assembly in Special Session met in New York in 1997, where we listened to statements from world leaders and others (including me) about the importance of reducing emissions. That meeting was followed by the UN Kyoto conference, at which the Kyoto Protocol was adopted. It was agreed that Annex 1 countries (37 developed countries) would reduce their emissions during two commitment periods by an average of 5.2% below their respective 1990 levels. Canada's commitment was a 6% decrease from 1990 levels by 2012. By 2008 Canada's emissions had increased by 24.1% over 1990 levels, and Canada withdrew from the protocol.

<u>So, the past should tell us that Madrid and COP 25 are examples of the present simply continuing failed international public policy and coordination from 1972!</u>

I ask you, is it not time for your generation to adopt new approaches if we are to succeed in saving the planet as we know it?

Your generation must step up to very serious and difficult challenges. I hope that many of you here will accept this challenge. Doing so does not necessarily mean a lifetime in public service, but it means connecting you with the challenges, opportunities, and satisfaction of changing our societies for the better.

I. Background Information

Donald Johnston, (1936—2022) was a Canadian economist, lawyer and politician who was Secretary-General of the Organization for Economic Cooperation and Development (OECD) from 1996 to 2006. While at the helm of the OECD, he helped to establish the Principles of Corporate Governance, OECD recommendations for good practice in corporate behavior, that have been adopted as a benchmark around the world. Johnston held key cabinet positions under two prime ministers of Canada. He was president of the Treasury Board and later minister of state for economic development under Pierre-Elliot Trudeau and briefly served as justice minister in John Turner's short-lived government.

II. Notes

1. **Blurb:** *n.* a short description of a book, a new product, etc., written by the people who have produced it, that is intended to attract people's interests

2. **Philanthropist:** *n.* a rich person who helps the poor and those in need, especially by giving money

3. **Bard:** *n.* a person who writes poems, here refers to Shakespeare

4. **Mantra:** *n.* a statement or slogan repeated frequently

5. **Yoke:** *v.* to bring two people, countries, ideas, etc. together so that they are forced into a close relationship

6. **Debris:** *n.* pieces from something that has been destroyed

7. **Shambolic:** *adj.* chaotic or disorganized

8. **Augur well:** to portend a good outcome

III. Discussion

Comment briefly on the following opinions and compare the primary purpose of education in China and Western countries.

1. In foreign countries, civil servants work under ordinary contracts; but in China, historically the purpose of education has been described as "to cultivate oneself in order to rule". (Source: *Civil Servant: A Popular Career Choice for Young Chinese*)

2. We have a good, flexible education system in this country, particularly in higher education. You can take a physics degree, but that doesn't mean you have to be a physicist. And while effective careers advice is a good idea, do we really want 18 year-olds to be set on a firm career path already? I'm not sure that's a good idea in a rapidly-changing jobs market, when they'll still be working 50 years from now. We need them to be flexible and able to turn their hand to a range of jobs. (Source: *Reality Check: Are Young People's Career Aspirations Unrealistic?*)

IV. Questions for Further Thought

1. What factors should students consider when looking for a job?
2. What challenges will the rapidly-changing jobs market bring to university students?
3. What suggestions will you give to your university to help meet the demand of the changing world?

[Mini-task for Chapter 2]

Discussion

Watch the movie *Steve Jobs* (2015) and discuss the question, "which factor should be given priority in choosing a job, money-oriented or ideal-oriented?"

[Further Reading]

1. Paul D. Tieger, Barbara Barron-Tiege, *Do What You Are*, New York: Little, Brown and Company, 2007.

2. Richard N. Bolles, *What Color is Your Parachute*? New York: Random House, 2010.

3. (美)约瑟夫·奈著，吴晓辉，钱程译，软力量：世界政坛成功之道，北京：东方出版社，2005.

4. 钱乘旦主编，英国社会转型研究丛书，南京：南京师范大学出版社，2021.

3 Love

Passage 1 Annabel Lee / 78
Passage 2 *Jane Eyre*: Chapter 23   / 82
Passage 3 Audrey Hepburn's Statement to Members of the United Nations Staff   / 92
Passage 4 Of Love / 100

3　Love

[本章导读]

"爱"（Love）是温暖的，是人们的共同追求。在全球化时代，"爱"变得更为重要，它不仅关乎个人幸福，更深刻影响着世界的和平与发展。

那么，如何理解"爱"？怎样学会"去爱"？为此，本章从不同文体选择了四篇文章。第一篇是诗歌体裁，选取的是美国著名诗人埃德加·爱伦坡（Allan Edgar Poe）的诗歌《安娜贝尔·李》（"Annabel Lee"），以帮助读者体会爱情的隽永。第二篇选自经典小说《简·爱》（Jane Eyre），帮助读者思考真爱赖以维系的前提。如果说爱情需要个体的自尊以及彼此的尊重，那么推演至国与国或地区与地区之间的友爱又需要怎样的基础？第三篇是奥黛丽·赫本（Audrey Hepburn）作为联合国儿童基金会亲善大使，应"百分之一发展基金"（1 Percent for Development Fund）邀请，在日内瓦（Geneva）会议上的一次演讲。她呼吁全世界要团结起来，以大爱的精神关心爱护儿童，尤其是第三世界国家的孩子们。第四篇是散文体裁，选取的是英国著名哲学家和文学家弗朗西斯·培根（Francis Bacon）的《论爱》（"Of Love"），读者可以体会虽然世事变迁，但"爱"的真谛是否仍然能跨越时空乃至文化的差异而得以永存？

综上所述，"爱"既是个体的人生课题，也是国家和民族发展面临的要务。学习理解"爱"、尊重"爱"并收获"爱"虽不容易，但值得努力。正如法国著名哲学家德尼·狄德罗（Denis Diderot）所指出的，"只有情感，而且只有伟大的情感，才能使灵魂达到伟大的成就"（Only passions, and great passions, can raise the soul to great things.）。

[Passage 1]

Annabel Lee[1]

It was many and many a year ago,
In a kingdom by the sea,
That a maiden there lived whom you may know
By the name of ANNABEL LEE;
And this maiden she lived with no other thought
Than to love and be loved by me.

She was a child and I was a child,
In this kingdom by the sea;
But we loved with a love that was more than love
I and my Annabel Lee;
With a love that the winged **seraphs** of heaven
Coveted her and me.

And this was the reason that, long ago,
In this kingdom by the sea;
A wind blew out of a cloud by night
Chilling my Annabel Lee;
So that her highborn kinsman came
And **bore** her **away** from me,
To shut her up in a **sepulcher**

Illustrate the rhyme of this poem.

Why did the poet emphasize where and when he met his Annabel Lee?

Paraphrase the sentence.

---

[1] Poe, Edgar Allan, *Annabel Lee* 1853, Poetry Foundation, https://www.poetryfoundation.org/poems/44885/annabel-lee accessed February 20, 2017.

In this kingdom by the sea.

The angels, not half so happy in the heaven,
Went envying her and me
Yes! That was the reason (as all men know, in this kingdom by the sea)
That the wind came out of the cloud,
Chilling and killing my Annabel Lee.

But our love it was stronger by far than the love
Of those who were older than we
Of many far wiser than we
And neither the angels in heaven above,
Nor the demons down under the sea,
Can ever **dissever** my soul from the soul
Of the beautiful Annabel Lee.

For the moon never **beams** without bringing me dreams
Of the beautiful Annabel Lee;
And the stars never rise but I see the bright eyes
Of the beautiful Annabel Lee;
And so, all the night-tide, I lie down by the side
Of my darling, my darling, my life and my bride,
In the sepulcher there by the sea,
In her tomb by the side of the sea.

3 Love

Passage 1

Why did the poet emphasize that again in this part?

Did Annabel Lee die of chilly weather?

Why was their love stronger?

Paraphrase the sentence.

Discern the relationships among "darling" "life" and "bride" with examples.

I. Background Information

Edgar Allan Poe (1809—1849) was an American poet, critic and father of detective stories. Born in Boston in 1809, Poe became orphaned after his father abandoned the family in 1810 and his mother died in 1811. Thus, he became the foster child (he was never adopted) of childless John and Frances Valentine Allan (hence the middle name Allan). Poe went to University of Virginia at 17 and the West Point later. At the age of 27, Poe married Clemm Poe, who was believed to be his cousin and only 13 then. His famous works includes: "Raven"; *The Death of the House of Usher*; "To Helen" etc.

Published in 1853, "Annabel Lee" shows how deep the narrator loves his bride, who passed away and was buried near the sea. Edgar Poe's wife Virginia Eliza Clemm Poe is commonly believed to be the inspiration for Annabel Lee by the critics. She died of the tuberculosis. The narrator recalled his bride and the love between them when they were young in a kingdom by the sea. Their love was so strong and ideal that even the angels envied this and thus killed the narrator's wife. However, even this could not separate the narrator from his bride, for their souls are still entwined.

II. Notes

1. **Seraphs:** *n.* an angel of the first order; usually portrayed as the winged head of a child

2. **Sepulcher:** *n.* a small room or building in which the bodies of dead people were put

3. **Dissever:** *v.* to separate

4. **Beams:** *v.* to emit light, to be bright

5. **Bear away:** take away

III. Translation

Translate the lyric of the traditional song "Greensleeves" into Chinese.

Greensleeves[1]

Alas, my love, you do me wrong

To cast me off discourteously,

And I have loved you so long,

Delighting in your company.

Greensleeves was all my joy,

Greensleeves was my delight,

Greensleeves was my heart of gold,

And who but my lady Greensleeves?

---

1 England, *The Songs of England and Scotland*, London: James Cochrane and Co, 1835, p.26. Google book, https://books.google.com.sg/books?id=pYB0Lwhd8BcC&printsec=frontcover&hl=zh-CN#v=onepage&q&f=false, accessed November 1, 2021.

3 Love

Passage 1

I have been ready at your hand
to grant whatever you would crave,
I have both waged life and land,
Your love and goodwill for to have.

I bought thee petticoats of the best,
the cloth so fine as it might be,
I gave thee jewels for thy chest,
And all this cost I spent on thee.

Well I will pray to God on high
that thou my constancy may'st see,
For I am still thy lover true,
Come once again and love me.

IV. Questions for Further Thought

1. Why did the poet think that even death cannot end his love for Annabel Lee?

2. Compare the emotions expressed in this poem with that in Tang Dynasty poet Bai Juyi's "The Everlasting Regret"(长恨歌).

[Passage 2]

Jane Eyre: Chapter 23[1]

A great moth goes humming by me; it alights on a plant at Mr. Rochester's foot: he sees it, and bends to examine it.

"Now, he has his back towards me" thought I, "and he is occupied too; perhaps, if I walk softly, I can slip away unnoticed."

I strode on an edging of **turf** that the crackle of the pebbly gravel might not betray me: he was standing among the beds at a yard or two distant from where I had to pass; the moth apparently engaged him. "I shall get by very well," I meditated. As I crossed his shadow, thrown long over the garden by the moon, not yet risen high, he said quietly, without turning—

"Jane, come and look at this fellow."

I had made no noise: he had not eyes behind—could his shadow feel?

I started at first, and then I approached him.

"Look at his wings," said he, "he reminds me rather of a West Indian insect; one does not often see so large and gay a night-rover in England; there! He is flown."

The moth roamed away. I was sheepishly retreating also; but Mr. Rochester followed me, and when we reached the wicket, he said— "Turn back: on so lovely a night it is a shame to sit in the house; and surely no one can wish to go to bed while sunset is thus at meeting with moonrise."

It is one of my faults, that though my tongue is sometimes prompt enough at an answer, there are times when it sadly fails me in framing an excuse; and always the lapse occurs at some crisis, when a **facile** word or plausible pretext is specially wanted

---

1 Brontë, Charlotte, *Jane Eyre*, San Diego: ICON Classics, 2005, pp. 314—323.

> **3** Love
>
> Passage 2

to get me out of painful embarrassment. I did not like to walk at this hour alone with Mr. Rochester in the shadowy orchard; but I could not find a reason to allege for leaving him. I followed with lagging step, and thoughts busily bent on discovering a means of extrication; but he himself looked so composed and so grave also, I became ashamed of feeling any confusion: the evil—if evil existent or prospective there was—seemed to lie with me only; his mind was unconscious and quiet.

"Jane," he recommenced, as we entered the laurel walk, and slowly strayed down in the direction of the sunk fence and the horse-chestnut, "Thornfield is a pleasant place in summer, is it not?"

"Yes, sir."

"You must have become in some degree attached to the house,—you, who have an eye for natural beauties, and a good deal of the organ of Adhesiveness?" *Paraphrase the sentence.*

"I am attached to it, indeed"

"And though I don't comprehend how it is, I perceive you have acquired a degree of regard for that foolish little child **Adele**, too; and even for simple dame **Fairfax**?" *Is Mr. Rochester discontent with Jane's opinion of Adele and Fairfax?*

"Yes, sir; in different ways, I have an affection for both."

"And would be sorry to part with them?"

"Yes."

"Pity!" he said, and sighed and paused. "It is always the way of events in this life," he continued presently: "no sooner have you got settled in a pleasant resting-place, than a voice calls out to you to rise and move on, for the hour of repose is expired."

"Must I move on, sir?" I asked. "Must I leave Thornfield?"

"I believe you must, Jane. I am sorry, Janet, but I believe indeed you must."

This was a blow: but I did not let it **prostrate** me. *Explain Jane's response.*

"Well, sir, I shall be ready when the order to march comes."

"It is come now—I must give it to-night."

"Then you are going to be married, sir?"

"Ex-act-ly—pre-cise-ly: with your usual acuteness, you have hit the nail straight on the head."

"Soon, sir?"

"Very soon, my—that is, Miss Eyre: and you'll remember, Jane, the first time I, or Rumour, plainly intimated to you that it was my intention to put my old bachelor's

文化智慧阅读

Paraphrase the sentence.

neck into the sacred noose, to enter into the holy estate of matrimony—to take Miss **Ingram** to my bosom, in short (she's an extensive armful: but that's not to the point—one can't have too much of such a very excellent thing as my beautiful **Blanche**): well, as I was saying—listen to me, Jane! You're not turning your head to look after more moths, are you? That was only a lady-clock, child, 'flying away home.' I wish to remind you that it was you who first said to me, with that discretion I respect in you—with that foresight, prudence, and humility which befit your responsible and dependent position—that in case I married Miss Ingram, both you and little Adele had better trot forthwith. I pass over the sort of slur conveyed in this suggestion on the character of my beloved; indeed, when you are far away, Janet, I'll try to forget it: I shall notice only its wisdom; which is such that I have made it my law of action. Adele must go to school; and you, Miss Eyre, must get a new situation."

What does Thornfield mean for Jane?

"Yes, sir, I will advertise immediately: and meantime, I suppose—" I was going to say, "I suppose I may stay here, till I find another shelter to betake myself to": but I stopped, feeling it would not do to risk a long sentence, for my voice was not quite under command.

"In about a month I hope to be a bridegroom," continued Mr. Rochester; "and in the interim, I shall myself look out for employment and an **asylum** for you."

"Thank you, sir; I am sorry to give—"

"Oh, no need to apologize! I consider that when a dependent does her duty as well as you have done yours, she has a sort of claim upon her employer for any little assistance he can conveniently render her; indeed I have already, through my future mother-in-law, heard of a place that I think will suit: it is to undertake the education of the five daughters of Mrs. Dionysius O'Gall of Bitternutt Lodge, Connaught, Ireland. You'll like Ireland, I think: they're such warmhearted people there, they say."

What can be inferred from "such warmhearted people"?

"It is a long way off, sir."

"No matter—a girl of your sense will not object to the voyage or the distance."

"Not the voyage, but the distance: and then the sea is a barrier—"

"From what, Jane?"

"From England and from Thornfield: and—"

"Well?"

Why does Jane feel sad?

"From you, sir." I said this almost involuntarily, and, with as little **sanction** of free will, my tears gushed out. I did not cry so as to be heard, however; I avoided sobbing. The thought of Mrs. O'Gall and Bitternutt Lodge struck cold to my heart; and colder the thought of all the brine and foam, destined, as it seemed, to rush between me and the master at whose side I now walked, and coldest the remembrance of the wider ocean—wealth, caste, custom intervened between me and what I naturally and inevitably loved.

"It is a long way," I again said.

"It is, to be sure; and when you get to Bitternutt Lodge, Connaught, Ireland, I shall never see you again, Jane: that's morally certain. I never go over to Ireland, not having myself much of a fancy for the country. We have been good friends, Jane; have we not?"

"Yes, sir."

"And when friends are on the eve of separation, they like to spend the little time that remains to them close to each other.

Come! we'll talk over the voyage and the parting quietly half an hour or so, while the stars enter into their shining life up in heaven yonder: here is the chestnut tree: here is the bench at its old roots.

Come, we will sit there in peace to-night, though we should never more be destined to sit there together." He seated me and himself.

"It is a long way to Ireland, Janet, and I am sorry to send my little friend on such weary travels: but if I can't do better, how is it to be helped? Are you anything akin to me, do you think, Jane?"

I could risk no sort of answer by this time: my heart was still.

"Because", he said, "I sometimes have a queer feeling with regard to you—especially when you are near me, as now: it is as if I had a string somewhere under my left ribs, tightly and inextricably knotted to a similar string situated in the corresponding quarter of your little frame. And if that **boisterous** Channel and two hundred miles or so of land come broad between us, I am afraid that cord of communion will be snapt; and then I've a nervous notion I should take to bleeding inwardly. As for you,—you'd forget me."

"That I never should, sir: you know—" Impossible to proceed.

"Jane, do you hear that nightingale singing in the wood? Listen!"

In listening, I sobbed convulsively; for I could repress what I endured no longer; I was

文化智慧阅读

Why does Jane have such a wish?

obliged to yield, and I was shaken from head to foot with acute distress. When I did speak, it was only to express an impetuous wish that I had never been born, or never come to Thornfield.

"Because you are sorry to leave it?"

The vehemence of emotion, stirred by grief and love within me, was claiming mastery, and struggling for full sway, and asserting a right to predominate, to overcome, to live, rise, and reign at last: yes, —and to speak.

Why does Jane love Thornfield?

"I grieve to leave Thornfield: I love Thornfield:—I love it, because I have lived in it a full and delightful life, —momentarily at least. I have not been trampled on. I have not been petrified. I have not been buried with inferior minds, and excluded from every glimpse of communion with what is bright and energetic and high. I have talked, face to face, with what I reverence, with what I delight in, —with an original, a vigorous, an expanded mind. I have known you, Mr. Rochester; and it strikes me with terror and anguish to feel I absolutely must be torn from you for ever. I see the necessity of departure; and it is like looking on the necessity of death."

"Where do you see the necessity?" he asked suddenly.

"Where? You, sir, have placed it before me."

"In what shape?"

Why does Jane emphasize "noble" and "beautiful" in speaking of Miss Ingram?

"In the shape of Miss Ingram; a noble and beautiful woman, —your bride."

"My bride! What bride? I have no bride!"

"But you will have."

"Yes; —I will!—I will!" He set his teeth.

"Then I must go: —you have said it yourself."

"No: you must stay! I swear it—and the oath shall be kept."

Comment on Jane's view of love.

"I tell you I must go!" I retorted, roused to something like passion. "Do you think I can stay to become nothing to you? Do you think I am an automaton? —a machine without feelings? and can bear to have my morsel of bread snatched from my lips, and my drop of living water dashed from my cup? Do you think, because I am poor, obscure, plain, and little, I am soulless and heartless? You think wrong! — I have as much soul as you, —and full as much heart! And if God had gifted me with some beauty and much wealth, I should have made it as hard for you to leave me, as it is now for me to leave you. I am not talking to you now through the medium of custom, conventionalities, nor

3 Love

Passage 2

even of mortal flesh; —it is my spirit that addresses your spirit; just as if both had passed through the grave, and we stood at God's feet, equal, —as we are!"

"As we are!" repeated Mr. Rochester— "so," he added, enclosing me in his arms, gathering me to his breast, pressing his lips on my lips:

"So, Jane!"

"Yes, so, sir," I rejoined: "and yet not so; for you are a married man—or as good as a married man, and wed to one inferior to you—to one with whom you have no sympathy—whom I do not believe you truly love; for I have seen and heard you sneer at her. I would scorn such a union: therefore I am better than you—let me go!"

Why does Jane wish to leave?

"Where, Jane? To Ireland?"

"Yes—to Ireland. I have spoken my mind, and can go anywhere now."

"Jane, be still; don't struggle so, like a wild frantic bird that is rending its own plumage in its desperation."

"I am no bird; and no net ensnares me; I am a free human being with an independent will, which I now exert to leave you."

What is Jane's understanding of being independent?

Another effort set me at liberty, and I stood erect before him.

"And your will shall decide your destiny," he said: "I offer you my hand, my heart, and a share of all my possessions."

"You play a farce, which I merely laugh at."

"I ask you to pass through life at my side—to be my second self, and best earthly companion."

How does Mr. Rochester interpret marriage?

"For that fate you have already made your choice, and must abide by it."

"Jane, be still a few moments: you are over-excited: I will be still too."

A waft of wind came sweeping down the laurel-walk and trembled through the boughs of the chestnut: it wandered away—away—to an indefinite distance—it died. The nightingale's song was then the only voice of the hour: in listening to it, I again wept. Mr. Rochester sat quiet, looking at me gently and seriously. Some time passed before he spoke; he at last said—

"Come to my side, Jane, and let us explain and understand one another."

"I will never again come to your side: I am torn away now, and cannot return."

"But, Jane, I summon you as my wife: it is you only I intend to marry."

I was silent: I thought he mocked me.

> 文化智慧阅读

"Come, Jane—come hither."

"Your bride stands between us."

He rose, and with a stride reached me.

"My bride is here," he said, again drawing me to him, "<u>because my equal is here, and my likeness. Jane</u>, will you marry me?"

Paraphrase the sentence.

Still I did not answer, and still I writhed myself from his grasp: for I was still incredulous.

"Do you doubt me, Jane?"

"Entirely."

"You have no faith in me?"

"Not a whit."

"Am I a liar in your eyes?" he asked passionately. "Little sceptic, you shall be convinced. What love have I for Miss Ingram? None: and that you know. What love has she for me? <u>None: as I have taken pains to prove: I caused a rumor to reach her that my fortune was not a third of what was supposed, and after that I presented myself to see the result; it was coldness both from her and her mother. I would not, I could not, marry Miss Ingram.</u> You, you strange, you almost unearthly thing! I love as my own flesh. You—poor and obscure, and small and plain as you are—I entreat to accept me as a husband."

Discuss Miss Ingram's understanding of love.

"What, me!" I ejaculated, beginning in his earnestness—and especially in his incivility—to credit his sincerity: "me who have not a friend in the world but you—if you are my friend: not a shilling but what you have given me?"

"You, Jane, I must have you for my own—entirely my own. Will you be mine? Say yes, quickly."

"Mr. Rochester, let me look at your face: turn to the moonlight."

"Why?"

"Because I want to read your countenance—turn!"

"There! You will find it scarcely more legible than a crumpled, scratched page. Read on: only make haste, for I suffer."

His face was very much agitated and very much flushed, and there were strong workings in the features, and strange gleams in the eyes.

"Oh, Jane, you torture me!" he exclaimed. "With that searching and yet faithful and generous look, you torture me!"

"How can I do that? If you are true, and your offer real, my only feelings to you must be gratitude and devotion—they cannot torture."

"Gratitude!" he ejaculated; and added wildly— "Jane, accept me quickly. Say, Edward—give me my name—Edward—I will marry you."

"Are you in earnest? Do you truly love me? Do you sincerely wish me to be your wife?"

"I do; and if an oath is necessary to satisfy you, I swear it."

"Then, sir, I will marry you."

"Edward—my little wife!"

"Dear Edward!"

I. Background Information

Charlotte Brontë (1816—1855) was an English novelist and poet. Her masterpiece *Jane Eyre* tells of a story about an orphaned girl, Jane Eyre's pursuit of happiness and independence. The story is set in Britain in the 19th century. Poor and plain, Jane Eyre began her life as an orphan. She did not have a happy childhood time both in her uncle's family and later in the boarding school. She fell into love with Edward Rochester, her employer, when she worked as a governess in Thornfield Hall without knowing that he was already married. Jane left Thornfield Hall when she found the truth. In the end Jane went back to Thornfield Hall and married her beloved Mr. Rochester despite St John River's proposal to her and Rochester's blindness.

In this chapter, Jane Eyre knew that she had to leave Thornfield Hall because Mr. Rochester would marry a girl who was from the upper class. Jane could not bear the bitterness when Mr. Rochester was discussing her leaving, so she confessed her love to Mr. Rochester but to her surprise, Mr. Rochester asked her to be his wife. Finally, she found that Mr. Rochester was teasing her and she accepted the love bravely.

II. Notes

1. **Turf:** *n.* short grass and the surface layer of soil bound together by its roots
2. **Facile:** *adj.* easily obtained or achieved
3. **Prostrate:** *v.* to make sb. helpless

---

3 Love

Passage 2

Paraphrase the sentence.

4. **Asylum:** *n.* safety or refuge

5. **Sanction:** *n.* permission or approval for an action

6. **Boisterous:** *adj.* stormy and rough

7. **Vehemence:** *n.* the showing or the cause of the strong feeling

8. **Blanche Ingram:** A socialite whom Mr. Rochester temporarily courts to make Jane jealous. She is described as having great beauty, but displays callous behavior and avaricious intent

9. **Adele:** Adele Varens, Mr. Rochester's illegitimate French daughter, a young girl to whom Jane is governess at Thornfield

10. **Fairfax:** Mrs. Alice Fairfax, an elderly widow and the housekeeper of Thornfield Manor. She cares for both Jane and Mr. Rochester

III. Translation

Translate the following excerpt from *Jane Eyre*[1] into Chinese.

FIVE o'clock had hardly struck on the morning of the 19th of January, when Bessie brought a candle into my closet and found me already up and nearly dressed. I had risen half an hour before her entrance, and had washed my face, and put on my clothes by the light of a half-moon just setting, whose rays streamed through the narrow window near my crib. I was to leave Gateshead that day by a coach which passed the lodge gates at six a.m. Bessie was the only person yet risen; she had lit a fire in the nursery, where she now proceeded to make my breakfast. Few children can eat when excited with the thoughts of a journey; nor could I. Bessie, having pressed me in vain to take a few spoonful of the boiled milk and bread she had prepared for me, wrapped up some biscuits in a paper and put them into my bag; then she helped me on with my pelisse and bonnet, and wrapping herself in a shawl, she and I left the nursery. As we passed Mrs. Reed's bedroom, she said, "Will you go in and bid Missis good-bye?"

"No, Bessie: she came to my crib last night when you were gone down to supper, and said I need not disturb her in the morning, or my cousins either; and she told me to remember that she had always been my best friend, and to speak of her and be grateful to her accordingly."

---

1 Brontë, Charlotte, *Jane Eyre*, San Diego: ICON Classics, 2005, pp. 51—52.

"What did you say, Miss?"

"Nothing: I covered my face with the bedclothes, and turned from her to the wall."

"What was wrong, Miss Jane."

"It was quite right, Bessie. Your Missis has not been my friend: she has been my foe."

"O Miss Jane! Don't say so!"

"Good-bye to Gateshead!" cried I, as we passed through the hall and went out at the front door.

IV. Questions for Further Thought

1. Do you agree with Jane Eyre's interpretation of love? Why or why not?
2. In your opinion, what are the critical factors for true love?

[Passage 3]

Audrey Hepburn's Statement to Members of the United Nations Staff[1]

Up until some eighteen months ago before I was given the great **privilege** of becoming a volunteer for UNICEF, I used to be overwhelmed by a sense of desperation and helplessness when watching television or reading about the indescribable misery of the developing world's children and their mothers.

If I feel less helpless today, it is because I have now seen what can be done and what is being done by UNICEF, by many other organizations and agencies, by the churches, by governments, and most of all, with very little help, by <u>people themselves.</u> And yet, we must do more about the alarming state of the children in the developing world—many are only just surviving, especially when we know that the finances needed are minimal compared to the global expenditure of this world, and when we know that less than half of one percent of today's world economy would be the total required to **eradicate** the worst aspects of poverty and to meet basic human needs over the next ten years. <u>In other words, there is no deficit in human resources—the deficit is in human will.</u>

The question I am most frequently asked is: "What do you really do for UNICEF?" Clearly, my <u>task</u> is to inform, to create awareness of the need of children. To fully understand the problems of the state of the world's children, it would be nice to be an expert on education, economics, politics, religious traditions, and cultures. I am none of these things, but I am a mother. There is unhappily a need for greater advocacy for children—children **haunted** by undernourishment, disease and death. You do not have to be a "financial **whiz**" to look into so many little faces with diseased, glazed eyes and to know that this is the result of critical malnutrition, one of the worst symptoms of which is vitamin A deficiency that causes corneal lesions resulting in partial or total

---

1 Audrey Hepburn, *Statement to Members of the United Nations Staff*, June 13, 1989.

blindness, followed within a few weeks by death. Every year there are as many as 500,000 such cases in countries like Indonesia, Bangladesh, India, the Philippines, and Ethiopia. Today there are in fact, millions of children at risk of going blind. Little wonder that I and many other UNICEF volunteers travel the world to raise funds before it is too late, but also to raise awareness and to combat a different kind of darkness, a darkness people find themselves in through lack of information on how easy it is to reach out and keep these children. It costs eighty-four cents a year to stop a child from going blind—the price of two vitamin A capsules.

I have known UNICEF for a long time. For, almost forty-five years ago, I was one of the tens of thousands of starving children in war-ravaged Europe to receive aid from UNICEF, immediately after our Liberation. That liberation freed us from hunger, repression, and constant violence. We were reduced to near total poverty, as is the developing world today. For it is poverty that is at the root of all their suffering, the-not-having: not having the means to help themselves. That is what UNICEF is all about—helping people to help themselves and giving them the aid to develop. The effect of the monstrous burden of debt in the developing world has made the poor even poorer, and has fallen most heavily on the neediest. Those whom it has damaged the most have been the women and children.

Unlike droughts, floods, or earthquakes, the tragedy of poverty cannot easily be captured by the media and brought to the attention of the public worldwide. It is happening not in any one particular place, but in slums and shanties and neglected rural communities across two continents. It is happening not at any one particular time, but over long years of increasing poverty, which have not been featured in the nightly news but which have changed the lives of many millions of people. And it is happening not because of any one visible cause, but because of an unfolding economic drama in which the industrialized nations play a leading part, which is spreading human misery and hardship on a scale and of a severity unprecedented in the postwar era.

In Africa, for instance, in spite of national reforms, improved weather conditions, and a surge of their agricultural output, all their hard-earned gains have been **undermined** by international economic trends and a drastic fall in commodity prices. They are now compelled to return four times as much money as they were loaned! But the poorest sectors of society in the developing world are also suffering as a result of all too frequent

> 文化智慧阅读
>
> Explain it with examples.
>
> How do you understand the differences?

misappropriation of funds, as well as <u>the tremendous inequality</u> in the distribution of land and other productive resources.

<u>UNICEF's business is children, not the workings of the international economy.</u> In its everyday work in over 100 developing nations, UNICEF is brought up against a face of today's international economic problems that is not seen in the corridors of financial power, not reflected in the statistics of debt service ratios, not seated at the conference tables of debt negotiations—it is in the face of a child. It is the young child whose growing mind and body is susceptible to permanent damage from even temporary deprivation. The human brain and body are formed within the first five years of life, and there is no second chance. It is the young child whose individual development today, and whose social contribution tomorrow, are being shaped by the economics of now. It is the young child who is paying the highest of all prices. We cannot therefore ignore the economic issues which for so many millions of the world's poorest families have made the 1980s into a decade of despair.

> What is "the heaviest burden" today?

<u>Today the heaviest burden</u> of a decade of frenzied borrowing is falling, not on the military, nor on those foreign bank accounts, nor on those who conceived the years of waste, but on the poor who are having to do without the bare necessities, on the women who do not have enough food to maintain their health, on the infants whose minds and bodies are being **stunted** because of untreated illnesses and malnutrition, and on children who are being denied their only opportunity ever to go to school. When the impact becomes visible in the rising death rates among children, then what has happened is simply an outrage against a large section of humanity. Nothing can justify it. The consensus now beginning to take shape is that the burden of debt must be lifted to a degree where the developing countries can cope with debt repayment, to the point where their economies can grow out of their overwhelming indebtedness, and set them on the road to recovery and real development.

> Are they still the "fundamental problems"?

World population growth is beginning to be brought under control. Change is in prospect everywhere, and if at this time there is the vision to use this opportunity creatively to see a brave new world and to dare to reach for it, there is a real possibility over the next ten years to begin to come to grips with the triad of fundamental problems which threaten mankind: <u>the presence and the threat of war, the **deterioration** of the environment, and the persistence of the worst aspects of absolute poverty.</u>

3 Love

Passage 3

Many of the great social changes of modern history—the abolition of slavery, the ending of colonial rule, the isolation of apartheid, the increasing consensus on the environment, or the growing recognition of the rights of women—have begun with rhetorical commitment which has eventually turned into action. In the 1990s it may at last be the turn of the child, and our dream for an international summit for children and ratification of the Convention on the Rights of the Child could become a reality.

Forty thousand (35,000 in 2003) children still die every day, 280,000 a week (245,000 in 2003). No natural calamity, be it flood or earthquake, has ever claimed as many children's lives. And this happens every week mostly in the silent emergency of preventable diseases like polio, tetanus, tuberculosis, measles, and the worst killer of all, dehydration from diarrhea caused by unclean drinking water and malnutrition. It costs five dollars to vaccinate a child for life, 6 cents will prevent death from dehydration, and 84 cents per year will stop a child from going blind. How is it that governments spend so much on warfare and bypass the needs of their children, their greatest capital, their only hope for peace?

What is your opinion on the statement?

I must admit to you that the **magnitude** of the task that UNICEF has undertaken sometimes overwhelms me, and I am saddened and frustrated when I stop to think of what we cannot do, like change the world overnight, or when I have to deal with the cynics of this world who argue. Is it morally right to save the lives of children who will only grow up to more suffering and poverty due to overpopulation? Letting children die is not the remedy to overpopulation; family planning and birth spacing is. Rapid population growth can be slowed by giving the world's poor a better life, giving them health, education, housing, nutrition, civil rights. These things are not free but available at a cost that developing countries can afford, given the assistance they need. China, Indonesia, Thailand, and Mexico have already proven that population can be slowed by working on public health education and family planning.

How do you answer the question?

The World Bank now forecasts that by the early 1990s the world should reach the historic turning point at which the annual increase in global population begins to decline. It is also true that in no country has the birth rate declined before infant deaths have declined. In other words, parents can plan to have two children if they know they will survive, rather than having six in the hopes that two will survive. That is why UNICEF is also so dedicated to educating and informing mothers in child care.

Are the forecasts verified to be true?

文化智慧阅读

For it is the mother who is still the best "caretaker" of her child, and UNICEF supports any amount of educational projects for women in the developing countries that relate directly to health and nutrition, sanitation and hygiene, education and literacy.

What will you speak for the children in need if there is a chance?

So today I speak for those children who cannot speak for themselves: children who are going blind through lack of vitamins; children who are slowly being mutilated by polio; children who are wasting away in so many ways through lack of water; for the estimated 100 million street children in this world who have no choice but to leave home in order to survive, who have absolutely nothing but their courage and their smiles and their dreams; for children who have no enemies yet are invariably the first tiny victims of war—wars that are no longer confined to the battlefield but which are being waged through terror and *intimidation* and massacre—children who are therefore growing up surrounded by the horrors of violence for the hundreds of thousands of children who are refugees. The task that lies ahead for UNICEF is ever greater, whether it be *repatriating* millions of children in Afghanistan or teaching children how to play who have only learned how to kill. Charles Dickens wrote, "In their little world, in which children have their existence, nothing is so finely perceived and so finely felt as injustice". Injustice which we can avoid by giving more of ourselves, yet we often hesitate in the face of such apocalyptic tragedy. Why, when the way and the low-cost means are there to safeguard and protect these children? It is for leaders, parents, and young people—young people, who have the purity of heart which age sometimes tends to obscure—to remember their own childhood and come to the rescue of those who start life against such heavy odds.

Paraphrase the sentence.

Children are our most vital resource, our hope for the future. Until they not only can be assured of physically surviving the first fragile years of life, but are free of emotional, social and physical abuse, it is impossible to *envisage* a world that is free of tension and violence. But it is up to us to make it possible.

What are the differences between "a humanitarian institution" and "a charitable organization"?

UNICEF is a humanitarian institution, not a charitable organization. It deals in development, not in welfare, giving handouts to those waiting with their hands outstretched. On my travels to Ethiopia, Venezuela, Ecuador, Central America, Mexico, and the Sudan, I have seen no out-stretched hands, only a silent dignity and a longing to help themselves, given the chance.

UNICEF's mandate is to protect every child against famine, thirst, sickness, abuse, and death. But today we are dealing with an even more ominous threat, "man's inhumanity to man"; with the dark side of humanity that is polluting our skies and our oceans, destroying our forests and extinguishing thousands of beautiful animals. Are our children next?

That is what we are up against. For it is no longer enough to vaccinate our children, to give them food and water, and only cure the symptoms of man's tendency to destroy—to destroy everything we hold dear, everything life depends on, the very air we breathe, the earth that sustains us, and the most precious of all, our children. Whether it be famine in Ethiopia, excruciating poverty in Guatemala and Honduras, civil strife in El Salvador, or ethnic massacre in the Sudan, I saw but one glaring truth. These are not natural disasters, but man-made tragedies, for which there is only one man-made solution—peace.

Even if this mammoth Operation Life-Line Sudan were only to achieve half its goal, due to the countless odds it is up against, in a vast country with no infrastructure, few roads to speak of, no communication system, it will have succeeded, for not only will it have saved thousands of lives, but it will also have given the Sudan hope. The United Nations will have shown the world that only through corridors of tranquility can children be saved, that only through peace can man survive, and only through development will they survive, with dignity and a future. A future in which we can say we have fulfilled our human obligation.

Your 1 percent is an example of 100 percent but all together a beautiful example to us of love and caring. Together there is nothing we cannot do.

I. Background Information

Audrey Hepburn (1929—1993) was a British actress and humanitarian. She was recognized as one of the greatest female film screen legend and fashion icon in the world. She starred in "Roman Holiday" "My Fair Lady" "Wait until Dark" etc. She won best Academy Award and Golden Globe Award for Best Actress in 1965. Hepburn was appointed to be the United Nations International Children's Emergency Fund (UNICEF) Goodwill Ambassador and devoted her later life to help children in African, Asia and South American countries.

This article was a speech delivered by Hepburn as UNICEF Goodwill Ambassador at the invitation of the 1 Percent for Development Fund in Geneva on 13 June 1989. In the speech Hepburn calls on people to be united and love the nature and the human ourselves—in particular children.

II. Notes

1. **Privilege:** *n.* special rights

2. **Eradicate:** *v.* to root out; to get rid of

3. **Haunt:** *v.* to cause problems for someone over a long period of time

4. **Whiz:** *n.* someone who is very intelligent

5. **Undermine:** *v.* to gradually make someone or something less strong

6. **Stunt:** *v.* to stop something or someone from growing or developing properly

7. **Deterioration:** *n.* getting worse

8. **Magnitude:** *n.* greatness of size or importance

9. **Intimidation:** *n.* threat

10. **Repatriate:** *v.* to send someone back to his homeland against his will, as of refugees

11. **Envisage:** *v.* to imagine something will happen in the future

12. **Vaccinate:** *v.* to perform vaccinations or produce immunity in by inoculation

13. **Infrastructure:** *n.* the basic systems and structures of a country or system or organization

14. **1 percent:** Referring 1% for Development Fund, a non-profit fund established in 1983 in Geneva aiming to give financial support to projects which can contribute to the alleviation of hunger and poverty in developing countries

III. Reading Comprehension

State whether the following statements are *True* or *False*.

1. ( ) To work for UNICEF, one does not have to be an expert on one certain field necessarily.

2. ( ) According to the article, Hepburn raised only funds for UNICEF.

3. ( ) It would not cost one much to stop one child from going blind.

4. ( ) From the article, it can be drawn that Hepburn believed the environmental issue was important for UNICEF too.

5. ( ) UNICEF is more like a charity organization.

IV. Questions for Further Thought

1. Compare the differences between "humanitarian institution" and "charitable organization", and explain why UNICEF is a "humanitarian institution".

2. In what ways can you devote your efforts to UNICEF?

[Passage 4]

Of Love[1]

Introduce your understanding of love.

The stage is more beholding to love, than the life of man. For as to the stage, love is ever matter of comedies; and now and then of tragedies; but in life it doth much mischief; sometimes like a siren, sometimes like a fury.

Is this view pessimistic or realistic?

You may observe, that amongst all the great and worthy persons (whereof the memory remaineth, either ancient or recent) there is not one that hath been transported to the mad degree of love: which shows that great spirits, and great business, do keep out this weak passion. You must except, nevertheless, **Marcus Antonius**, the half partner of the empire of Rome, and **Appius Claudius**, the **decemvir** and lawgiver; whereof the former was indeed a **voluptuous** man, and **inordinate**; but the latter was an **austere**

Might you accept this idea?

and wise man: and therefore it seems (though rarely) that love can find entrance, not only into an open heart, but also into a heart well-**fortified**, if watch be not well kept.

It is a poor saying of Epicurus, Satis magnum alter alteri theatrum sumus; as if man, made for the **contemplation** of heaven, and all noble objects, should do nothing but kneel before a little idol, and make himself a subject, though not of the mouth (as beasts are), yet of the eye; which was given him for higher purposes.

"Each is a theatre large enough to another." Do you agree with Epicurus?

It is a strange thing, to note the excess of this passion, and how it **braves** the nature, and value of things, by this; that the speaking in a perpetual hyperbole, is **comely** in nothing but in love. Neither is it merely in the phrase; for whereas it hath been well said, that the **arch-flatterer**, with whom all the petty flatterers have intelligence, is a man's self; certainly the lover is more. For there was never proud man thought so absurdly well of himself, as the lover doth of the person loved; and therefore it was well

---

1 Francis Bacon, *The Essay of Francis Bacon*, New York: Charles Scribner's Sons, 1908, pp. 42—45.

said, that it is impossible to love, and to be wise. Neither doth this weakness appear to others only, and not to the party loved; but to the loved most of all, except the love be **reciproque**. For it is a true rule, that love is ever rewarded, either with the reciproque, or with an inward and secret **contempt**.

By how much the more, men ought to beware of this passion, which loseth not only other things, but itself! As for the other losses, the poet's **relation** doth well figure them: that he that preferred Helena, quitted the gifts of Juno and Pallas. For whosoever esteemeth too much of amorous affection, quitteth both riches and wisdom.

This passion hath his floods, in very times of weakness; which are great prosperity, and great adversity; though this latter hath been less observed: both which times kindle love, and make it more fervent, and therefore show it to be the child of folly. They do best, who if they cannot but admit love, yet make it keep quarters; and sever it wholly from their serious affairs, and actions, of life; for if it check once with business, it troubleth men's fortunes, and maketh men, that they can no ways be true to their own ends.

I know not how, but **martial** men are given to love: I think, it is but as they are given to wine; for **perils** commonly ask to be paid in pleasures.

There is in man's nature, a secret inclination and motion, towards love of others, which if it be not spent upon someone or a few, doth naturally spread itself towards many, and maketh men become humane and charitable; as it is seen sometime in friars.

Nuptial love maketh mankind; friendly love perfecteth it; but wanton love corrupteth, and embaseth it.

I. Background Information

Francis Bacon (1561—1626) was an English philosopher, statesman, scientist, jurist, orator, essayist, and author in the 17th century. He made great contribution to the development of literature, science and philosophy. As an essayist, Bacon's wrote many essays, which have diverse topics and famous for Bacon's philosophical ideas and eloquence. The most well-known essays are "Of Study" (1597), "Of Truth" (1625), "Of Marriage and Single Life" (1612) and so on.

"Of Love" was written in 1612 and has been considered as one of Bacon's most famous essays. Bacon showed his disapproval of the sublunary lover's love and thought

---

3 Love

Passage 4

Compare the opinion to the statement that "Love is blind".

What do you think of the idea?

Paraphrase the sentence.

How to understand the meaning of universal love? Discern the differences between the love towards many and the love given to one person.

Discuss Bacon's view of love.

it is noble to have universal love for the world instead of loving one individual.

II. Notes

1. **Marcus Antonius (83—30BC):** a Roman politician and general, who assassinated Caesar in 44BC and controlled Rome. He was criticized for his relationship with Cleopatra, the Egyptian queen

2. **Appius Claudius (340—173BC):** a distinguished Roman politician and reformer, who made laws in Rome

3. **Decemvir:** *n.* a member of a body of ten Roman magistrates

4. **Voluptuous:** *adj.* devoted to pleasure and entertainment

5. **Inordinate:** *adj.* excessive without limit

6. **Austere:** *adj.* severely and strictly moral

7. **Fortified:** *adj.* strengthened

8. **Contemplation:** *n.* a long and thoughtful observation

9. **Braves:** *v.* to make something splendid

10. **Comely:** *adj.* pleasing

11. **Arch-flatterer:** *n.* biggest flatter

12. **Reciproque:** *adj.* of or relating to the multiplicative inverse of a quantity or function

13. **Contempt:** *n.* a manner that is generally disrespectful and contemptuous

14. **Relation:** *n.* narrative poem

15. **Martial:** *adj.* (of persons) befitting a warrior

16. **Perils:** *n.* a state of danger involving risk

III. Writing

Read the following article, and write an approximately 300-word essay, discussing why a father's love is more influential.

A father's Love is one of the greatest influences on personality development[1]

Looking at 36 studies from around the world that together involved more than 10,000 participants, Rohner and co-author Abdul Khaleque found that in response to rejection

---

1 Society for Personality and Social Psychology, *A father's love is one of the greatest influences on personality development*, June 12, 2012, *Science Daily*, www.sciencedaily.com/releases/2012/06/120612101338.htm, accessed May 20, 2022.

by their parents, children tend to feel more anxious and insecure, as well as more hostile and aggressive toward others. The pain of rejection—especially when it occurs over a period of time in childhood—tends to linger into adulthood, making it more difficult for adults who were rejected as children to form secure and trusting relationships with their intimate partners. The studies are based on surveys of children and adults about their parents' degree of acceptance or rejection during their childhood, coupled with questions about their personality dispositions.

Moreover, Rohner says, emerging evidence from the past decade of research in psychology and neuroscience is revealing that the same parts of the brain are activated when people feel rejected as are activated when they experience physical pain. "Unlike physical pain, however, people can psychologically re-live the emotional pain of rejection over and over for years," Rohner says.

When it comes to the impact of a father's love versus that of a mother, results from more than 500 studies suggest that while children and adults often experience more or less the same level of acceptance or rejection from each parent, the influence of one parent's rejection—oftentimes the father's—can be much greater than the other's. A 13-nation team of psychologists working on the International Father Acceptance Rejection Project has developed at least one explanation for this difference: that children and young adults are likely to pay more attention to whichever parent they perceive to have higher interpersonal power or prestige. So if a child perceives her father as having higher prestige, he may be more influential in her life than the child's mother. Work is ongoing to better understand this potential relationship.

One important take-home message from all this research, Rohner says, is that fatherly love is critical to a person's development. The importance of a father's love should help motivate many men to become more involved in nurturing child care. Additionally, he says, widespread recognition of the influence of fathers on their children's personality development should help reduce the incidence of "mother blaming" common in schools and clinical setting. "The great emphasis on mothers and mothering in America has led to an inappropriate tendency to blame mothers for children's behavior problems and maladjustment when, in fact, fathers are often more implicated than mothers in the development of problems such as these."

IV. Questions for Further Thought

1. Give your evidence to support the statement "wanton love corrupteth, and embaseth it (mankind)"?

2. How could college students balance campus love and college study?

[Mini-task for Chapter 3]

Writing

Read the following news headings about marriage from four countries, and write an approximately 500-word essay to discuss the changing attitudes toward marriage and love.

British, *BBC News*, September 13, 2020:

"Divorce boom" forecast as lockdown sees advice queries rise[1]

The coronavirus pandemic is creating an "enormous strain" on relationships, an advice charity has warned, with family lawyers predicting a "post-lockdown divorce boom".

Canada, *CTV News*, March 13, 2022:

Divorce activity in Canada hit 47-year low during pandemic, StatCan says[2]

The first year of the COVID-19 pandemic saw the fewest divorces in Canada since 1973, but according to Statistics Canada, that low figure may be tied to public health measures.

China, *People's Daily Online*, March 21, 2022:

Marriages fall in 2021 leading to lower birth rates in China, despite declining divorce rate[3]

The number of Chinese couples tying the knot dropped sharply in 2021 which an expert said would continue to cause a decline in China's birth rate, despite that the

---

1 Michael Race, "Divorce boom" forecast as lockdown sees advice queries rise, *BBC News*, September 13, 2020.
2 Matthew Talbot, Divorce activity in Canada hit 47-year low during pandemic, StatCan says, *CTV News*, March 13, 2022.
3 Du Qiongfang, Marriages fall in 2021 leading to lower birth rates in China, despite declining divorce rate, People's Daily Online, March 21, 2022.

number of Chinese couples who got divorced in 2021 also dropped, a temporary effect caused by the cooling-off period stipulated by the newly enacted Civil Code last year.

South Africa, *Statistics South Africa*, March 24, 2022:

Is marriage an old-fashioned institution?[1]

Marriages are becoming less common in South Africa. Could this mean that marriage is becoming a fading tradition? According to the Marriages and Divorce, 2020 report released by Statistics South Africa, the total number of people getting married has fallen steadily from 2011 to 2020. Besides the high decline in 2020 that may have resulted from the restrictions on gatherings in that year, the number of civil marriages have been consistently declining. Civil marriages fell by 22.5% between 2011 and 2019 and declined by a further 31.1% in 2020.

[Further Reading]

1. (英)简·奥斯汀，傲慢与偏见（中英对照全译本），西安：世界图书出版公司，2008.
2. 金莉等，当代美国女权文学批评家研究，北京：北京大学出版社，2014.
3. 钱锺书，围城（英文版），北京：外语教学与研究出版社，2003.

---

1 Statistics South Africa, *Is marriage an old-fashioned institution?*, March 24, 2022.

4 Lifestyle

Passage 1 A Psalm of Life   / 110

Passage 2 My Father's Suitcase / 115

Passage 3 The Gift of the Magi / 122

Passage 4 What I Have Lived for / 130

[本章导读]

著名法国作家爱弥尔·左拉（Émile Zola）曾说过："生活的全部意义在于无穷地探索未知的东西，在于不断增加更多的知识。"（The only basis for living is believing in life, loving it, and applying the whole force of one's intellect to know it better.）可见，生活的过程是发现与追求之旅。然而，不同的目标决定了不同的人生态度，也由此形成了林林总总的生活方式。

诚然，生活方式千差万别，似乎难以简单地按照优劣进行评判。但是，其中所折射的一些根本性认识却是相似的，它们反映着生活的真谛。为此，本章以"如何生活"为主题，选择了四篇文章。第一篇《生命礼赞》（"A Psalm of Life"）来自美国著名诗人亨利·沃兹沃斯·朗费罗（Henry Wadsworth Longfellow）。诗中赞美了乐观与拼搏的生活态度。第二篇和第三篇相当于两个生活案例，具体说明开朗豁达和乐于奋斗的生活态度对于人生的影响。《父亲的手提箱》（"My Father's Suitcase"）选自2006年诺贝尔文学奖获奖者土耳其的奥尔汗·帕穆克（Orhan Pamuk）的获奖演说。作者通过亲身经历，阐释了生活方式与人生结局的深刻关联。《麦琪的礼物》（"The Gift of the Magi"）是美国短篇小说作家欧·亨利（O. Henry）的代表作之一。故事以黑色幽默的方式描写了贫困的小夫妻舍弃了自己最珍贵的东西为对方准备礼物，却仿佛未能如愿。但是，生活的作弄能够轻易摧毁真心相爱和憧憬幸福的人们吗？第四篇是英国哲学家伯特兰·罗素（Bertrand Russell）的散文《我为何而生？》（"What I Have Lived For?"），阐释了智慧的人生态度不仅是对自己负责，更加要努力为人类的幸福做出贡献。本篇从更高的层面反思生活态度的意义，作为这一章的小结。

毋庸置疑，每个人都有权利追求心仪的生活方式。但是，积极且达观应当成为选择的基本原则。在很大程度上，生活方式的形成如同中国哲学所说的"修身"，它是"齐家""治国"和"平天下"的起点。

[Passage 1]

A Psalm of Life[1]

What the Heart of Young Man Said to the **Psalmist**

Tell me not, in **mournful** numbers,
Life is but an empty dream! —
For the soul is dead that **slumbers**,
And things are not what they seem.

Life is real! Life is earnest!
And the grave is not its goal;
Dust thou art, to dust returnest,
Was not spoken of the soul.

Not enjoyment, and not sorrow,
Is our destined end or way;
But to act, that each to-morrow
Find us farther than to-day.

Art is long, and Time is fleeting,
And our hearts, though **stout** and brave,
Still, like **muffled** drums, are beating
Funeral marches to the grave.

Paraphrase the stanza.

Explain Longfellow's understanding of life with examples.

What does the poet imply?

Why does Longfellow think that "Art is long"?

---

1 Henry Wadsworth Longfellow, *A Psalm of Life*, 1838, Poetry Foundation, https://www.poetryfoundation.org/poems/44644/a-psalm-of-life accessed February 20, 2017.

4 Lifestyle

Passage 1

<u>In the world's broad field of battle,</u>
　　In the **bivouac** of Life,
　Be not like dumb, driven cattle!
　　<u>Be a hero in the **strife**</u>!

Trust no Future, howe'er pleasant!
Let the dead Past bury its dead!
<u>Act— act in the living Present!</u>
Heart within, and God o'erhead!
Lives of great men all remind us
We can make our lives sublime,
And, departing, leave behind us
Footprints on the sands of time;

<u>Footprints, that perhaps another,</u>
　　<u>Sailing o'erlife's solemn main,</u>
A **forlorn** and shipwrecked brother,
　　Seeing, shall take heart again.

Let us, then, be up and doing,
　With a heart for any fate;
Still achieving, still pursuing,
<u>Learn to labor and to wait.</u>

Do you agree with this viewpoint? Why or why not?

State the virtues that a hero should have.

Comment on the attitude to life.

What does "footprint" imply?

Discuss how people can "learn to wait" while "learn to labor".

I. Background Information

Henry Wadsworth Longfellow (1807—1882) was one of the greatest American Romantic poets in 20th century. He was born in a lawyer family. In 1822, he studies at Bowdoin College where he met Nathaniel Hawthorne who later became his lifelong friend. After graduation, he was offered a job as professor of modern languages at alma mater. He had to travel in Europe to study Italian, French and Spanish. In 1836, Longfellow returned to the United States. He taught Europe culture and Romanticism in Harvard College. In 1939 he published his first poetry collection, *Voices of the Night*, and Romantic fiction, *Hyperion, a Romance*. The publication of *Ballads and Other Poems* in 1941 established his status of a poet. He was honored in March 2007 when the United States Postal Service issued a stamp commemorating him.

"A Psalm of Life" conveys the author's idea about life from a perspective of young people. It points out the character of time in life and the goal of life. People can surpass themselves through action. This poem gives people a sense of encouragement, which echoes the improvement of Industry Revolution when it was written.

II. Notes

1. **Psalmist:** *n.* a writer or composer of especially biblical psalms
2. **Mournful:** *adj.* feeling or expressing sorrow or grief; sorrowful
3. **Slumber:** *v.* to sleep lightly; *n.* sleep; a light sleep
4. **"Dust thou art, to dust returnest":** these are the remarks that Lord speaks to Adam in Genesis of the Old Testament
5. **Stout:** *adj.* having or marked by boldness, bravery, or determination; firm and resolute
6. **Muffle:** *v.* to wrap up so as to conceal or protect; to keep down; to suppress
7. **Bivouac:** *n.* a temporary camp built outside without any tents
8. **Strife:** *adj.* angry or violent disagreement between two people or groups of people
9. **Forlorn:** *adj.* sad and lonely because of isolation or desertion

III. Reading Comprehension

Read the poem, and choose the best answer to each question.

The Road Not Taken[1]

Two roads diverged in a yellow wood,
And sorry I could not travel both
And be one traveler, long I stood
And looked down one as far as I could
To where it bent in the undergrowth;

Then took the other, as just as fair,

---

1 Robert Lee Frost, The Road Not Taken, *Mountain Interval*, New York: Holt, 1916.

4 Lifestyle

Passage 1

And having perhaps the better claim,
Because it was grassy and wanted wear;
Though as for that the passing there
Had worn them really about the same,

And both that morning equally lay
In leaves no step had trodden black.
Oh, I kept the first for another day!
Yet knowing how way leads on to way,
I doubted if I should ever come back.

I shall be telling this with a sigh
Somewhere ages and ages hence:
Two roads diverged in a wood, and I—
I took the one less traveled by,
And that has made all the difference.

1. What does the "two roads" symbolize?

(A) people who affect our lives.   (B) the beginnings of new journey in life

(C) paths that are hidden in secret   (D) important decisions one makes in life

2. Which word is closest in meaning to "diverged"?

(A) presented   (B) divided   (C) conformed   (D) unequaled

3. Which statement best indicates the poet's meaning?

(A) The poet was not worried he made a wrong choice because he is still young.

(B) The poet was worried he took the more traveled road and could not return to take the other one.

(C) The poet understood that taking one opportunity might prevent him from going back to take another.

(D) The poet believed that he could take the opportunities presented to him at some point in life.

4. Which statement best describes the theme of *The Road Not Taken*?

(A) When making decision, choosing the most common one can ensure that one will take the correct path through life.

(B) Sometimes one must make decision without knowing the results and live with the consequences.

(C) Since it is easier to follow one's heart than head, one would better follow their hearts.

(D) There will always be decisions in life; therefore, one may have chance to return and make a different decision someday.

IV. Questions for Further Thought

1. Regarding lifestyle, what matters more to you and why?

2. Do you believe that different attitudes to life may change one's fate? Why or why not?

[Passage 2]

My Father's Suitcase[1]

Two years before his death, my father gave me a small suitcase filled with his writings, manuscripts and notebooks. Assuming his usual joking, mocking air, he told me he wanted me to read them after he was gone, by which he meant after he died.

"Just take a look", he said, looking slightly embarrassed. "See if there's anything inside that you can use. Maybe after I'm gone you can make a selection and publish it".

We were in my study, surrounded by books. My father was searching for a place to set down the suitcase, wandering back and forth like a man who wished to rid himself of a painful burden. In the end, he deposited it quietly in an **unobtrusive** corner. It was a shaming moment that neither of us ever forgot, but once it had passed and we had gone back into our usual roles, taking life lightly, our joking, mocking personas took over and we relaxed. We talked as we always did, about the trivial things of everyday life, and Turkey's never-ending political troubles, and my father's mostly failed business ventures, without feeling too much sorrow.

I remember that after my father left, I spent several days walking back and forth past the suitcase without once touching it. I was already familiar with this small, black, leather suitcase, and its lock, and its rounded corners. My father would take it with him on short trips and sometimes use it to carry documents to work. I remembered that when I was a child, and my father came home from a trip, I would open this little suitcase and **rummage** through his things, savoring the scent of cologne and foreign countries. This suitcase was a familiar friend, a powerful reminder of my childhood, my past, but now I couldn't even touch it. Why? No doubt it was because of the **mysterious weight** of its contents.

---

[1] Pamuk Orhan, *The Nobel Prize Lecture,* 2006, https://www.newyorker.com/magazine/2006/12/25/my-fathers-suitcase accessed February 20, 2017.

Side questions:

- Explain why did author's father make such a request after reading the story.
- Why was it an unforgettable shaming moment for them?
- Why did the author feel hesitate to open the suitcase?
- What does "mysterious weight" imply?

I am now going to speak of this weight's meaning. It is what a person creates when he shuts himself up in a room, sits down at a table, and retires to a corner to express his thoughts—that is, the meaning of literature.

When I did touch my father's suitcase, I still could not bring myself to open it, but I did know what was inside some of those notebooks. I had seen my father writing things in a few of them. This was not the first time I had heard of the heavy load inside the suitcase. My father had a large library; in his youth, in the late 1940s, he had wanted to be an Istanbul poet, and had translated Valéry into Turkish, but he had not wanted to live the sort of life that came with writing poetry in a poor country with few readers. My father's father—my grandfather—had been a wealthy business man; my father had led a comfortable life as a child and a young man, and he had no wish to endure hardship for the sake of literature, for writing. He loved life with all its beauties—this I understood.

The first thing that kept me distant from the contents of my father's suitcase was, of course, the fear that I might not like what I read. Because my father knew this, he had taken the **precaution** of acting as if he did not take its contents seriously. After working as a writer for 25 years, it pained me to see this. But I did not even want to be angry at my father for failing to take literature seriously enough … My real fear, the crucial thing that I did not wish to know or discover, was the possibility that my father might be a good writer. I couldn't open my father's suitcase because I feared this. Even worse, I couldn't even admit this myself openly. If true and great literature emerged from my father's suitcase, I would have to acknowledge that inside my father there existed an entirely different man. This was a frightening possibility. <u>Because even at my advanced age I wanted my father to be only my father—not a writer.</u>

<u>A writer is someone who spends years patiently trying to discover the second being inside him, and the world that makes him who he is:</u> when I speak of writing, what comes first to my mind is not a novel, a poem, or literary tradition, it is a person who shuts himself up in a room, sits down at a table, and alone, turns inward; amid its shadows, he builds a new world with words. This man—or this woman—may use a typewriter, profit from the ease of a computer, or write with a pen on paper, as I have done for 30 years. As he writes, he can drink tea or coffee, or smoke cigarettes. From time to time he may rise from his table to look out through the window at the children playing in the street, and, if he is lucky, at trees and a view, or he can gaze out at a black

wall. He can write poems, plays, or novels, as I do. All these differences come after the crucial task of sitting down at the table and patiently turning inwards. To write is to turn this inward gaze into words, to study the world into which that person passes when he retires into himself, and to do so with patience, **obstinacy**, and joy. As I sit at my table, for days, months, years, slowly adding new words to the empty page, I feel as if I am creating a new world, as if I am bringing into being that other person inside me, in the same way someone might build a bridge or a dome, stone by stone. <u>The stones we writers use are words. As we hold them in our hands, sensing the ways in which each of them is connected to the others, looking at them sometimes from afar, sometimes almost caressing them with our fingers and the tips of our pens, weighing them, moving them around, year in and year out, patiently and hopefully, we create new worlds.</u>

The writer's secret is not inspiration—for it is never clear where it comes from—it is his stubbornness, his patience. That lovely Turkish saying—<u>to dig a well with a needle</u>—seems to me to have been said with writers in mind. In the old stories, I love the patience of Ferhat, who digs through mountains for his love—and I understand it, too. In my novel, **My Name is Red**, when I wrote about the old Persian miniaturists who had drawn the same horse with the same passion for so many years, memorizing each stroke, that they could recreate that beautiful horse even with their eyes closed, I knew I was talking about the writing profession, and my own life. If a writer is to tell his own story—tell it slowly, and as if it were a story about other people—if he is to feel the power of the story rise up inside him, if he is to sit down at a table and patiently give himself over to this art—this craft—he must first have been given some hope. The angel of inspiration (who pays regular visits to some and rarely calls on others) **favors** the hopeful and the confident, and it is when a writer feels most lonely, when he feels most doubtful about his efforts, his dreams, and the value of his writing—when he thinks his story is only his story—it is at such moments that the angel chooses to reveal to him stories, images and dreams that will draw out the world he wishes to build. <u>If I think back on the books to which I have devoted my entire life, I am most surprised by those moments when I have felt as if the sentences, dreams, and pages that have made me so ecstatically happy have not come from my own imagination—that another power has found them and generously presented them to me.</u>

I was afraid of opening my father's suitcase and reading his notebooks because I knew

4 Lifestyle

Passage 2

State the author's understanding of a writer's life. Do you enjoy a lifestyle of this kind? Why or why not?

Compare the idea with that of Chinese culture with examples.

Paraphrase the sentence.

that he would not tolerate the difficulties I had endured, that it was not **solitude** he loved but mixing with friends, crowds, salons, jokes, company. But later my thoughts took a different turn. These thoughts, these dreams of **renunciation** and patience, were prejudices I had derived from my own life and my own experience as a writer. There were plenty of brilliant writers who wrote surrounded by crowds and family life, in the glow of company and happy chatter. In addition, my father had, when we were young, tired of the monotony of family life, and left us to go to Paris, where—like so many writers—he'd sat in his hotel room filling notebooks. I knew, too, that some of those very notebooks were in this suitcase, because during the years before he brought it to me, my father had finally begun to talk to me about that period in his life. He spoke about those years even when I was a child, but he would not mention his vulnerabilities, his dreams of becoming a writer, or the questions of identity that had plagued him in his hotel room. He would tell me instead about all the times he'd seen Sartre on the pavements of Paris, about the books he'd read and the films he'd seen, all with the elated sincerity of someone **imparting** very important news. When I became a writer, I never forgot that it was partly thanks to the fact that I had a father who would talk of world writers so much more than he spoke of pashas or great religious leaders. So perhaps I had to read my father's notebooks with this in mind, and remembering how indebted I was to his large library. I had to bear in mind that when he was living with us, my father, like me, enjoyed being alone with his books and his thoughts—and not pay too much attention to the literary quality of his writing.

But as I gazed so anxiously at the suitcase my father had **bequeathed** me, I also felt that this was the very thing I would not be able to do. My father would sometimes stretch out on the **divan** in front of his books, abandon the book in his hand, or the magazine and drift off into a dream, lose himself for the longest time in his thoughts. When I saw on his face an expression so very different from the one he wore amid the joking, teasing, and **bickering** of family life—when I saw the first signs of an inward gaze—I would, especially during my childhood and my early youth, understand, with **trepidation**, that he was discontent. Now, so many years later, I know that this discontent is the basic trait that turns a person into a writer. To become a writer, patience and toil are not enough: we must first feel compelled to escape crowds, company, the stuff of ordinary, everyday life, and shut ourselves up in a room. We wish for patience and hope so that we can create a deep world in our writing. But the desire to shut oneself up in a room is what pushes us into action. The **precursor** of this sort of independent writer—who reads his books to his heart's content, and who, by listening only to the voice of his own conscience, disputes with other's words, who, by entering into conversation with his books develops his own thoughts, and his own world—was most certainly Montaigne, in the earliest days of modern literature. Montaigne was a writer to whom my father returned often, a writer he recommended to me. I would like to see myself as belonging to the tradition of writers who—wherever they are in the world, in the East or in the West—cut themselves off from society, and shut themselves up with their books in their room. The starting point of true literature is the man who shuts himself up in his room with his books.

But once we shut ourselves away, we soon discover that we are not as alone as we thought. We are in the company of the words of those who came before us, of other people's stories, other people's books, other people's words, the thing we call tradition. I believe literature to be the most valuable **hoard** that humanity has gathered in its quest to understand itself. Societies, tribes, and peoples grow more intelligent, richer, and more advanced as they pay attention to the troubled words of their authors, and, as we all know, the burning of books and the **denigration** of writers are both signals that dark and improvident times are upon us. But literature is never just a national concern. The writer who shuts himself up in a room and first goes on a journey inside himself will, over the years, discover literature's eternal rule: he must have the artistry to tell his own stories as if they were other people's stories, and to tell other people's stories as if they were his own, for this is what literature is. But we must first travel through other people's stories and books.

I. Background Information

This passage is an extract of "My Father's Suitcase", which was lectured by Orhan Pamuk when he was awarded the Nobel Prize in 2006.

Orhan Pamuk (born June 7, 1952) is a Turkish novelist, screenwriter. He won the 2006 Nobel Prize in Literature for his work, *My Name Is Red*. He is the first Turkish citizen to win this prize. He is thought to be one of the prominent European writers at present. Pamuk grew up in a wealthy and Western-oriented family. He went to Istanbul

Technical University to study architecture. In 1974, he started his writing career and became a full-time writer. He thinks himself is a Cultural Muslim who combines the historical and cultural identification with the religion while not believing in a personal connection to God. His first novel *Cevdet Beyve Oğulları* (*Mr. Cevdet and His Sons*) was finished in 1979 and was published in 1982. It won the Orhan Kemal Novel Prize in 1983.Pamuk's fifth novel Yeni Hayat (*New Life*) caused a sensation in Turkey upon its 1995 publication and became the fastest-selling book in Turkish history.

"My Father's Suitcase" talks about how the author developed his interest in writing when he was a child. The author's father influenced him a lot on writing. How the author regarded the function of his father was written in this article.

II. Notes

1. **Unobtrusive:** *adj.* not noticeable; seeming to fit in well with the background

2. **Rummage:** *v.* to search for something by moving things around in a careless or hurried way

3. **Precaution:** *n.* something you do in order to prevent something dangerous or unpleasant from happening

4. **Obstinacy:** *n.* stubbornness; the quality of being unwilling to be reasonable and change your behavior, plans, or ideas

5. **My Name is Red**: it is a Turkish book written by Orhan Pamuk in 1998, and translated into English in 2001. It describes stories in Ottoman Empire in 1959. The novel contributed Orhan Pamuk's Nobel Prize in Literature in 2006.

6. **Favor:** *v.* to agree with sth.; to treat with partiality

7. **Solitude:** *n.* a state of social isolation; the state or situation of being alone

8. **Renunciation:** *n.* rejecting or disowning or disclaiming as invalid; the act of renouncing; sacrificing or giving up or surrendering (a possession or right or title or privilege etc.)

9. **Impart:** *v.* to give (qualities, knowledge, etc.); to inform

10. **Bequeath:** *v.* to leave or give by will after one's death

11. **Divan:** *n.* a bed with a thick base; a long low soft seat without a back or arms

12. **Bicker:** *v.* to argue, especially about something very unimportant

13. **Trepidation:** *n.* a feeling of anxiety or fear about something that is going to happen

14. **Precursor:** *n.* something that happened or existed before something else and influenced its development

15. **Hoard:** *n.* a collection of things that someone hides somewhere, especially so they can use them later

16. **Denigration:** *n.* the action to say things to make someone or something seem less important or good

III. Discussion

Read the following sentences, and give your comments on them about life.

Don't run through life so fast that you forget not only where you've been, but also where you're going. Life is not a race, but a journey to be savored each step of the way.

Life doesn't always give us the joys we want. We don't always get our hopes and dreams, and we don't always get our own way.

A great life is the result of creating priorities. It's easy to spend your days just responding to the next thing that gets your attention, instead of intentionally using the time, energy and money you have in a way that's important to you.

Difficulties arise in the lives of us all. What is most important is dealing with the hard times, coping with the changes, and getting through to the other side where the sun is still shining just for you.

Life is about growing, learning, and being a better person. Never trying to improve yourself is a guaranteed path to living a completely average life. Can anyone honestly say they want an average life? Of course not.

IV. Questions for Further Thought

1. Why did the father fail to make his dream come true while his son succeeded?

2. Why the lifestyle like shutting oneself up in a room and sitting down at a table may not lead to a successful career?

[Passage 3]

The Gift of the Magi[1]

<u>One dollar and eighty-seven cents.</u> That was all. And sixty cents of it was in pennies. Pennies saved one and two at a time by **bulldozing** the grocer and the vegetable man and the butcher until one's cheeks burned with the silent imputation of **parsimony** that such close dealing implied. Three times Della counted it. One dollar and eighty-seven cents. And the next day would be Christmas.

There was clearly nothing to do but flop down on the shabby little couch and howl. So Della did it. <u>Which **instigates** the moral reflection that life is made up of sobs, sniffles, and smiles, with sniffles predominating.</u>

While the mistress of the home is gradually subsiding from the first stage to the second, take a look at the home. A furnished flat at $8 per week. It did not exactly beggar description, but it certainly had that word on the lookout for the **mendicancy** squad.

<u>In the vestibule below was a letter-box into which no letter would go, and an electric button from which no mortal finger could coax a ring.</u> Also appertaining **thereunto** was a card bearing the name "Mr. James Dillingham Young".

The "Dillingham" had been flung to the breeze during a former period of prosperity when its possessor was being paid $30 per week. Now, when the income was shrunk to $20, though, they were thinking seriously of contracting to a modest and unassuming D. But whenever Mr. James Dillingham Young came home and reached his flat above he was called "Jim" and greatly hugged by Mrs. James Dillingham Young, already introduced to you as Della. <u>Which is all very good.</u>

Della finished her cry and attended to her cheeks with the powder rag. She stood by

---

1 Henry O., The Gift of the Magi, *The Four Million*, New York: McClure, Phillips & Co., 1906.

the window and looked out dully at a gray cat walking a gray fence in a gray backyard. Tomorrow would be Christmas Day, and she had only $1.87 with which to buy Jim a present. She had been saving every penny she could for months, with this result. Twenty dollars a week doesn't go far. Expenses had been greater than she had calculated. They always are. Only $1.87 to buy a present for Jim. Her Jim. Many a happy hour she had spent planning for something nice for him. Something fine and rare and sterling—something just a little bit near to being worthy of the honor of being owned by Jim.

There was a **pier** glass between the windows of the room. Perhaps you have seen a pier glass in an $8 flat. A very thin and very **agile** person may, by observing his reflection in a rapid sequence of longitudinal strips, obtain a fairly accurate conception of his looks. Della, being **slender**, had mastered the art.

Suddenly she **whirled** from the window and stood before the glass. Her eyes were shining brilliantly, but her face had lost its color within twenty seconds. Rapidly she pulled down her hair and let it fall to its full length.

Now, there were two possessions of the James Dillingham Young's in which they both took a mighty pride. One was Jim's gold watch that had been his father's and his grandfather's. The other was Della's hair. Had the queen of Sheba lived in the flat across the airshaft, Della would have let her hair hang out the window someday to dry just to depreciate Her Majesty's jewels and gifts. Had King Solomon been the **janitor**, with all his treasures piled up in the basement, Jim would have pulled out his watch every time he passed, just to see him pluck at his beard from envy.

So now Della's beautiful hair fell about her rippling and shining like a cascade of brown waters. It reached below her knee and made itself almost a garment for her. And then she did it up again nervously and quickly. Once she **faltered** for a minute and stood still while a tear or two splashed on the worn red carpet.

On went her old brown jacket; on went her old brown hat. With a whirl of skirts and with the brilliant sparkle still in her eyes, she fluttered out the door and down the stairs to the street.

Where she stopped the sign read: "Mme. Sofronie. Hair Goods of All Kinds." One flight up Della ran, and collected herself, panting. Madame, large, too white, chilly, hardly looked the "Sofronie".

"Will you buy my hair?" asked Della.

---

4 Lifestyle

Passage 3

Does Della love Jim? Why or why not?

What does the plot imply?

Why does the writer exaggeratedly describe Della's hair and Jim's watch?

What do you think of their life through the subtle plot?

文化智慧阅读

"I buy hair," said Madame. "Take your hat off and let's have a sight at the looks of it".

Down rippled the brown cascade.

"Twenty dollars," said Madame, lifting the mass with a practiced hand.

"Give it to me quick," said Della.

Oh, and the next two hours tripped by on rosy wings. Forget the hashed metaphor. She was **ransacking** the stores for Jim's present.

She found it at last. It surely had been made for Jim and no one else. There was no other like it in any of the stores, and she had turned all of them inside out. It was a platinum **fob** chain simple and chaste in design, properly proclaiming its value by substance alone and not by **meretricious** ornamentation—as all good things should do. It was even worthy of The Watch. As soon as she saw it, she knew that it must be Jim's. It was like him. Quietness and value—the description applied to both. Twenty-one dollars they took from her for it, and she hurried home with the 87 cents. With that chain on his watch Jim might be properly anxious about the time in any company. Grand as the watch was, he sometimes looked at it on the sly on account of the old leather strap that he used in place of a chain.

Imagine what a young woman Della is according to the plot.

When Della reached home her intoxication gave way a little to prudence and reason. She got out her curling irons and lighted the gas and went to work repairing the **ravages** made by generosity added to love. Which is always a tremendous task, dear friends—a mammoth task.

What does the plot imply?

Within forty minutes her head was covered with tiny, close-lying curls that made her look wonderfully like a truant schoolboy. She looked at her reflection in the mirror long, carefully, and critically.

"If Jim doesn't kill me," she said to herself, "before he takes a second look at me, he'll say I look like a Coney Island chorus girl. But what could I do—oh! What could I do with a dollar and eighty-seven cents?"

At 7 o'clock the coffee was made and the frying-pan was on the back of the stove hot and ready to cook the chops.

What does the plot imply?

Jim was never late. Della doubled the fob chain in her hand and sat on the corner of the table near the door that he always entered. Then she heard his step on the stair away down on the first flight, and she turned white for just a moment. She had a habit of saying a little silent prayer about the simplest everyday things, and now she whispered: "Please God, make him think I am still pretty".

The door opened and Jim stepped in and closed it. He looked thin and very serious. Poor fellow, he was only twenty-two—and to be burdened with a family! He needed a new overcoat and he was without gloves.

Jim stopped inside the door, as immovable as a setter at the scent of quail. <u>His eyes were fixed upon Della, and there was an expression in them that she could not read, and it terrified her. It was not anger, nor surprise, nor disapproval, nor horror, nor any of the sentiments that she had been prepared for. He simply stared at her fixedly with that peculiar expression on his face.</u>

> Why does Jim have this reaction?

Della wriggled off the table and went for him.

"Jim, darling," she cried, "don't look at me that way. I had my hair cut off and sold because I couldn't have lived through Christmas without giving you a present. It'll grow out again—you won't mind, will you? I just had to do it. My hair grows awfully fast. Say 'Merry Christmas!' Jim, and let's be happy. You don't know what a nice—what a beautiful, nice gift I've got for you".

"You've cut off your hair?" asked Jim, laboriously, as if he had not arrived at that patent fact yet even after the hardest mental labor.

"Cut it off and sold it," said Della. "Don't you like me just as well, anyhow? I'm me without my hair, ain't I?"

Jim looked about the room curiously.

"You say your hair is gone?" he said, with an air almost of **idiocy**.

"You needn't look for it," said Della. "It's sold, I tell you—sold and gone, too. It's Christmas Eve, boy. Be good to me, for it went for you. Maybe the hairs of my head were numbered," she went on with sudden serious sweetness, "<u>but nobody could ever count my love for you.</u> Shall I put the **chops** on, Jim?"

> Is this your dream love? Why or why not?

Out of his trance Jim seemed quickly to wake. He enfolded his Della. For ten seconds let us regard with discreet **scrutiny** some inconsequential object in the other direction. Eight dollars a week or a million a year—what is the difference? A mathematician or a wit would give you the wrong answer. The magi brought valuable gifts, but that was not among them. This dark **assertion** will be illuminated later on.

Jim drew a package from his overcoat pocket and threw it upon the table.

"Don't make any mistake, Dell," he said, "about me. I don't think there's anything in

文化智慧阅读

the way of a haircut or a shave or a shampoo that could make me like my girl any less. But if you'll unwrap that package you may see why you had me going a while at first."

White fingers and nimble tore at the string and paper. And then an **ecstatic** scream of joy; and then, alas! A quick feminine change to **hysterical** tears and wails, necessitating the immediate employment of all the comforting powers of the lord of the flat.

For there lay The Combs—the set of combs, side and back, that Della had worshipped long in a Broadway window. Beautiful combs, pure tortoise shell, with jeweled rims— just the shade to wear in the beautiful vanished hair. They were expensive combs, she knew, and her heart had simply craved and yearned over them without the least hope of possession. And now, they were hers, but the tresses that should have **adorned** the coveted adornments were gone.

What do you think about the end of this story?

But she hugged them to her bosom, and at length she was able to look up with dim eyes and a smile and say: "My hair grows so fast, Jim!"

And then Della leaped up like a little singed cat and cried, "Oh, oh!"

Comment on Della's answer to the regret.

Jim had not yet seen his beautiful present. She held it out to him eagerly upon her open palm. The dull precious metal seemed to flash with a reflection of her bright and ardent spirit.

"Isn't it a dandy, Jim? I hunted all over town to find it. You'll have to look at the time a hundred times a day now. Give me your watch. I want to see how it looks on it."

Instead of obeying, Jim tumbled down on the couch and put his hands under the back of his head and smiled.

Imagine Della's reaction.

"Dell," said he, "let's put our Christmas presents away and keep them a while. They're too nice to use just at present. I sold the watch to get the money to buy your combs. And now suppose you put the chops on."

The magi, as you know, were wise men—wonderfully wise men—who brought gifts to the Babe in the manger. They invented the art of giving Christmas presents. Being wise, their gifts were no doubt wise ones, possibly bearing the privilege of exchange in case of duplication. And here I have **lamely** related to you the uneventful chronicle of two foolish children in a flat who most unwisely sacrificed for each other the greatest treasures of their house. But in a last word to the wise of these days let it be said that of all who give gifts these two were the wisest. Of all who give and receive gifts, such as they are wisest. Everywhere they are wisest. They are the magi.

Why are they "the magi"?

4 Lifestyle

Passage 3

I. Background Information

O. Henry is the pen name of William Sydney Porter (1862—1910), who was an American writer. He is famous for short stories with surprising endings.

"The Gift of the Magi" is a representative work of O. Henry. The motivation of writing is believed to reflect the hardship of life among lower-class people through it. The other essential factor is the author wanted to memorize his wife, Athol Estes. She was weak and suffered from tuberculosis when they got married. They had a daughter, Margaret Worth Porter. In 1896, the bank Porter worked for was audited by federal auditors and Porter was suspected to conduct the embezzlement shortages. He fled first to New Orleans and later to Honduras in order to avoid the federal indictment. Next year, when Porter learned that his wife was dying, he went back to see her. The pain of losing his beloved and the absence when she was ill contributed to his regret, which account for the motivation of writing "the Gift of the Magi".

This novel reflects the harsh life of American low-level people. It reveals the gap between the rich and the poor. Another important reason O. Henry wrote this love story is that he wanted to memorize his wife—Athol Estes.

O. Henry also had many other famous short stories which are worth reading, such as "A Retrieved Reformation" (1903), "The Cop and the Anthem" (1904), "The Ransom of Red Chief" (1907).

II. Notes

1. **Bulldoze:** *v.* to force someone to do something that they do not really want to do; to push objects such as earth and rocks out of the way with a bulldozer

2. **Parsimony:** *n.* the quality of being careful with money or resources

3. **Instigate:** *v.* to make a process start, especially one relating to law or politics; to persuade someone do something bad or violent

4. **Mendicancy:** *n.* the condition of being a beggar

5. **Thereunto:** *adv.* to that, this, or it; thereto

6. **Pier:** *n.* a thick stone, wooden, or metal post that is used to support something

7. **Agile:** *adj.* able to move quickly and easily

8. **Slender:** *adj.* thin in an attractive or graceful way

9. **Whirl:** *v.* to turn or spin around very quickly, or to make someone or something

do this

10. **Janitor:** *n.* doorkeeper; someone whose job is to look after a school or other large building

11. **Falter:** *v.* to become weaker and unable to continue in an effective way; to speak in a voice that sounds weak and uncertain, and keeps stopping; to stop walking or to walk in an unsteady way because you suddenly feel weak or afraid

12. **Ransack:** *v.* to go through a place, stealing things and causing damage; to search a place very thoroughly, often making it untidy

13. **Fob:** *n.* a short chain that is attached to a watch that is carried in a pocket

14. **Meretricious**: *adj.* seeming attractive but really false or of little value

15. **Ravage:** *v.* to damage something very badly

16. **Idiocy:** *n.* very stupid behavior; the state of being very stupid

17. **Chops:** *n.* the area of the face surrounding the mouth of a person or an animal

18. **Scrutiny:** *n.* careful and thorough examination; the careful and detailed examination of something in order to obtain information about it

19. **Assertion:** *n.* a statement that you strongly believe is true

20. **Ecstatic:** *adj.* feeling extremely happy and excited

21. **Hysterical:** *adj.* unable to control your behavior or emotions because you are very upset, afraid, excited etc.

22. **Adorn:** *v.* to add something decorative to a person or thing

23. **Lamely:** *adv.* in a way that does not sound very confident or that does not persuade other people

III. Translation

Translate the following sentences into Chinese.

1. Somehow, I can't believe that there are any heights that can't be scaled by a man who knows the secrets of making dreams come true. This special secret, it seems to me, can be summarized in four Cs. They are curiosity, confidence, courage, and constancy, and the greatest of all is confidence. When you believe in a thing, believe in it all the way, implicitly and unquestionable. (By Walt Disney)

2. The heights by great men reached and kept were not attained by sudden flight, but they, while their companions slept, were toiling upward in the night. (By Henry

Wadsworth Longfellow)

3. However mean your life is, meet it and live it; do not shun it and call it hard names. It is not so bad as you are. Things do not change; we change. Sell your clothes and keep your thoughts. (By Jean-Jacques Rousseau)

IV. Questions for Further Thought

1. If Della did not sell her hair, would the story still be moving? What would the end be?

2. There is a popular saying that a girl would rather cry in a BMW than laugh at the back of a bicycle. What is attitude to life hidden within the saying?

[Passage 4]

What I Have Lived for[1]

What are the three passions?

Three passions, simple but **overwhelmingly** strong, have **governed** my life: the longing for love, the search for knowledge, and unbearable pity for the suffering of mankind. These passions, like great winds, have blown me hither and thither, in a wayward course, over a deep ocean of **anguish**, reaching to the very **verge** of despair.

Paraphrase the sentence.

I have sought love, first, because it brings **ecstasy**—ecstasy so great that I would often have sacrificed all the rest of life for a few hours of this joy. I have sought it, next, because it **relieves** loneliness—that terrible loneliness in which one shivering consciousness looks over the rim of the world into the cold **unfathomable** lifeless **abyss**. I have sought it, finally, because in the union of love I have seen, in a mystic **miniature**, the prefiguring vision of the heaven that saints and poets have imagined. This is what I sought, and though it might seem too good for human life, this is what-at last-I have found.

Why do people need knowledge in life?

With equal passion I have sought knowledge. I have wished to understand the hearts of men. I have wished to know why the stars shine. And I have tried to **apprehend** the Pythagorean power by which number holds sway above the **flux**. A little of this, but not much, I have achieved.

Why do people need pity in life?

Love and knowledge, so far as they were possible, led upward toward the heavens. But always pity brought me back to earth. Echoes of cries of pain **reverberate** in my heart. Children in famine, victims tortured by oppressors, helpless old people a hated burden to their pain make a mockery of what human life should be. I long to **alleviate** the evil, but I can't, and I too suffer.

---

1 Bertrand Russell, Prologue: What I Have Lived For, *Autobiography of Bertrand Russell*. London: Routledge, 1998.

This has been my life. I have found it worth living, and would gladly live it again if the chance were offered me.

I. Background Information

Bertrand Russell (1872—1970) was a British philosopher, mathematician, educator, social critic and political activist. He authored over 70 books and thousands of essays and letters which are focused on a diverse of topics. In 1950, he, at age 78, was awarded the Nobel Prize in Literature. His Principal publications include *German Social Democracy* (1896), *The Problems of Philosophy* (1912), *The Analysis of Mind* (1921) and *The Problem of China* (1922) and so on.

The article is the prologue to *Bertrand Russell's Autobiography*. It talks about the elements that the author thinks are important in his life. From the three passions, readers can think about the classic questions about philosophy—who are we? Where are we from? Where are we going? Having a deep consideration about life is the aim of this article.

II. Notes

1. **Overwhelmingly:** *adv.* extremely; mostly by far
2. **Govern:** *v.* to control or influence sb/sth or how sth happens, functions, etc.
3. **Anguish:** *n.* severe pain, mental suffering or unhappiness
4. **Verge:** *n.* the edge or border of something; the strip of land which borders a road or path
5. **Ecstasy:** *n.* a feeling of extreme happiness
6. **Relieve:** *v.* to reduce someone's pain or unpleasant feelings; to make a problem less difficult or serious
7. **Unfathomable:** *adj.* difficult or impossible to understand or measure; incomprehensible
8. **Abyss:** *n.* a very dangerous or frightening situation; a deep empty hole in the ground; a very big difference that separates two people or groups
9. **Miniature:** *n.* a very small example or model of something that is usually much larger
10. **Apprehend:** *v.* (formal) (of the police) to catch sb and arrest them; to understand

or recognize sth.

11. **Flux:** *n.* a situation in which things are changing a lot and you cannot be sure what will happen

12. **Reverberate:** *v.* (of a sound) to be repeated several times as it bounces off different surfaces; (of a place) to seem to shake because of a loud noise; (formal) to have a strong effect on people for a long time or over a large area

13. **Alleviate:** *v.* to make something less painful or difficult to deal with

III. Writing

Read the following article, and write an approximately 400-word essay, discussing the important qualities that a person should live with.

Our Family Creed[1]

They are the principles on which my wife and I have tried to bring up my family. They are the principles in which my father believed, and by which he governed his life. They are the principles, many of them, which I learned at my mother's knee.

They point the way to usefulness and happiness in life, to courage and peace in death.

If they mean to you what they mean to me, they may perhaps be helpful also to our sons for their guidance and inspiration.

Let me state them:

I believe in the supreme worth of the individual and his right to life, liberty and the pursuit of happiness.

I believe that every right implies a responsibility, every opportunity, an obligation, every possession, a duty.

I believe that the law was made for the man, but not man for the law. The government is the servant of the people, but not their master.

I believe in the dignity of the labor, whether with head or hand. That the world owns no man a living, but that it owns every man an opportunity to make a living.

I believe that thrift is essential to well-ordered living and economy is a prime requisite of sound financial structure, whether in government, business or personal affairs.

I believe that truth and justice are fundamental to an enduring social order.

I believe in the sacredness of a promise, that a man's word should be as good as his

---

1 John Davison Rockefeller, Our Family Creed, *The New York Times*, July 9, 1941.

bond, that character—not wealth, power and position—is of supreme worth.

I believe that the rendering of useful service is the common duty of mankind, that only in the purifying fire of sacrifice is the dross of selfishness consumed and the greatness of the human soul set free.

I believe that love is the greatest thing in the world, that it alone can overcome hate, that right can and will triumph over might.

These are the principles, however formulated, for which all good men and women throughout the world, irrespective of race or creed, education, social position or occupation, are standing, and for which many of them are suffering and dying.

These are the principles upon which alone a new world recognizing the brotherhood of man can be established.

IV. Questions for Further Thought

1. Life is more than having a good income and a stable job. Many things inspire us to live and fight for. What qualities or passions can you find to inspire your life?

2. Discuss how we can achieve a life that we "have found it worth living, and would gladly live it again if the chance were offered".

[Mini-task for Chapter 4]

Questionnaire and report

Design a questionnaire for your fellow classmates or students in your university, focusing on the following three topics and write an approximately 500-word report.

1. Describe your lifestyle.

2. Are you satisfied with your current lifestyle? Why or why not?

3. What types of lifestyle do you wish to form and foster?

[Further Reading]

1. Michaela Benson, Karen O'Reilly, *Lifestyle Migration: Expectations, Aspirations and Experiences*, England: Burlington, VT: Ashgate, 2009.

2. Isaacson Walter, *Steve Jobs*, New York: Simon & Schuster, 2011.

3. (法)克劳德·拉朋特，(法)西尔维特·甘多勒，陶然译，定格时光·幸福规画，北京：中信出版社，2013.

4. 张剑，英语文学的社会历史分析，北京：人民出版社，2020.

5 Mindset

Passage 1　*The Little Prince*　/ 138

Passage 2　Dare to Feel Joy　/ 145

Passage 3　Breaking Bad　/ 149

Passage 4　How to Grow Old　/ 156

[本章导读]

英国前首相"铁娘子"（Irion Lady）玛格丽特·撒切尔夫人（Margaret Thatcher）曾这样总结，"小心你的想法，因为它们会成为言辞。小心你的言辞，因为它们会成为行动。小心你的行动，因为它们会成为习惯。小心你的习惯，因为它们会成为性格。小心你的性格，因为它会成为你的命运"（Watch your thoughts, for they become words. Watch your words, for they become actions. Watch your actions, for they become habits. Watch your habits, for they become character. Watch your character, for it becomes your destiny.）。可见，"命运"是一个环环相扣的过程，而其中的核心要素则是每个人的心态。

如果说，心态决定姿态，而姿态关乎结果，那么如何才能培养健全的人格并维护心理的健康呢？或许，这对于青年学子来说是一个非常重要的青春课题。因此，本章选篇的主题是贯穿一生的心态培养。根据人生的不同阶段，四篇选文有针对性地介绍人在青少年、青年与中年，直至生命步入晚年的不同时期该如何形成良好心态并维护自身心理健康。本章第一篇选自法国著名作家安东尼·德·圣—埃克苏佩里）（Antoine de Saint-Exupéry）的佳作《小王子》（The Little Prince），节选了书中的第 21 章、22 章和 23 章。在这部分故事中，因目睹了各类残缺人格而深感困惑的小王子遇到了生命中的导师狐狸（Fox），并从它那里开始领悟何为正确的人生态度。第二篇和第三篇解答的是青年和中年人的普遍心理问题。事业的压力、生活的负担以及由此带来的复杂的情绪变化，面对种种难题，该如何保有从容、乐观和淡然的成熟态度？第四篇选了伯特兰·罗素（Bertrand Russel）的名篇《论衰老》（"How to Grow Old"）。文章剖析了幸福晚年所不能或缺的心理状态，并从中折射出一个道理——心态，尤其是心理的健康，是一生的课业，修得好与不好不仅深刻地影响着人生沿途的风景，更预示着晚年时的境遇。

诚然，一个人若想达到庄子《逍遥游》（"A Happy Excursion"）中所揭示的人生境界并非易事。然而，青年人能够懂得"至人无己，神人无功，圣人无名"（The perfect man ignores self; the divine man ignores achievement; the true Sage ignores reputation.）的修养感悟仍然是有意义的。

文化智慧阅读

[Passage 1]

The Little Prince[1]

Chapter XXI

IT WAS THEN that the fox appeared.

"Good morning," said the fox.

"Good morning," the little prince responded politely, although when he turned around he saw nothing.

"I am right here," the voice said, "under the apple tree."

"Who are you?" asked the little prince, and added, "You are very pretty to look at."

"I am a fox," the fox said.

"Come and play with me," proposed the little prince. "I am so unhappy."

"I cannot play with you," the fox said. "I am not **tamed**."

> What does "tame" imply?

"Ah! Please excuse me," said the little prince.

But, after some thought, he added:

"What does that mean— 'tame'?"

"You do not live here," said the fox. "What is it that you are looking for?"

"I am looking for men," said the little prince. "What does that mean— 'tame'?"

"Men," said the fox. "They have guns, and they hunt. It is very disturbing. They also raise chickens. These are their only interests. Are you looking for chickens?"

"No," said the little prince. "I am looking for friends. What does that mean—'tame'?"

"It is an act too often neglected," said the fox. "It means to establish ties."

> What has caused the perplexity that people are concerned about "ties", but often ignore the maintenance of relationships?

"'To establish ties'?"

"Just that," said the fox. "To me, you are still nothing more than a little boy who is

---

1 Antoine de Saint-Exupéry, Translated by Katherine I. Woods, *The Little Prince*, Orlando, Florida: Harcourt Brace Company, 1995, pp. 127—144.

just like a hundred thousand other little boys. And I have no need of you. And you, on your part, have no need of me. To you, I am nothing more than a fox like a hundred thousand other foxes. But if you tame me, then we shall need each other. To me, you will be unique in all the world. To you, I shall be unique in all the world…"

"I am beginning to understand," said the little prince. "There is a flower…I think that she has tamed me…"

"It is possible," said the fox. "On the Earth one sees all sorts of things."

"Oh, but this is not on the Earth!" said the little prince.

The fox seemed **perplexed**, and very curious.

"On another planet?"

"Yes."

"Are there hunters on that planet?"

"No."

"Ah, that is interesting! Are there chickens?"

"No."

"Nothing is perfect," sighed the fox.

But he came back to his idea.

"My life is very **monotonous**," he said. "I hunt chickens; men hunt me. All the chickens are just alike, and all the men are just alike. And, in consequence, I am a little bored. But if you tame me, it will be as if the sun came to shine on my life. I shall know the sound of a step that will be different from all the others. Other steps send me hurrying back underneath the ground. Yours will call me, like music, out of my **burrow**. And then look: you see the grain fields down **yonder**? I do not eat bread. Wheat is of no use to me. The wheat fields have nothing to say to me. And that is sad. But you have hair that is the color of gold. Think how wonderful that will be when you have tamed me! The grain, which is also golden, will bring love to listen to the wind me back the thought of you. And I shall in the wheat…"

The fox gazed at the little prince, for a long time.

"Please—tame me!" he said.

"I want to, very much," the little prince replied. "But I have not much time. I have friends to discover, and a great to understand."

"One only understands the things that one tames," said the fox. "Men have no more

> **5** Mindset
>
> Passage 1
>
> What does "tame" mean?
>
> What does the rule imply?
>
> Why does the fox feel sad?

文化智慧阅读

time to understand anything. They buy things already made at the shops. But there is no shop anywhere where one can buy friendship, and so men have no friends any more. If you want a friend, tame me…"

"What must I do, to tame you?" asked the little prince.

What factors are critical to establishing ties? In doing so, what sort of mindset is demanded?

"You must be very patient," replied the fox. "<u>First you will sit down at a little distance from me—like that—in the grass. I shall look at you out of the corner of my eye, and you will say nothing. Words are the source of misunderstandings. But you will sit a little closer to me, every day…</u>"

The next day the little prince came back.

"It would have been better to come back at the same hour," said the fox. "If, for example, you come at four o'clock in the afternoon, then at three o'clock I shall begin to be happy. I shall feel happier and happier as the hour advances. At four o'clock, I shall already be worrying and jumping about. I shall show you how happy I am! But if you come at just any time, I shall never know at what hour my heart is to be ready to greet you…One must observe the proper rites…"

"What is a rite?" asked the little prince.

What does "rite" mean? Why is it meaningful for life?

"Those also are actions too often neglected," said the fox. "They are what make one day different from other days, one hour from other hours. <u>There is a rite</u>, for example, among my hunters. Every Thursday they dance with the village girls. So Thursday is a wonderful day for me! I can take a walk as far as the vineyards. But if the hunters danced at just any time, every day would be like every other day, and I should never have any vacation at all."

So the little prince tamed the fox. And when the hour of his departure drew near—

"Ah," said the fox, "I shall cry."

"It is your own fault," said the little prince. "I never wished you any sort of harm; but you wanted me to tame you…"

"Yes, that is so," said the fox.

"But now you are going to cry!" said the little prince.

"Yes, that is so," said the fox.

"Then it has done you no good at all!"

"It has done me good," said the fox, "because of the color of the wheat fields." And then he added:

5 Mindset

"Go and look again at the roses. <u>You will understand now that yours is unique in all the world.</u> Then come back to say goodbye to me, and I will make you a present of a secret."

Passage 1
What will make the Rose unique?

The little prince went away, to look again at the roses.

"You are not at all like my rose," he said. "As yet you are nothing. No one has tamed you, and you have tamed no one. You are like my fox when I first knew him. He was only a fox like a hundred thousand other foxes. But I have made him my friend, and now he is unique in all the world."

And the roses were very much embarrassed.

"<u>You are beautiful, but you are empty</u>," he went on. "One could not die for you. To be sure, an ordinary passerby would think that my rose looked just like you—the rose that belongs to me. But in herself alone she is more important than all the hundreds of you other roses: because it is she that I have watered; because it is she that I have put under the glass globe; because it is she that I have sheltered behind the screen; because it is for her that I have killed the caterpillars (except the two or three that we saved to become butterflies); because it is she that I have listened to, when she **grumbled**, or boasted, or even sometimes when she said nothing. <u>Because she is my rose</u>."

Paraphrase the sentence.

How does the Little Prince develop an understanding of "ties"?

And he went back to meet the fox.

"Goodbye," he said.

"Goodbye," said the fox. "And now here is my secret: <u>It is only with the heart that once can see rightly; what is essential is invisible to the eye.</u>"

Comment on the point.

"What is essential is invisible to the eye," the little prince repeated, so that he would be sure to remember.

"<u>It is the time you have devoted to your rose that makes your rose so important.</u>"

What does the sentence imply?

"It is the time I have devoted to my rose—" said the little prince, so that he would be sure to remember.

"Men have forgotten this truth," said the fox. "But you must not forget it. You become responsible, forever, for what you have tamed. You are responsible for your rose…"

"I am responsible for my rose," the little prince repeated, so that he would be sure to remember.

Chapter XXII

"GOOD MORNING," said the little prince.

141

"Good morning," said the railway switchman.

"What do you do here?" the little prince asked.

"I sort out travelers, in bundles of a thousand," said the switchman. "I send off the trains that carry them: now to the right, now to the left."

And a brilliantly lighted express train shook the switchman's cabin as it rushed by with a roar like thunder.

"They are in a great hurry," said the little prince. "What are they looking for?"

"Not even the locomotive engineer knows that," said the switchman.

And a second brilliantly lighted express thundered by, in the opposite direction.

"Are they coming back already?" demanded the little prince.

"These are not the same ones," said the switchman. "It is an exchange."

"Were they not satisfied where they were?" asked the little prince.

"No one is ever satisfied where he is," said the switchman.

And they heard the roaring thunder of a third brilliantly lighted express.

"Are they pursuing the first travelers?" demanded the little prince?

"They are pursuing nothing at all," said the switchman. "They are asleep in there, or if they are not asleep they are yawning. Only the children are flattening their noses against the windowpanes."

"Only the children know what they are looking for," said the little prince. "They devote their time to a rag doll and it becomes very important to them; and if anybody takes it away from them, they cry…"

"They are lucky," the switchman said.

Chapter XXIII

"GOOD MORNING," said the little prince.

"Good morning," said the merchant.

This was a merchant who sold pills that had been invented to quench thirst. You need only swallow one pill a week, and you would feel no need of anything to drink.

"Why are you selling those?" asked the little prince.

"Because they save a tremendous amount of time," said the merchant. "Computations have been made by experts. With these pills, you save fifty-three minutes in every week."

"And what do I do with those fifty-three minutes?"

"Anything you like…"

<u>"As for me," said the little prince to himself, "if I had fifty-three minutes to spend as I liked, I should walk at my leisure toward a spring of fresh water."</u>

I. Background Information

The Little Prince tells of the story that a pilot encounters a young boy when he crashes his plane in Sahara Desert.

The narrator refers to him as "little Prince". During the following eight days, the prince recounts his story that he is from a tiny planet and has visited six other asteroids in order to add to his knowledge. Sadly, all adults he met are narrow-minded including a king to whom all men are subjects, a conceited man who never hearing anything but praise, a tippler drinking to forget the shame of drinking, a businessman who is naturally interested in matters of consequence, a lamplighter who mindlessly puts on and relights street lamps because orders are orders, and an old geographer who never leaves his desk. On Earth, he met a yellow snake, a dessert flower, a fox and a railway switchman. They helped Little Prince in different ways reflect on life and human nature. The Fox, in particular, explained why one needs to feel responsible for what he or she owns. In the end, the Little Prince decides to come back to his home planet and bids an emotional farewell to the narrator stating though he shall look as if he was dead, it is only because the body is too heavy to carry, and there is nothing sad about abandoning "old shells".

The Little Prince is the most read and most translated book in the French language. It is a book actually dedicated to adults for that "all grown-ups were once children, although few of them remember it".

II. Notes

1. **Tame:** *v.* to train a wild animal to obey you and not to attack people
2. **Perplexed:** *adj.* confused and worried by something that you do not understand
3. **Monotonous:** *adj.* boring because there is no variety
4. **Burrow:** *n.* a passage in the ground made by a rabbit or fox as a place to live
5. **Yonder:** *adv.* used for telling someone which place or direction you mean

---

5 Mindset

Passage 1

Discuss the Little Prince's mindset.

6. **Grumble:** *v.* to keep complaining in an unhappy way

7. **Locomotive:** *n.* technical or a railway engine

8. **Yawn:** *v.* to open our mouth wide and breathe in deeply, usually because you are tired or bored

9. **Quench:** *v.* to stop yourself from feeling thirsty

10. **Computation:** *n.* the process of calculating or the result of calculating

III. Discussion

Make brief comments on the following statements from *The Little Prince*.

1. All of them are lonely. They do not know how to love.

2. People no longer have the time to understand anything. They buy everything ready-made from the shops. But there is no shop where friends can be bought, so people no longer have friends.

3. Go and look at the rose again. You will understand that yours is, after all, unique in the world.

IV. Questions for Further Thought

1. How is one's mindset changed from children to grow-ups, according to *The Little Prince*?

2. What can adults learn from children regarding mindset?

[Passage 2]

Dare to Feel Joy[1]

If you are always <u>waiting for the other shoe to drop</u>, says Brené Brown, you're **missing out**.

I used to stand over my two kids while they slept, and <u>just as a profound sense of love and joy washed over me, I'd imagine horrible things happening to them: car crashes, **tsunamis**.</u> Do other mothers do this, I'd wonder, or am I **unhinged**? I now know from my research that 95 percent of parents can relate to my constant disaster planning. When we're overwhelmed by love, we feel vulnerable—so we dress-rehearse tragedy.

Though I study scary emotions like anger and shame for a living, <u>I think the most terrifying human experience is joy</u>. It's as if we believe that by truly feeling happiness, we're setting ourselves up for a **sucker punch**. <u>The problem is, worrying about things that haven't happened doesn't protect us from pain.</u> Ask anyone who has experienced a tragedy; they'll tell you there is no way to prepare. Instead, **catastrophizing**, as I call it, squanders the one thing we all want more of in life. We simply cannot know joy without embracing vulnerability—and the way to do that is to focus on gratitude, not fear.

The good news is that joy, collected over time, fuels **resilience**—ensuring we'll have reservoirs of emotional strength when hard things do happen.

THE DARE:

Stop the train. <u>The next time you're traumatized by "What ifs," say aloud, "I am feeling vulnerable"</u>. This sentence changed my life. It takes me out of my fear brain—i.e., off the crazy train—and puts me back on the platform, where I can make a conscious

---

1 Brené Brown, *Daring Greatly: How the Courage to Be Vulnerable Transforms the Way We Live, Love, Parent, and Lead,* New York: Penguin, 2012.

Sidebar questions:

Discuss Brené Brown's illustration of mindset.

Why do some people often feel vulnerable in happiness?

Comment on the statement.

Do you agree with the opinion? Why or why not?

How do you restore and keep your peace of mind?

choice not tore board.

Be thankful. Recently, when a turbulent flight caused me to start planning my own funeral, I remembered something I'd learned in my research: Joyous people are grateful people. So I used the fear alarm in my head as are minder to feel grateful for my kids, my husband, and my work. Even more effective: Speak your gratitude aloud to others, or write it in your journal.

Start a practice. I believe joy is a spiritual practice we have to work at. For me, that means appreciating everyday moments: a walk with my husband, fishing with my kids on the Gulf Coast. It means not living in fear of what I could lose, but softening into the moments I have.

> Which habit looks more acceptable to you?
>
> What does "spiritual practice" refer to?

I. Background Information

Brené Brown (born November 18, 1965), PhD, researches vulnerability, shame, courage, and worthiness at the University of Houston Graduate College of Social Work. She is concerned "Researcher and thought leader [who] offers a powerful new vision that encourages us to dare greatly: to embrace vulnerability and imperfection, to live wholeheartedly, and to courageously engage in our lives" (Book Description, *Daring Greatly: How the Courage to Be Vulnerable Transforms the Way We Live, Love, Parent, and Lead*).

In the Preface of *Daring Greatly* entitled "What It Means to Dare Greatly", Dr. Brown noted that "The phrase Daring Greatly is from Theodore Roosevelt's speech 'Citizenship in a Republic'. The speech sometimes referred to as 'The Man in the Arena,' was delivered at the Sorbonne in Paris, France, on April 23, 1910. This is the passage that made speech famous 'It is not the critic who counts; not the man who points out how the strong man stumbles, or where the doer of deeds could have done them better. The credit belongs to the man who is actually in the arena, whose face is marred by dust and sweat and blood; who strives valiantly; ... who at best knows in the end the triumph of high achievement, and who at worst, if he fails, at least fails while daring greatly'".

II. Notes

1. **Tsunami:** *n.* a very large wave, often caused by an earthquake that flows onto the land and destroys things

2. **Unhinged:** *adj.* be critical of some behavior because it seems wild and uncontrollable

3. **Catastrophize:** *v.* to view an event or situation as worse than it actually is, or as if it were a disaster

4. **Resilience:** *n.* the power or ability to return to the original form, position, etc., after being bent, compressed, or stretched

5. **Miss out:** If you miss out on something that would be enjoyable or useful to you, you are not involved in it or do not take part in it.

6. **A sucker punch:** an unexpected blow with fist

III. Reading Comprehension

Read the following article, and choose the best answer to each question.

Everyone feels overwhelmed at some point—it's completely normal. Meditating daily for ten minutes is one of the best things you can do to manage stress and quell anxiety. There are also a few habits you can learn that will allow you to collect your thoughts and remain calm.

Take a deep breath. Fear and anxiety cause your breathing to become short and shallow. If you lengthen your breath, you can in turn affect your emotions. Deep breathing signals to your brain that your body is calming down. Your mind will follow.

Be in the moment. When you have a coffee, take two minutes to sit down and drink it. Notice the warmth, the smell, and the taste. Or if you're walking down the street, pay attention to your soles hitting the pavement. By focusing your brain on physical sensations for just a few minutes, you short-circuit the thinking mind. You immediately quiet your thoughts, which will help you think more clearly for the rest of your day.

Jot it down. If there are things you're worried about forgetting, write them down before bed. But then try this: make the last item on the list something you are grateful for that day. I know it sounds cheesy, but there is strong science to show that doing this evokes feelings of well-being, so you enter a happier state of mind—and get more restful sleep.

1. When you feel overwhelmed, it is suggested that you _____.

(A) should try to get rid of the abnormal feeling

(B) would better concentrate and think intently for a few minutes

(C) should forget about what happened

(D) should take actions immediately to eliminate stress and anxiety

2. You are advised to take a deep breath because_____.

(A) your breath is short and shallow

(B) deep breathing calms you down

(C) you brain stops working

(D) deep breathing helps blood circulation

3. All the following statements are correct EXCEPT _____.

(A) you can use the coffee time to relax your mind

(B) listening to the soles hitting the pavement calls off your attention from the thinking

(C) you'd better read the sensational news rather than focusing on the work at hand

(D) a short-time mental rest can improve the efficiency of thinking

4. In case you forget the things you have to do, you'd better _____.

(A) write them down immediately after you get up the next morning

(B) get more restful sleep

(C) jot them down in a cheesy way

(D) write them down and make the item cheering you up the last

IV. Questions for Further Thought

1. In *Daring Greatly: How the Courage to Be Vulnerable Transforms the Way We Live, Love, Parent, and Lead*, Dr. Brené Brown asked a question that "what drives our fear of being vulnerable?" Share your reflections on the question.

2. How can people protect themselves from feeling vulnerable?

[Passage 3]

Breaking Bad[1]

Nail biting, midnight snacking.... Unlocking the causes of a bad habit is the first step toward forming a good One.

Each morning you brush your teeth, turn on the *Today* show, and stop by the Starbucks around the corner without thinking about it. As humans, it's only natural that we believe we're in control of these and all of our actions at all times. It's what separates us from apes (aside from reality TV and $200 haircuts). But when Immanuel Kant praised the power of human **autonomy**, he probably didn't realize that more than 40 percent of the tasks we perform each day—like the ones in our morning routine—aren't conscious decisions, but mere habits. "Habits are a very basic way of learning," says Wendy Wood, a professor of psychology at the University of Southern California. "They teach us to associate actions with certain contexts, so whenever we're in that situation again, the same result automatically comes to mind".

This **neurological** auto pilot saves the time and energy needed to make constant decisions, but it can also cause problems when we aren't aware of our behavior and fail to notice the circumstances that act as cues. Inhaling a few rookies one afternoon might be relatively harmless the day you need a sugar boost to meet a deadline, but if you start doing that regularly, your brain begins to expect the snack whether your body needs it or not. Once habits form, sheer willpower often isn't enough to change them. The good news: Scientific studies have revealed ways to recognize the impulses you'd like to change and create new, better routines. "Habits aren't deeply **ingrained** psychodynamic needs," says Wood. "They're simple associative patterns,

---

1 Alexandra Owens, Breaking Bad, *Allure,* October 2013, pp. 184—188.

文化智慧阅读

Have you tried a similar strategy?

so the mechanisms to break them are equally simple." <u>Repetition is key for all of these techniques—and once you establish the behavior you want, it will actually become a habit.</u>

1 Take notes.

It's not exactly a secret that our memory is selective. "Even though we make promises to change a habit, when the situation arises we often don't take action because we've forgotten or are tired or distracted." says Jeremy Dean, a psychologist and the author of *Making Habits. Breaking Habits* (Da Capo). If there's a pattern of behavior you'd like to change—say, staying up too late on Facebook—keep a record of everything about that habit. Write down how you're feeling and what time you go on your nightly social-media **binge**. "<u>The more you understand your habit, the more you can use that information to be vigilant at the appropriate times to make sure the behavior isn't triggered.</u>" says Wood. Once you know the triggers, making a chance can be as simple as scolding yourself: Say "Don't do it" at the moments when you sense that you're back tracking.

Paraphrase the sentence.

2 Get strong.

What does the sentence imply?

Developing a new habit often requires plenty of self-control, and your willpower, like a muscle needs exercise. <u>Megan Oaten and Ken Cheng, psychologists at Macquarie University in Sydney, Australia, have found through a series of studies that self-control in one area breeds self-control in others.</u> In one example, students who enrolled in a program to improve their study habits found that they cut back on smoking, drinking, and television. Meditation may also be an effective way to strengthen willpower. For an easy five-minute practice, try closing your eyes and focusing on your breath. If you get distracted by a thought, acknowledge it without **chastising** yourself and refocus. "There is interesting work saying that certain types of meditation can help you pay more attention to your environment and break repeated tasks," Wood says, "Meditation has been shown to boost activity in the executive part of the brain, the area that decides what we're going to do, which improves self-control," says Dean.

How do you build up your self-control?

3 Plan ahead.

Sometimes your willpower is strong—and sometimes you're feeling weak and really want to go to Chipotle. <u>The more decisions you can make when you're focused, calm,</u>

Paraphrase the sentence.

and well-rested—in other words, when your self-control is at its peak, the better. "It's putting your executive brain in charge rather than your impulsive brain," says Joe Frascella, director of the Division of Clinical Neuroscience and Behavioral Research at the National Institute on Drug Abuse in Bethesda, Maryland. If you know you're going out for dinner but you want to keep the calories under control, pick a Japanese restaurant rather than Mexican. Or if you always stop at Zara to see what's new on your way to the gym, leave your credit card at home.

4 Distract yourself.

Habits seem **tenacious**, but they actually suffer from a little ADD. They are so reliant on external cues that they can be disrupted by a simple visual reminder. To kick a habit, remove any visual triggers that might cause you to slip, and replace them with eye-catching objects to remind you of your resolution. "I've found that people who are trying to stop biting their nails can paint them a bright color," says Dean. "When their hand comes up, they remember their plan and often decide immediately to stop." A physical roadblock can also help you snap out of it. In experiments at Duke University, Wood and her colleagues had people eat stale popcorn while watching a movie. If they ate with their dominant hand, they kept snacking during the film, even though they later acknowledged that the popcorn was stale. But if they ate with their non-dominant hand, it seemed to disrupt the habit, and they paid attention to how the popcorn tasted. "It's the same principle behind swapping your fork for chopsticks: Using an unfamiliar tool is another way to ensure that you only eat what you really want," says Wood. If you find you get caught up tweezing your eyebrows or picking at blackheads, try using your non dominant hand to make the action more difficult and less hypnotic before you do any damage.

5 Link up.

When a company wants you to fall for something new, like the latest song on the radio, it's not uncommon for it to use a technique called "sand-wicking," surrounding the unfamiliar material with what already feels comfortable—for example, playing a new release between two hits. Experts have found the same approach works when adopting a habit. "I think of all our activities during the day as a chain," says Dean. "So if you want to create a new habit, look for a spot in your routine where you can fit in the new action conveniently and with minimal effort." For example, if you want to exercise more, plan to hit the gym before your weekly manicure. If you need to **floss** daily but tend to put it off, do it at night between washing your face and brushing your teeth, instead of during the morning rush. "You want to make a habit part of the context in which you live," says Wood. "It takes work initially, but eventually it will happen automatically. That's the beauty of habits."

> *Discuss "the beauty of habits".*

6 Make a trade.

Like preventing your dog from destroying your Manolos by giving him a new bone (presumably one that doesn't cost $900), there's evidence that smart substitution is an effective way to break a habit. Wood suggests choosing something that gives a similar type of response to satisfy the craving-think smokers chewing gum, or squeezing a stress ball instead of picking at your split ends. This solution is especially useful in situations where you can't avoid potent cues such as social settings. If you're trying to snack less and are invited to a friend's engagement party, make sure you have something in your hand as you **mingle**, even if it's a glass of sparkling water or a few carrot sticks-something to put in your mouth instead of the fried spring rolls.

> *Explain the advice with examples.*

7 Accentuate the positive.

There really is power in positive thinking and writing. In a study led by psychologist Pablo Briñol at the Universidad Autónoma de Madrid, test subjects were asked to make a list of the good and bad things they had heard about the Mediterranean diet. Some kept what they had written in their pockets; others threw the lists away. Those who held on to the page with positive thoughts were more likely to adopt the diet they had described than those who didn't, suggesting that the influence of our intentions can be magnified by carrying them with us—literally—as a reminder. According to Dean, just the very step of listing pros and cons on paper can increase motivation as well. "You want to visualize all the positives outweighing the negatives to pull you toward your goal," he says. "It helps to make an actual written list."

> *What does the "power" of "positive thinking and writing" mean?*
>
> *What would you do in this situation?*

8 Be specific.

While most of us have made a New Year's resolution at some point, only 40 percent succeed in keeping them, according to new research from the University of Scranton. So why is that determination to be on time, to save money, and to always be kind to strangers so often a bust? Those goals are too broad, say the experts. "To create a habit, your mind has to link a situation to a specific action", says Dean. You need what's called an "implementation intention"—a detailed strategy of how you will form and maintain a new habit. This is easier to follow than a resolution that's too vague or ambitious, because it involves a particular, productive action. So instead of telling yourself, "I'm going to get organized," try, "I'm going to clean out my handbag every Sunday night before bed."

9 Consider the big picture.

It seems a little melodramatic, but when you're fighting the urge to turn on Bravo instead of turning in for the night, thinking about what is really important to you, like your family, friends, freedom, or religious beliefs, has been shown to boost resolve. Researchers at Florida State University asked test subjects to submerge their hand in a bucket of freezing water. The average person lasted for 27 seconds, but those who had first written an essay about their higher ideals managed an average of 62 seconds. Strangely, the thought doesn't have to be connected to the habit you're trying to change, says Dean. He speculates this is because when we're tempted by something, we tend to think in the moment, while contemplating high-minded thoughts makes us think abstractly and perhaps more nobly. To give yourself a boost, remember why a particular value or person matters to you, or look at a photo of him of her.

I. Background Information

Most of life is habitual. As for habits without which no one can succeed, Benjamin Franklin famously stated 13 virtues, namely, Temperance, Silence, Order, Resolution, Frugality, Industry, sincerity Justice, Moderation, Cleanliness, Tranquility, Chastity, and Humility.

Habits, good or bad, make you who you are. Therefore, it is virtually important to control them. If you know how to change your habits, then even a small effort can create big changes. Try to find some techniques to get you started.

II. Notes

1. **Autonomy:** *n.* the control or government of a country, organization, or group by itself rather than by others

2. **Neurological:** *adj.* related to the nervous system

3. **Ingrained:** *adj.* ingrained habits and beliefs are difficult to change or remove

4. **Binge:** *n.* a short period to do too much of something, such as drinking alcohol, eating, or spending money

5. **Chastise:** *v.* to speak to people angrily or punish them for something wrong that they have done

6. **Tenacious:** *adj.* something tenacious has a strong influence on people and is difficult to change or remove

7. **Floss:** *v.* to use a thread to remove food particles and plaque from between the teeth and under the gums

8. **Mingle:** *v.* to move around at a party and talk to people

III. Translation

Read Benjamin Franklin's statements on virtues and translate them into Chinese[1].

TEMPERANCE: Eat not to dullness; drink not to elation.

SILENCE: Speak not but what may benefit others or yourself; avoid trifling conversation.

ORDER: Let all your things have their places; let each part of your business have its time.

RESOLUTION: Resolve to perform what you ought; perform without fail what you resolve.

FRUGALITY: Make no expense but to do good to others or yourself; that is, waste nothing.

INDUSTRY: Lose no time; be always employed in something useful; cut off all unnecessary actions.

SINCERITY: Use no hurtful deceit; think innocently and justly, and, if you speak, speak accordingly.

---

1 Benjamin Franklin, *Autobiography of Benjamin Franklin*, New York: The Quinn & Boden Co. Press, 1916, p.146.

JUSTICE: Wrong none by doing injuries; or omitting the benefits of your duty.

MODERATION: Avoid extremes; forbear resenting injuries so much as you think they deserve.

CLEANLINESS: Tolerate no uncleanliness in body, clothes, or habitation.

TRANQUILITY: Be not disturbed at trifles or at accidents common or unavoidable.

IV. Questions for Further Thought

1. How could the tips that Passage Three provides help to break your entrenched bad habits?

2. How could you unlock the causes of bad habits and form good habits?

[Passage 4]

How to Grow Old[1]

What does Russell intend to illustrate?

In spite of the title, this article will really be on how not to grow old, which, at my time of life, is a much more important subject. My first advice would be to choose your ancestors carefully. Although both my parents died young, I have done well in this respect as regards my other ancestors. My maternal grandfather, it is true, was cut off in the flower of his youth at the age of sixty-seven, but my other three grandparents all lived to be over eighty. Of remoter ancestors I can only discover one who did not live to a great age, and he died of a disease which is now rare, namely, having his head cut off. A great-grandmother of mine, who was a friend of Gibbon, lived to the age of ninety-two, and to her last day remained a terror to all her descendants. My maternal grandmother, after having nine children who survived, one who died in infancy, and many miscarriages, as soon as she became a widow devoted herself to women's higher education. She was one of the founders of Girton College, and worked hard at opening the medical profession to women. She used to tell of how she met in Italy an elderly gentleman who was looking very sad. She asked him why he was so melancholy and he said that he had just parted from his two grandchildren. "Good gracious," she exclaimed, "I have seventy-two grandchildren, and if I were sad each time I parted from one of them, I should have a miserable existence!" "Madre snaturale!" he replied. But speaking as one of the seventy-two, I prefer her recipe. After the age of eighty she found she had some difficulty in getting to sleep, so she habitually spent the hours from midnight to 3 a.m. in reading popular science. I do not believe that she ever had time to notice that she was growing old. This, I think, is the proper recipe for remaining young.

What does "terror" imply in this sentence?

How does Russell's maternal grandmother respond to growing old?

---

1 Bertrand Arthur William Russell, How to Grow Old, *Portraits from Memory: And Other Essays*, California: G. Allen & Unwin, 1956, pp. 50—52.

5 Mindset

Passage 4

If you have wide and keen interests and activities in which you can still be effective, you will have no reason to think about the merely statistical fact of the number of years you have already lived, still less of the probable shortness of your future.

As regards health, I have nothing useful to say as I have little experience of illness. <u>I eat and drink whatever I like, and sleep when I cannot keep awake. I never do anything whatever on the ground that it is good for health, though in actual fact the things I like doing are mostly **wholesome**.</u>

Psychologically there are two dangers to be guarded against in old age. One of these is undue absorption in the past. It does not do to live in memories, in regrets for the good old days, or in sadness about friends who are dead. One's thoughts must be directed to the future, and to things about which there is something to be done. This is not always easy; one's own past is a gradually increasing weight. It is easy to think to oneself that one's emotions used to be more vivid than they are, and one's mind more keen. If this is true it should be forgotten, and if it is forgotten it will probably not be true.

<u>The other thing to be avoided is clinging to youth in the hope of sucking **vigor** from its vitality.</u> When your children are grown up they want to live their own lives, and if you continue to be as interested in them as you were when they were young, you are likely to become a burden to them, unless they are unusually **callous**. I do not mean that one should be without interest in them, but one's interest should be contemplative and, if possible, **philanthropic**, but not unduly emotional. Animals become indifferent to their young as soon as their young can look after themselves, but human beings, owing to the length of infancy, find this difficult.

I think that a successful old age is easiest for those who have strong <u>impersonal interests</u> involving appropriate activities. It is in this sphere that long experience is really fruitful, and it is in this sphere that the wisdom born of experience can be exercised without being oppressive. It is no use telling grownup children not to make mistakes, both because they will not believe you, and because mistakes are an essential part of education. But if you are one of those who are incapable of impersonal interests, you may find that your life will be empty unless you concern yourself with your children and grandchildren. <u>In that case you must realize that while you can still render them material services, such as making them an allowance or knitting them jumpers, you must not expect that they will enjoy your company.</u>

Comment on Russell's mindset.

Paraphrase the sentence.

Explain the "impersonal interests" with examples from your personal experience.

What is your opinion on the point?

文化智慧阅读

Why are some old people "oppressed by the fear of death"?

Paraphrase the sentence.

<u>Some old people are oppressed by the fear of death.</u> In the young there is a justification for this feeling. Young men who have reason to fear that they will be killed in battle may justifiably feel bitter in the thought that they have been cheated of the best things that life has to offer. But in an old man who has known human joys and sorrows, and has achieved whatever work it was in him to do, the fear of death is somewhat **abject** and **ignoble**. <u>The best way to overcome it -so at least it seems to me- is to make your interests gradually wider and more impersonal, until bit by bit the walls of the ego recede, and your life becomes increasingly merged in the universal life. An individual human existence should be like a river: small at first, narrowly contained within its banks, and rushing passionately past rocks and over waterfalls. Gradually the river grows wider, the banks recede, the waters flow more quietly, and in the end, without any visible break, they become merged in the sea, and painlessly lose their individual being.</u> The man who, in old age, can see his life in this way, will not suffer from the fear of death, since the things he cares for will continue. And if, with the decay of vitality, **weariness** increases, the thought of rest will not be unwelcome. I should wish to die while still at work, knowing that others will carry on what I can no longer do and content in the thought that what was possible has been done.

I. Background Information

Russell had an uneventful life behind the glories and successes. For instances, he was deprived of his lectureship in 1916 by his college. Then, he received an offer from Harvard, but was refused a passport. Mainly as a result of his opposition against World War I, he was sentenced a six-month-imprisonment in 1918.

II. Notes

1. **Melancholy:** *adj.* very sad
2. **Wholesome:** *adj.* good for health
3. **Vigor:** *n.* active strength of body or mind
4. **Callous:** *adj.* a callous person or action is very cruel and shows no concern for other people or their feelings
5. **Philanthropic:** *adj.* generous in assistance to the poor
6. **Abject:** *adj.* If you describe someone as abject, you think they have no courage or

respect for themselves.

7. **Ignoble:** *adj.* completely lacking nobility in character or quality or purpose

8. **Weariness:** *n.* temporary loss of strength and energy resulting from hard physical or mental work

III. Writing

Read the two poems, and write an approximately 300-word essay, comparing their answers to getting old.

《酬乐天咏老见示》

刘禹锡

人谁不顾老，老去有谁怜？

身瘦带频减，发稀冠自偏。

废书缘惜眼，多灸为随年。

经事还谙事，阅人如阅川。

细思皆幸矣，下此便翛然。

莫道桑榆晚，为霞尚满天。

When You Are Old[1]

When you are old and grey and full of sleep,

And nodding by the fire, take down this book,

And slowly read, and dream of the soft look,

Your eyes had once, and of their shadows deep;

How many loved your moments of glad grace,

And loved your beauty with love false or true,

But one man loved the pilgrim soul in you,

And loved the sorrows of your changing face;

And bending down beside the glowing bars,

Murmur, a little sadly, how Love fled,

---

1 William Butler Yeats, When You Are Old, *The Collected Poems of W. B. Yeats*, Collier Books, 1989.

And paced upon the mountains overhead,

And hid his face amid a crowd of stars.

IV. Questions for Further Thought

1. What should be avoided in old age, according to Russell?

2. How does Chinese culture interpret "How to grow old"?

[Mini-task for Chapter 5]

Discussion

Read the two quotations about the fixed mindset and the growth mindset, and discuss the following two questions.

Fixed mindset: "This is hard because I'm not smart."

Growth Mindset: "This is hard because I'm learning!"

1. What is your mindset for now, fixed or growth? Explain your answer with examples.

2. How can teachers support students to develop a Growth Mindset?

[Further Reading]

1. Carol Dweck, *Mindset: the New Psychology of Success*, New York: The Random House Publishing Group, 2007.

2. Tal Ben-Shahar, *Happier*, New York: McGraw-Hill, 2007.

3. 冯友兰，冯友兰文集（全10卷），长春：长春出版社，2007.

6 Cultivation

- **Passage 1** The University's Mission, Reaffirmed   / 165
- **Passage 2** Industry and Educational Readjustment   / 169
- **Passage 3** A Culture of Curiosity   / 175
- **Passage 4** Containing of the Coronavirus Outbreak: Truth and Trust   / 182

[本章导读]

习近平总书记在 2018 年全国教育大会上指出,"教育是民族振兴、社会进步的重要基石,是功在当代、利在千秋的德政工程,对提高人民综合素质、促进人的全面发展、增强中华民族创新创造活力、实现中华民族伟大复兴具有决定性意义"[1]。在全球化背景下,由于国家间和地区间的联系日益密切,教育事关人类共同的未来。那么,新环境下的高等教育的精神与本位是什么?时代的变革带给教育和青年学子怎样的新挑战?

为了探讨上述问题,本章选取了四篇文章。第一篇文章来自德鲁·吉尔平·福斯特教授(Drew Gilpin Faust)在波士顿大学建校 150 周年庆典上的演讲,阐述当前高等教育的新使命。福斯特曾任美国哈佛大学第二十八任校长(2007—2018),也是该校历史上第一位女校长。在演讲中,她从历史研究的视角分析社会变革带来的挑战,指出大学的责任在于"点亮过往、塑造未来,明确人类长远的抱负"(to illuminate the past and shape the future, to define human aspirations for the long term)。社会的变革考验着教育的使命与担当,如何科学平衡教育的独立精神与服务时代需求?针对这个问题,第二篇文章节选自著名的教育学家约翰·杜威(John Dewey)与女儿伊芙琳·杜威(Evelyn Dewey)合著的《明日之学校》(*Schools of To-morrow*)第九章。本书聚焦百年前处于快速工业化进程中的美国社会。以剧变的大时代为背景,杜威尝试解释教育应如何适应新的时代特征,在"传统的书本教育(inherited bookish education)和实践教育(practical education)中找到平衡"。当前,"百年变局"成为理解当今时代的关键词。如果百年变局会不可避免地带给年轻人更多的未知与不确定性,我们该如何积极应对?第三篇来自耶鲁大学校长苏必德(Peter Salovey)2019 年的开学演讲,尝试从国际视野给出一个注脚。在演讲中,苏必德结合不同文化背景的案例,剖析了耶鲁的"好奇心文化"(culture of curiosity),他鼓励青年学子面对未知要满怀自信,保持好奇心,有勇气走出舒适区。宏大的时代命题最终需要从一个个具体的实际问题中找寻答案,凝聚

---

[1] 习近平,2018 年全国教育大会讲话,《习近平总书记教育重要论述讲义》,北京:高等教育出版社,2020,第 78 页。

智慧。因此,第四篇针对数字时代以及新冠肺炎疫情带来的深刻变化中,最为全球普遍关注的新时期国际交流合作能力培养。

综上所述,教育是个任重而道远的过程,需要各方面都付出真诚、努力与智慧,而这也正是教育的使命担当。正如美国作家赛珍珠(Pearl Buck)所总结的,"教育的意旨并非知识的累积,而是心智上的能力的发育"(The purpose of education is not the accumulation of knowledge but the development of mental abilities.)。

6 Cultivation

Passage 1

[Passage 1]

The University's Mission, Reaffirmed[1]

"Our task is to illuminate the past and shape the future, to define human aspirations for the long term," President Drew Faust told a crowd of **trustees**, faculty, **alumni**, and friends in Boston College's Robsham Theater.

Show More

By Katie Koch, Harvard Staff Writer

Harvard neighbor Boston College (BC) celebrates its 150th anniversary this year, providing an **opportune** time for the Jesuit institution to reflect on the enduring, necessary <u>struggle</u> between scholarship for social good and inquiry for its own sake, President Drew Faust said on Wednesday.

> What does the "struggle" refer to?

"At their best, universities maintain a creative tension, tackling the purposeful and the apparently pointless with equal delight," she told a crowd of trustees, faculty, alumni, and friends in BC's Robsham Theater. Harvard and BC must keep sight of that goal "in a world where the measure of things so often trumps the meaning of things, and the practical, immediate uses of knowledge so often overshadow the larger, more enduring purposes of education".

Faust had crossed the Charles River to the Heights to kick off the college's Sesquicentennial Speaker Series and to receive the first of three Sesquicentennial Medals that BC will award this year in celebration of its **milestone**.

She spoke following the college's celebratory Mass for 20,000 guests at Fenway Park—"a hard act to follow," she said.

---

1 Drew Gilpin Faust, Faust speaks at Boston College as it celebrates its 150th year, Edited by Kris Snibbe, *Editor's Pick,* October 11, 2012.

文化智慧阅读

Faust was honored for her leadership in higher education and for her Civil War scholarship, work that "has illuminated events of the past, enhancing our understanding of the present," said Kathleen M. McGillycuddy, chair of BC's board of trustees, as BC President William P. Leahy presented Faust with her award.

What does "myopic present" imply?

Faust echoed that aim in her lecture, calling for a broad effort among institutions of higher education to look beyond the "myopic present" and address questions of how to live and how to shape a better future for civilization.

"Certainly, our budgets must balance, our operations must be efficient— but we are not about the bottom line, not about just the next quarter, not even about who our graduates are the day they leave our walls," she said. "Our task is to illuminate the past and shape the future, to define human aspirations for the long term".

What is President Pusey's thinking about the higher education purpose? Why is it described as "call-to-arms"?

Her message wasn't so different from the call-to-arms that Harvard President Nathan M. Pusey delivered to the BC community 50 years ago for its centennial, when he lamented that the two schools' "common task ... does not get easier with the passing centuries." Indeed, the debate over both who and what higher learning is for extends back to BC's founding during the Civil War, Faust said.

Then, as now, Americans were pursuing higher education in unprecedented numbers. As college leaders dealt with this new demand, they struggled to integrate a newfound research agenda with a traditional model of education that aimed to cultivate character.

Explain the different functions of the two kinds of knowledge.

"In what was widely seen to be an increasingly materialistic age, the affirmation of the transcendent purposes of learning came to seem imperative," Faust said, citing leading Catholic thinker Cardinal John Henry Newman's characterization of the struggle between "useful knowledge" and "liberal knowledge".

"In Boston, the argument played out between Boston College and Harvard, in a battle of words whose fierceness would have done the Bean pot rivalry proud," she added to laughter, mentioning Boston's annual hockey tournament.

What is your opinion on the phenomenon? Explain the importance of "curiosity" for university students with examples.

Today, as a college degree becomes an ever-more-necessary credential for success— and as universities continue to play a central role in producing cutting-edge research— leaders must not lose sight of the aim of learning and teaching for its own sake, Faust said.

"The scholarship that has served as the beating heart of the research university is exploration based on curiosity," she said. "Without such scholarship, without zones of contemplation, with only **prescribed** purposes and goals, we will underemphasize the questions that most concern us, our lives, our mysteries".

As the decades have passed, BC's founding principle—"that an education is not just about knowledge, but also about how to live a life"—seems more relevant than ever, Faust concluded.

"Yours is a great university, an institution that in a century and a half has never lost sight of its larger purposes," Faust said. "It is a privilege to celebrate with you that singular achievement and to honor the Jesuit commitment to scholarship, justice, and service. They are all needed today just as urgently as they were 150 years ago".

I. Background Information

Catharine Drew Gilpin Faust (born September 18, 1947) is an American historian, college administrator and the 28th president of Harvard University. Faust is the first woman to serve as Harvard's president.

The above speech was given by Catharine Drew Gilpin Faust when Harvard neighbor Boston College (BC) celebrated its 150th anniversary. In her speech, she stated her viewpoint about the task of higher education, namely to illuminate the past and shape the future.

Harvard College strives to attain the aim for "the advancement of all good literature, arts, and sciences; the advancement and education of youth in all manner of good literature, arts, and sciences; and all other necessary provisions that may conduce to the education of the ... youth of this country..." In other words, Harvard spares no effort to "create knowledge, to open the minds of students to that knowledge, and to enable students to take the best advantage of their educational opportunities". Education at Harvard is to stimulate students' ability to explore, to develop critical thought, to pursue excellence in a spirit of productive cooperation; and to assume responsibility for the consequences of personal action, to challenge, and to lead. All these outstanding capabilities will qualify them for their later lives to advance knowledge, to promote understanding, and to serve society.

II. Notes

1. **Trustee:** *n.* a trustee is someone with legal control of money or property that is

kept or invested for another person, company, or organization

2. **Alumni:** *n.* a person who has received a degree from a school (high school or college or university)

3. **Opportune:** *adj.* suitable or at a time that is suitable or advantageous especially for a particular purpose

4. **Milestone:** *n.* a milestone is an important event in the history or development of something or someone

5. **Centennial:** *n.* a period of 100 years

6. **Lament:** *v.* to mourn or grieve for

7. **Unprecedented:** *adj.* having no precedent; novel

8. **Affirmation:** *n.* a statement asserting the existence or the truth of something

9. **Transcendent:** *adj.* beyond and outside the ordinary range of human experience or understanding

10. **Rivalry:** *n.* the act of competing as for profit or a prize

11. **Hockey:** *n.* an outdoor game played between two teams of 11 players who use long curved sticks to hit a small ball and try to score goals

12. **Tournament:** *n.* a sports competition in which players who win a match continue to play further matches in the competition until just one person or team is left

13. **Prescribed:** *adj.* set down as a rule or guide

III. Discussion

Comment on the following excerpts from "The University's Mission, Reaffirmed."

1. In a world where the measure of things so often trumps the meaning of things, and the practical, immediate uses of knowledge so often overshadow the larger, more enduring purposes of education.

2. As college leaders dealt with this new demand, they struggled to integrate a newfound research agenda with a traditional model of education that aimed to cultivate character.

IV. Questions for Further Thought

1. What might happen if "an education is just about knowledge"?

2. What should be the university's mission for a shared future?

[Passage 2]

Industry and Educational Readjustment[1]

These are some of the reasons for saying that the general problem of readjustment of education to meet present conditions is most acute at the angle of industry. The various details may be summed up in <u>three general moral principles</u>. First, never before was it as important as it is now that each individual should be capable of self-respecting, self-supporting, intelligent work—that each should make a living for himself and those dependent upon his efforts, and should make it with an intelligent recognition of what he is doing and an intelligent interest in doing his work well. Secondly, never before did the work of one individual affect the welfare of others on such a wide scale as at present. Modern conditions of production and exchange of commodities have made the whole world one to a degree never approximated before. A war today may close banks and paralyze trade in places thousands of miles away from the scene of action. <u>This</u> is only a **coarse** and sensational manifestation of an interdependence which is quietly and persistently operating in the activity of every farmer, manufacturer, laborer, and merchant, in every part of the civilized globe. Consequently, there is a demand which never existed before that all the items of school instruction shall be seen and appreciated in their bearing upon the network of social activities which bind people together. When men lived in small groups which had little to do with each other, the harm done by an education which pursued exclusively intellectual and theoretic aims was comparatively slight. Knowledge might be isolated because men were isolated. But today the accumulation of information, just as information, apart from its social bearings, is worse than **futile**. <u>Acquisition of modes of skill apart from realization of</u>

> Are the three moral principles suitable for a globalizing world?

> What does "this" refer to?

> Paraphrase the sentence.

---

1 John Dewey, Evelyn Dewey. *Schools of To-morrow*. New York: Dutton, 1915, pp. 244—250.

> 文化智慧阅读

the social uses to which they may be put is fairly criminal. In the third place, industrial methods and processes depend today upon knowledge of facts and laws of natural and social science in a much greater degree than ever before. Our railways and steamboats, **traction** cars, telegraphs, and telephones, factories and farms, even our ordinary household appliances, depend for their existence upon **intricate** mathematical, physical, chemical, and biological insight. They depend for their best ultimate use upon an understanding of the facts and relationships of social life. Unless the mass of workers are to be blind **cogs** and **pinions** in the **apparatus** they employ, they must have some understanding of the physical and social facts behind and ahead of the material and appliances with which they are dealing.

> Why does Dewey analogize "worker" to "cogs and pinions"?

Thus put, the problem may seem to be so vast and complicated as to be impossible of solution. But we must remember that we are dealing with a problem of readjustment, not of original creation. It will take a long time to complete the readjustment which will be brought about gradually. The main thing now is to get started, and to start in the right direction. Hence the great importance of the various experimental steps which have already been taken. And we must also remember that the essential thing to be brought about through the change is not amassing more information, but the formation of certain attitudes and interests, ways of looking at things and dealing with them. If accomplishment of the **educational readjustment** meant that pupils must become aware of the whole scope of scientific and social material involved in the occupations of daily life, the problem would be absolutely impossible of solution. But in reality accomplishing the reform means less attention than under present conditions to mere bulk of knowledge.

> Do you agree with the statement? Why or why not?

> What kinds of readjustments may work?

What is wanted is that pupils shall form the habit of connecting the limited information they acquire with the activities of life, and gain ability to connect a limited sphere of human activity with the scientific principles upon which its successful conduct depends. The attitudes and interests thus formed will then take care of themselves. If we take **arithmetic** or geography themselves as subjects isolated from social activities and uses, then the aim of instruction must be to cover the whole ground. Any failure to do so will mark a defect in learning. But not so if what we, as educators, are concerned with is that pupils shall realize the connection of what they learn about number, or about the earth's surface, with vital social activities. The question ceases to be a matter simply of quantity and becomes one of motive and purpose. The problem is not the impossible

> Discuss what educators can do and must do.

one of acquainting the pupil with all the social uses to which knowledge of number is put, but of teaching him in such a way that each step which he takes in advance in his knowledge of number shall be connected with some situation of human need and activity, so that he shall see the bearing and application of what is learnt. Any child who enters upon the study of number already has experiences which involve number. Let his instruction in arithmetic link itself to these everyday social activities in which he already shares, and, as far as it goes, the problem of socializing instruction is solved.

The industrial phase of the situation comes in, of course, in the fact that these social experiences have their industrial aspect. This does not mean that his number work shall be crassly **utilitarian**, or that all the problems shall be in terms of money and **pecuniary** gain or loss. On the contrary, it means that the pecuniary side shall be **relegated** to its proportionate place, and emphasis put upon the place occupied by knowledge of weight, form, size, measure, numerical quantity, as well as money, in the carrying on of the activities of life. The purpose of the readjustment of education to existing social conditions is not to substitute the acquiring of money or of bread and butter for the acquiring of information as an educational aim. It is to supply men and women who as they go forth, from school shall be intelligent in the pursuit of the activities in which they engage. That a part of that intelligence will, however, have to do with the place which bread and butter actually occupy in the lives of people today, is a necessity. Those who fail to recognize this fact are still **imbued**, consciously or unconsciously, with the intellectual prejudices of an **aristocratic** state. But the primary and fundamental problem is not to prepare individuals to work at particular callings, but to be vitally and sincerely interested in the calling upon which they must enter if they are not to be social **parasites**, and to be informed as to the social and scientific bearings of that calling. The aim is not to prepare bread-winners. But since men and women are normally engaged in bread-winning vocations, they need to be intelligent in the conduct of households, the care of children, the management of farms and shops, and in the political conduct of a democracy where industry is the prime factor.

The problem of educational readjustment thus has to steer between the extremes of an inherited bookish education and a narrow, so-called practical, education. It is comparatively easy to **clamor** for a **retention** of traditional materials and methods on the ground that they alone are liberal and cultural. It is comparatively easy to urge the

6 Cultivation

Passage 2

How is the socializing problem solved?

What does it refer to?

Introduce your thinking of the purpose of education.

Explain "practical education" with examples.

文化智慧阅读

Is it the "question" for today's China?

addition of narrow vocational training for those who, so it is assumed, are to be the drawers of water and the **hewers** of wood in the existing economic régime, leaving intact the present bookish type of education for those fortunate enough not to have to engage in manual labor in the home, shop, or farm. But since <u>the real question</u> is one of reorganization of all education to meet the changed conditions of life—scientific, social, political—accompanying the revolution in industry, the experiments which have been made with this wider end in view are especially deserving of sympathetic recognition and intelligent examination.

I. Background Information

John Dewey (1859—1952) was an American philosopher, psychologist, and educational reformer whose ideas have been influential in education and social reform. He was one of the most prominent American scholars in the first half of the twentieth century.

Dewey was also a major educational reformer for the 20th century. A well-known public intellectual, he was a major voice of progressive education and liberalism. While a professor at the University of Chicago, he founded the University of Chicago Laboratory Schools, where he was able to apply and test his progressive ideas on pedagogical method. Although Dewey is known best for his publications about education, he also wrote about many other topics, including epistemology, metaphysics, aesthetics, art, logic, social theory, and ethics. Dewey was also one of the primary figures associated with the philosophy of pragmatism and is considered one of the fathers of functional psychology. His paper *The Reflex Arc Concept in Psychology* (1896), is regarded as the first major work in the (Chicago) functionalist school of psychology. *A Review of General Psychology Survey* (2002), ranked Dewey as the 93rd-most-cited psychologist of the 20th century.

II. Notes

1. **Coarse:** *adj.* rough
2. **Futile:** *adj.* pointless; having no purpose because there is no chance of success
3. **Traction:** *n.* motive power provided for such movement, especially on a railway
4. **Intricate:** *adj.* very complicated or detailed

5. **Cog:** *n.* one of a series of teeth on the edge of a wheel

6. **Pinion:** *n.* a cogwheel that engages with a larger wheel or rack

7. **Apparatus:** *n.* equipment, such as tools and machines, which is used to do a particular job or activity

8. **Arithmetic:** *n.* a part of mathematics that is concerned with the addition, subtraction, multiplication, and division of numbers

9. **Utilitarian:** *adj.* based on the idea that the morally correct course of action is the one that produces benefit for the greatest number of people

10. **Pecuniary:** *adj.* relating to or connected with money

11. **Relegate:** *v.* to give sb. a lower or less important position, rank, etc., than before

12. **Imbue:** *v.* to be filled with strong feelings, opinions or values

13. **Aristocratic:** *adj.* being born in the highest social class, who have special titles

14. **Parasites:** *n.* a person who always relies on or benefits from other people and gives nothing back

15. **Clamor:** *v.* to demand sth. loudly

16. **Retention:** *n.* the action of keeping sth. rather than losing it or stopping it

17. **Hewer:** *n.* a person who cuts wood

III. Translation

Translate the following paragraph into English.

古之学者必有师。师者，所以传道受业解惑也。人非生而知之者，孰能无惑？惑而不从师，其为惑也，终不解矣。生乎吾前，其闻道也固先乎吾，吾从而师之；生乎吾后，其闻道也亦先乎吾，吾从而师之。吾师道也，夫庸知其年之先后生于吾乎？是故无贵无贱，无长无少，道之所存，师之所存也。

传道: to propagate the doctrine.

受业: to impart professional knowledge.

解惑: to resolve doubts.

无惑: claim to have no doubts.

从师: to learn from a teacher.

无贵无贱: be high or low in position.

IV. Questions for Further Thought

1. What are the similarities or differences between Dewey and Confucius in the role of teachers?

2. Does China's ongoing education reform need to steer between the "inherited bookish education" and "practical education"? Explain your answers with examples from your experience.

6 Cultivation

Passage 3

[Passage 3]

A Culture of Curiosity[1]

Good morning! To all Eli Whitney students, transfer students, visiting international students, and first-year Yale College students: Welcome to Yale! On behalf of my colleagues here on stage, I extend a warm greeting to the families here today and thank you for joining us. Please enjoy these first moments of your loved one's college career.

Usually in an opening address, university presidents tell undergraduates that they are amazing individuals, selected from among the most talented high school students in the world today. That is, of course, true, but it is not <u>the point I want to make</u>. Instead, I want to encourage you to approach college unimpressed by how impressive you are; have more questions than answers; admit to being puzzled or confused; be willing to say, "I don't know...but I want to find out." And, most important, have the courage to say, "Perhaps I am wrong, and others are right."

That is how you will learn the most from your teachers and classmates. And that is why we have all come to this place. We are here to ask questions—questions about one another and about the world around us. <u>We are at Yale to nurture a culture of curiosity</u>.

This summer I read a story about **Isidor Isaac Rabi**, one of this country's most extraordinary scientists. He remembered an important question his mother asked him. Brought to this country as an infant, Rabi conducted research into particle beams that led to the development of the **MRI** and many other scientific advances. He won the Nobel Prize for Physics in 1944.

<u>Rabi's parents</u> ran a small grocery store in Brooklyn. His mother had no formal education. The other moms, he remembered, asked their children every afternoon if

> What is the core message that Salovey wishes to deliver?

> Why is "a culture of curiosity" so important for Yale?

> How do Rabi's parents help him?

---

1 Peter Salovey, *A Culture of Curiosity*, August 24, 2019, https://president.yale.edu/president/speeches/culture-curiosity accessed November 1, 2021.

文化智慧阅读

they had learned anything in school. "Not my mother," he recalled. "She always asked me a different question. 'Izzy,' she would say, 'did you ask a good question today?'" He believed her reminder to ask good questions helped set him on a path to becoming a distinguished scientist.

So, to all the families here today, when you call your Yale students—when you ask them about their classes and their roommates and the food—remember also to ask about their questions.

Comment on the statement.

Imagine <u>all the great discoveries that have come from asking a question</u>—from Newton's theory of gravity to the astonishing breakthroughs in quantum science—some of which are happening at Yale. When a musician experiments with a new melody, or a sociologist observes a social interaction, they ask "why" and "what would happen if...?" Their curiosity lights up our world and points us in new directions. Self-discoveries come from asking questions, too. What do you learn when you ask yourself, "Why do I believe that?" or "Why did I do that?"

I think of these lines from the poet Billy Collins: "the trouble with poetry is / that it encourages the writing of more poetry."

I would say the same of asking questions. One leads to another, which opens doors to still another. <u>Sometimes our questions lead us to a dead end</u>. We realize the question we asked wasn't quite right, and a door closes. But along the way we have learned something. Perhaps in the future we will ask better questions.

How will you deal with "a dead end"?

What does the scene in the movie imply?

In <u>a well-known scene in the movie</u> "**The Pink Panther**", Inspector Clouseau checks into a hotel in Germany. He sees a **dachshund** in the lobby and asks the hotel owner, "Does your dog bite?" The owner replies, "No." When Clouseau goes to pet the dog, it bites his hand—hard! Shocked, he tells the hotel owner, "I thought you said your dog doesn't bite!" The owner responds, "That is not my dog." Clouseau simply hadn't asked the right question.

Comment on the statement.

Years ago, I co-taught an undergraduate seminar. One of the questions on the application to the course was, "What is the most important thing you've changed your mind about?" <u>We were surprised that quite a few students had not changed their minds about anything at all!</u> We decided to accept to the class only students who had changed their minds about something important.

So, be willing to change your mind. Ask questions and embrace Yale's culture of curiosity. Be open to different viewpoints and experiences, and see them as opportunities to learn—even if sometimes you get your hand bit.

I am a social psychologist. As a graduate student at Yale, my curiosity was sparked by the study of emotions, and by a question my undergraduate advisor first asked me: "Peter, why do you think humans even have emotions? What do they do for us?" One of my major areas of research almost ever since then has been emotional intelligence.

In our earliest work, we described emotional intelligence as a set of skills that one could learn that would help a person extract the information—the "data"—contained in emotions, either one's own or those of another person. After a few years of research, it was obvious to me and my collaborators that we weren't asking exactly the right questions. We needed to be able to show that emotional intelligence predicted outcomes in life—the ability to form friendships, succeed in school, work as part of a team, and the like.

Trouble was, <u>how do you measure the skills of emotional intelligence?</u> We asked ourselves a series of questions starting with, "How are personal characteristics typically measured by psychologists? The answer is by asking people to rate themselves—what are called "self-reports." But this led to approaches that disappointed us: How would someone know if they were the kind of person who was especially good at identifying, understanding, managing, and using emotions? Perhaps thinking you had spectacular emotional intelligence was a sign of not having much of it at all!

<u>That door closed</u>, and so we asked ourselves another question: If we wanted to know if someone possessed the skills of a great baseball player—hitting, throwing, and catching a ball; running bases effectively—how confident would we be of self-report? Not very: All ball players think they are the next A-Rod! As a child, I thought I would be the next **Carl Yastrzemski** when playing in the backyard with my brother, but, in fact, I barely got out of Little League with my pride intact.

Why would emotional intelligence be any different than baseball? If we wanted to know whether someone had high E.I., we needed to assess these skills as abilities. And what would an ability measure of emotional intelligence look like? Asking ourselves these questions led to an answer that made sense, and our ability-based measure of emotional intelligence has now been used in hundreds of studies. Knowing we didn't have all the answers and taking an inquisitive, curious attitude allowed us the

6 Cultivation

Passage 3

How will you deal with the problem?

What does "that door" refer to?

文化智慧阅读

opportunity to create something new.

So, what questions will you ask? What will spark your curiosity?

What could students learn from the 77 speakers?

Not long ago, I received an email from a very proud Yale College parent. He told me about his son, who heard <u>seventy-seven different speakers</u> during his first year at Yale. Seventy-seven! He had learned from thinkers and leaders across the political spectrum and attended events organized by a wide range of campus organizations. What a way to spend your first year! Could you do this and not change your mind about something important?

And it turns out this student is also very good at asking questions: in the past year, he has interviewed dozens of people—scholars and activists, journalists and entrepreneurs from many different sectors. Like so many students, faculty, and staff, he is nurturing a culture of curiosity at Yale.

Explain "coeducation".

Indeed, the Yalies who have come before you have asked a dazzling array of questions. I think of the pioneers of <u>coeducation</u>. Fifty years ago, in 1969, 575 women came to study in Yale College. They entered what had long been an all-male institution, and they asked questions that hadn't been asked before. We will commemorate this milestone—along with the 150th anniversary of women enrolling at Yale in the School of Art—throughout this year.

I think of Margaret Warner, Class of 1971. An award-winning journalist, she knows how to ask brilliant questions. She has reported from warzones for decades, witnessing history firsthand and trying to understand our world.

I think, too, of Alice Young, Class of 1971. She looked around this campus and asked why there weren't more students from public schools, so she became an ambassador for Yale back in her home state of Hawaii. And she was one of the founders of the Asian American Students Alliance, which also celebrates its 50th anniversary this year.

Why does Salovey mention the pioneers?

And we remember other important anniversaries and the curious students who were part of these changes. In 1969, thanks to student efforts, the Afro-American Cultural Center, known as "the House," opened, and what is now the Department of African American Studies was created. And that same year, students established the Yale chapter of Movimiento Estudiantil Chicano de Aztlán, also known as MEChA. <u>I believe we owe a debt of gratitude to all the courageous pioneers, throughout our history, who have made Yale what it is today.</u>

178

What questions will you ask? And how will your questions transform Yale and improve our world?

Your time at Yale is an unparalleled opportunity to engage with a wide range of people, ideas, and experiences. More than at any other point in your life, you will have the means and the opportunity to hear from—and converse with—world-renowned experts in many fields. You will have the chance to create knowledge through rigorous research, and attend arts, literary, and athletic events that challenge and inspire you. You will spend time with peers whose lives have been wildly different from your own.

What if you nurtured your own curiosity by <u>pushing yourself beyond the familiar and the comfortable?</u> What would that look like?

> List some strategies helping for "pushing yourself".

It might mean attending a talk on a topic you don't know much about or by someone who doesn't share your beliefs. Or conducting research in a Yale laboratory or collaborating on an exhibit at one of our amazing museums. Or perhaps your curiosity will be sparked having coffee with a classmate who comes from a different part of the world or a different place on the political spectrum.

And when you do these things, when you take advantage of the opportunities Yale makes possible, what questions will you ask?

There is so much we do not know. Let us embrace, together, our humility—our willingness to admit what we have yet to discover. After all, if you knew all the answers, you would not need Yale. And if humanity knew all the answers, the world would not need Yale.

<u>So, what questions will you ask today? Tomorrow? The next day?</u> And in the days, months, and years after I have shaken your hand at Commencement, let me know what questions you've asked that have changed your life.

> What questions will you ask?

Good luck, Class of 2023!

I. Background Information

Peter Salovey (born February 21, 1958) is an American social psychologist and the twenty-third President of Yale University. He previously served as Yale's Provost, Dean of Yale Graduate School of Arts and Sciences, and Dean of Yale College. With John D. Mayer, he developed the broad framework of Emotional Intelligence, the theory that just as people have a wide range of intellectual abilities, they also have a wide range of measurable emotional skills that profoundly affect their thinking and action. Salovey has authored or edited over a dozen books translated into 11 languages and published hundreds of journal articles and essays, primarily on human emotion and health behavior.

II. Notes

1. **Isidor Isaac Rabi:** (1898—1988) was an American physicist who won the Nobel Prize in Physics in 1944 for his discovery of nuclear magnetic resonance, which is used in magnetic resonance imaging. He was also one of the first scientists in the United States to work on the cavity magnetron, which is used in microwave radar and microwave ovens.

2. **MRI:** magnetic resonance imaging

3. **The Pink Panther:** The Pink Panther is an American media franchise primarily focusing on a series of comedy-mystery films featuring an inept French police detective, Inspector Jacques Clouseau. The franchise began with the release of the classic Pink Panther film in 1963. The role of Clouseau was originated by and is most closely associated with Peter Sellers.

4. **Dachshund:** *n.* a small dog with a long body, long ears and very short legs

5. **Carl Yastrzemski:** (nicknamed "Yaz", born August 22, 1939) is an American former Major League Baseball player

III. Translation

Translate the following excerpts from Passage Three into Chinese.

1. Instead, I want to encourage you to approach college unimpressed by how impressive you are; have more questions than answers; admit to being puzzled or confused; be willing to say, "I don't know...but I want to find out." And, most important, have the courage to say, "Perhaps I am wrong, and others are right."

2. I think of these lines from the poet Billy Collins: "the trouble with poetry is / that it encourages the writing of more poetry." I would say the same of asking questions. One leads to another, which opens doors to still another. Sometimes our questions lead us to a dead-end. We realize the question we asked wasn't quite right, and a door closes.

But along the way we have learned something. Perhaps in the future we will ask better questions.

3. What if you nurtured your own curiosity by pushing yourself beyond the familiar and the comfortable? What would that look like? It might mean attending a talk on a topic you don't know much about or by someone who doesn't share your beliefs. Or conducting research in a Yale laboratory or collaborating on an exhibit at one of our amazing museums. Or perhaps your curiosity will be sparked having coffee with a classmate who comes from a different part of the world or a different place on the political spectrum.

4. There is so much we do not know. Let us embrace, together, our humility—our willingness to admit what we have yet to discover. After all, if you knew all the answers, you would not need Yale. And if humanity knew all the answers, the world would not need Yale.

IV. Questions for Further Thought

1. Have you ever done anything in your university life which pushed you beyond the familiar and the comfortable? Describe your experience.

2. If you have an opportunity to talk to your university president, what questions will you ask? How will your questions help transform your university and improve our world?

[Passage 4]

Containing of the Coronavirus Outbreak: Truth and Trust[1]

Share your COVID-19 experience at that time.

On any given day in February, you could watch the news about Coronavirus outbreak (COVID-19). Globally, 80,239 confirmed, outside of China 2,459 confirmed, and 35 countries throughout the world where COVID-19 is spreading, according to the World Health Organization's February 25 situation report. The virus is spreading swiftly, for instance, the globally confirmed cases rose by 33,242 within half a month from 46,997 on February 13. As it stands, the virus outbreak is negatively affecting the world economy. "The deadly coronavirus outbreak could choke global growth and **veer** the

Explain how it could happen.

U.S. toward a recession", former Federal Reserve Chair Janet Yellen warned at an event held by the Brookings Institution on February 26.

As coronavirus fears **pummel** the world, stocks of efforts have been launched in containment of the **epidemic**. As the vast majority of reported cases thus far, China

Why has China taken this approach?

has taken an all-of-people approach. For instance, the cutting of Wuhan in Hubei Province where confirmed most cases in order to protect the world from this disease. It is a heavy-handed decision as Wuhan is the largest city in central China, with a population of nearly 15 million. The movement restrictions apply to everybody, not just the **quarantined** people. The Wuhan people, however, take it as playing a role in saving life. Thus, they have the courage and determination to play the role.

Now, the important question is how can empower the strategy and tools in battling the coronavirus outbreak?

Give some examples of disinformation about COVID-19.

Decrease disinformation in public sphere. The rise of disinformation in public arena has been a hot-button issue in the world. The dramatic advances in information

---

[1] Liu Chen, Containing of the Coronavirus Outbreak: Truth and Trust, *Global Village Space*, March 9, 2020.

technology thrive social media such as Facebook, Twitter, WhatsAPP, Wechat and so on. As to positive points, there are more channels through which information flows, and that this makes information manipulation harder to address. The ease of creating and spreading bad information, and even lies, at the same time, shrinks the public trust in institutions. When disinformation outpaces the efforts to correct it, "the panic rears its ugly head whenever the media attaches an Internet angle to a breaking news story" noted by Mike Godwin in 1995.

Disinformation pollutes information environment, making public administration more difficult to address. In the situation of emergency such as the coronavirus outbreak, the awareness of distrust about government's ability leads to misunderstanding, cynicism, and disengagement in the end. According to a **Pew Research Center's** survey, two-thirds of Americans think that other Americans have little or no trust in the federal government.

In China's battling the coronavirus outbreak, the public discourse is complicated. In the beginning when the instant reaction system to the outbreak was not well established, the mass public would resort to their own **curated** information platform such as weibo, wechat in China and Facebook, Twitter outside China rather than the common public sphere. The disinformation increased the likelihood of panic, misunderstanding, and division.

When the official information publicity system at all levels was soon available including situation report, briefs, press conferences, and on-the-spot report, the control measures launched by government have much greater accesses to the public. The **transparency** of information holds governments more accountable, and that helps rebuild the faith in combating the virus outbreak China. A transparent information environment is not the only thing that matters in taming of the coronavirus outbreak, but no possibility to win the battle without it.

Strengthen mutual-trust for international cooperation. Globalization, the term was coined by Zbigniew Brzezinski, in his book *Between Two Ages: America's Role in the Technetronic Era* (1969) to refer to a new era that the world is proceeding. Professor Richard Cooper, Harvard University in his paper, "Economic Interdependence and War" documents three Globalizations in human history: The first globalization in the 16th century; the period 1870-1913 was the second globalization; the third globalization,

Paraphrase the quotation.

"the great period of globalization" since the 1970s. Regarding what makes the third globalization a "great period", British sociologist, Anthony Giddens' comments in his *Sociology* (3rd Edition) (2004) shed light on that "<u>globalization opens our eyes to the fact that the increasing ties between the local and global, it means [in the context of globalization], our actions and behavior will have the consequences for the others, and the world's problems will have the consequences for us</u>".

The coronavirus combat turns out, although the context is different the inseparability of international cooperation for the "global community with shared future" in China's President Xi Jinping's remarks. Since the virus outbreak, China has received varied supports from across the world. For instance, the medical supplies including face masks, medical gloves, and protective suits donated by Pakistan gave warmth to people in Wuhan. The support reminds the Chinese of the donation made by Pakistan in 2008 for Wenchuan earthquake.

What may be the challenges of building "mutual trust"?

China at the same time has made all-out efforts at home. For instance, China identified the genetic sequence of the virus "at a record time and immediately shared the sequence which helps other countries to prepare for the cases", said Tedros Ghebreyesus, director-general of the WHO in a press release on February 12. <u>The mutual trust is the foundation of international cooperation.</u>

From a historical perspective, the growing evidence shows that citizens can trust the possibility of progress. The transparency of public administration is improving before our eyes. However, disinformation remains **perplexing**. This is why the whole world shall work together in pursuit of a better information ecosystem.

Comment on the forecast.

<u>Looking into future, if international perspective surpasses political conflict, economic competition and cultural bias, trust will be strengthened, which give people hope.</u> Given the above, there is hope for containment of the coronavirus. Importantly, "In a moment, passes sorrow, That which passes will be dear" (by Alexander Pushkin in 1852).

I. Background Information

1. Liu Chen is a professor of Public Administration and Cultural Studies. Harvard Kennedy School Mason Fellow, Postdoctoral Fellow, Graduate School of Arts and Sciences, Harvard. Her research focuses on policy, practice, leadership, culture and

international cooperation.

2. Disinformation is false information that is spread deliberately to deceive. It is sometimes confused with misinformation, which is false information but is not deliberate.

II. Notes

1. **Veer:** *v.* to change in the way it develops
2. **Pummel:** *v.* to strike repeatedly
3. **Epidemic:** *n.* a particular disease affects a very large number of people there and spreads quickly to other areas
4. **Quarantine:** *v.* an animal or a person that has or may have a disease is kept away from others in order to prevent the disease from spreading
5. **Curated:** *adj.* be selected, organized
6. **Transparency:** *n.* open to public scrutiny
7. **Perplexing:** *adj.* complicated or confused
8. **Pew Research Center:** The Pew Research Center is a nonpartisan American think tank (referring to itself as a "fact tank") based in Washington, D.C.

III. Writing

Read the following article about World Health Organization (WHO), and write an approximately 200-word summary about WHO's position on "herd immunity" and "lockdown".

What is WHO's position on "herd immunity" as a way of fighting COVID-19?[1]

Attempts to reach "herd immunity" through exposing people to a virus are scientifically problematic and unethical. Letting COVID-19 spread through populations, of any age or health status will lead to unnecessary infections, suffering and death.

The vast majority of people in most countries remain susceptible to this virus. Seroprevalence surveys suggest that in most countries, less than 10% of the population have been infected with COVID-19.

We are still learning about immunity to COVID-19. Most people who are infected

---

[1] World Health Organization, Coronavirus disease (COVID-19): Herd immunity, lockdowns and COVID-19, Q&A, December 31, 2020, https://www.who.int/news-room/questions-and-answers/item/herd-immunity-lockdowns-and-covid-19 accessed November 1, 2021.

with COVID-19 develop an immune response within the first few weeks, but we don't know how strong or lasting that immune response is, or how it differs for different people. There have also been reports of people infected with COVID-19 for a second time.

Until we better understand COVID-19 immunity, it will not be possible to know how much of a population is immune and how long that immunity last for, let alone make future predictions. These challenges should preclude any plans that try to increase immunity within a population by allowing people to get infected.

Although older people and those with underlying conditions are most at risk of severe disease and death, they are not the only ones at risk.

Finally, while most infected people get mild or moderate forms of COVID-19 and some experience no disease, many become seriously ill and must be admitted into hospital. We are only beginning to understand the long-term health impacts among people who have had COVID-19, including what is being described as "Long COVID." WHO is working with clinicians and patient groups to better understand the long term effects of COVID-19.

What is WHO's position on "lockdowns" as a way of fighting COVID-19?

Large scale physical distancing measures and movement restrictions, often referred to as "lockdowns", can slow COVID19 transmission by limiting contact between people.

However, these measures can have a profound negative impact on individuals, communities, and societies by bringing social and economic life to a near stop. Such measures disproportionately affect disadvantaged groups, including people in poverty, migrants, internally displaced people and refugees, who most often live in overcrowded and under resourced settings, and depend on daily labor for subsistence.

WHO recognizes that at certain points, some countries have had no choice but to issue stay-at-home orders and other measures, to buy time.

Governments must make the most of the extra time granted by "lockdown" measures by doing all they can to build their capacities to detect, isolate, test and care for all cases; trace and quarantine all contacts; engage, empower and enable populations to drive the societal response and more.

WHO is hopeful that countries will use targeted interventions where and when needed, based on the local situation.

IV. Questions for Further Thought

1. What is "disinformation"? And why do people create and spread it?

2. How can you spot "disinformation"? What are the right things to do when you spot it?

[Mini-task for Chapter 6]

Reading Report

Read the lecture "The Chinese Renaissance" delivered by Hu Shi and write an approximately 500-word reading report about it.

The Chinese Renaissance[1]

"THE RENAISSANCE" was the name given by a group of Peking University students to a new monthly magazine which they published in 1918. They were mature students well trained in the old cultural tradition of the country, and they readily recognized in the new movement then led by some of their professors a striking similarity to the Renaissance in Europe. Three prominent features in the movement reminded them of the European Renaissance. First, it was a conscious movement to promote a new literature in the living language of the people to take the place of the classical literature of old. Second, it was a movement of conscious protest against many of the ideas and institutions in the traditional culture, and of conscious emancipation of the individual man and woman from the bondage of the forces of tradition. It was a movement of reason versus tradition, freedom versus authority, and glorification of life and human values versus their suppression. And lastly, strange enough, this new movement was led by men who knew their cultural heritage and tried to study it with the new methodology of modern historical criticism and research. In that sense it was also a humanist movement. In all these directions the new movement which began in 1917 and which was sometimes called the "New Culture Movement", the "New Thought" movement or "The New Tide" was capturing the imagination and sympathy of the youth of the nation as something which promised and pointed to the new birth of an old people and an old civilization.

Historically, there had been many periods of Chinese Renaissance. The rise of the great poets in the T'ang Dynasty, the simultaneous movement for a new prose literature

---

1 Hu Shi, *The Chinese Renaissance: The Haskell Lectures*, 1933.

modeled after the style of the Classical period, and the development of Zen Buddhism as a Chinese reformation of that Indian religion—these represented the First Chinese Renaissance. The great reform movements in the eleventh century, the subsequent development of a powerful secular neo-Confucianist philosophy which gradually overshadowed and finally replaced the medieval religions—all these important developments of the Sung Dynasty may be regarded as the Second Renaissance. The rise of the dramas in the thirteenth century, and the rise of the great novels in a later period, together with their frank glorification of love and the joys of life, may be called the Third Renaissance. And lastly, the revolt in the seventeenth century against the rational philosophy of the Sung and Ming dynasties, and the development of a new technique in classical scholarship in the last three hundred years with its philological and historical approach and its strict emphasis on the importance of documentary evidence—these, too, may be called the Fourth Renaissance.

Each of these historical movements had its important role to play and contributed to the periodic renewals of vitality in an old civilization. But all these great movements which rightly deserve the term of "renaissances", suffered from one common defect, namely, the absence of a conscious recognition of their historical mission. There was no conscious effort nor articulate interpretation: all of them were natural developments of historical tendencies and were easily overpowered or swept away by the conservative force of tradition against which they had only dimly and unconsciously combated. Without this conscious element, the new movements remained natural processes of revolution, and never achieved the work of revolutions; they brought in new patterns, but never completely dethroned the old, which continued to co-exist with them and in time absorbed them. The Zen movement, for instance, practically replaced all the other schools of Buddhism; and yet, when Zen became the officially recognized orthodoxy, it lost its revolutionary character and resumed all the features against which its founders had explicitly revolted. The secular philosophy of neo-Confucianism was to replace the medieval religions, but it soon made itself a new religion embodying unwittingly many of the features of medievalism. The new critical scholarship of the last three centuries began as a revolt against, and ended as a refuge for, the fruitless philosophizing and the sterile literary education, both of which continued to dominate and enslave the vast majority of the literati. The new dramas and the new novels came and went, but the

Government continued to hold the literary examinations on the classics, and the men of letters continued to write their poetry and prose in the classical language.

The Renaissance movement of the last two decades differs from all the early movements in being a fully conscious and studied movement. Its leaders know what they want, and they know what they must destroy in order to achieve what they want. They want a new language, a new literature, a new outlook on life and society, and a new scholarship. They want a new language, not only as an effective instrumentality for popular education, but also as the effective medium for the development of the literature of a new China. They want a literature that shall be written in the living tongue of a living people and shall be capable of expressing the real feelings, thoughts, inspirations, and aspirations of a growing nation. They want to instill into the people a new outlook on life which shall free them from the shackles of tradition and make them feel at home in the new world and its new civilization. They want a new scholarship which shall not only enable us to understand intelligently the cultural heritage of the past, but also prepare us for active participation in the work of research in the modern sciences. This, as I understand it, is the mission of the Chinese Renaissance.

The conscious element in this movement is the result of long contact with the people and civilization of the West. It is only through contact and comparison that the relative value or worthlessness of the various cultural elements can be clearly and critically seen and understood. What is sacred among one people may be ridiculous in another; and what is despised or rejected by one cultural group, may in a different environment become the cornerstone for a great edifice of strange grandeur and beauty. For ten long centuries, by a peculiar perversion of aesthetic appreciation, the bound feet of Chinese women were regarded as beautiful; but it took only a few decades of contact with foreign peoples and ideas to make the Chinese people see the ugliness and inhumanity of this institution. On the other hand, the novels which were read by the millions of Chinese but which were always despised by the Chinese literati, have in recent decades been elevated to the position of respectable literature, chiefly through the influence of the European literature. Contact with strange civilizations brings new standards of value with which the native culture is re-examined and re-evaluated, and conscious reformation and regeneration are the natural outcome of such transvaluation of values. Without the benefit of an intimate contact with the civilization of the West, there could not be the Chinese Renaissance.

In this lecture I propose to tell the story of one phase of this Renaissance as a case study of the peculiar manner of cultural response in which important changes in Chinese life and institutions have been brought about. This phase is sometimes known as the Literary Renaissance or Revolution.

Let me first state the problem for which the literary revolution offers the solution. The problem was first seen by all early reformers as the problem of finding a suitable language which could serve as an effective means of educating the vast millions of children and of illiterate adults. They admitted that the classical language which was difficult to write and to learn, and for thousands of years incapable of being spoken or verbally understood—was not suited for the education of children and the masses. But they never thought of giving up the classical language, in which was written and preserved all the cultural tradition of the race. Moreover, the classical language was the only linguistic medium for written communication between the various regions with different dialects, just as Latin was the universal medium of communication and publication for the whole of medieval Europe. For these reasons the language of the classics must be taught, and was taught, in the schools throughout the country. All the school texts, from the primary grades to the university, were written in this dead language; and teaching in the primary schools consisted chiefly in reading and memorizing the texts which had to be explained, word for word, in the local dialects of the pupils. When European literature began to be translated into Chinese, the translations were all in this classical language; and it was a tremendous task and exceedingly amusing to read the comic figures in the novels of Charles Dickens talking in the dead language of two thousand years ago!

There was much serious talk about devising an alphabet for transcribing Chinese sounds and for publishing useful information for the enlightenment of the masses. The Christian missionaries had devised a number of alphabets for translating the Bible into the local dialects for the benefit of illiterate men and women. Some Chinese scholars also worked out several alphabetical systems for the mandarin dialect, and publicly preached their adoption for the education of illiterate adults. Other scholars advocated the use of the pei-hua [baihua; literal: "white speech"], that is, the spoken tongue of the people, for publishing periodicals and newspapers in order to inculcate useful information and patriotic ideas in the people who could not read the literary language of the scholars.

But these scholar-reformers all agreed that such expedient measures as the use of the vulgar tongue or the adoption of an alphabet were only necessary for those adults who had had no chance to go to the regular schools. They never for a moment would consider the idea that these expedients should be so universally used as to replace the classical language altogether. The pei-hua was the vulgar jargon of the people, good enough only for the cheap novels, but certainly not good enough for the scholars. As to the alphabet, it was only intended for the illiterates. For, they argued, if the pupils in the schools were taught to read and write an alphabetical language, how could they ever hope to acquire a knowledge of the moral and cultural heritage of the past?

All such attempts of reform were bound to fail, because nobody wanted to learn a language which was despised by those who advocated it, which had no more use than the reading of a few cheap magazines and pamphlets that the reformers were kind enough to condescend to publish for the benefit of the ignorant and the lowly. Moreover, it was impossible for these reformers to keep up enough enthusiasm to continue writing and publishing in a language which they themselves considered to be beneath their dignity and intelligence to employ as their own literary medium. So the pei-hua magazines were always short-lived and never reached the people; and the alphabetical systems remained the fads of a few reformers. The schools continued to teach the language of the classics which had been dead over two thousand years; the newspapers continued to be written and printed in it; and the scholars and authors continued to produce their books and essays and poems in it. The language problem remained unsolved and insoluble.

The solution of this problem came from the dormitories in the American universities. In the year 1915 a series of trivial incidents led some Chinese students in Cornell University to take up the question of reforming the Chinese language. My classmate, Mr. Chao Yuen-ren, and I prepared a series of articles on this question. He took the position that it was possible to alphabetize the Chinese language; and he proposed certain details of procedure and answered all possible arguments against alphabetization. I took the position that, while an alphabetized language might be the ultimate goal, it was necessary to consider intermediate steps to make the ideographical characters more teachable in the elementary schools, and I also proposed certain methods of reform. These articles were read in English and published in the Chinese Students' Monthly. They attracted no comment and were soon forgotten.

But other disputes arose among some of my literary friends in the United States and led me to give more thought to the problem of Chinese language and literature. The original dispute was one of poetic diction; and a great many letters were exchanged between Ithaca, New York City, Cambridge, Poughkeepsie, and Washington, D.C. From an interest in the minor problem of poetic diction I was led to see that the problem was really one of a suitable medium for all branches of Chinese literature. The question now became: In what language shall the New China produce its future literature? My answer was: The classical language, so long dead, can never be the medium of a living literature of a living nation; the future literature of China must be written in the living language of the people. "No dead language can produce a living literature." And the living language I proposed as the only possible medium of the future literature of China, was the pei-hua, the vulgar tongue of the vast majority of the population, the language which, in the last 500 years, had produced the numerous novels read and loved by the people, though despised by the men of letters. I wanted this much despised vulgar tongue of the people and the novels to be elevated to the position of the national language of China, to the position enjoyed by all the modern national languages in Europe.

With the exception of a Chinese girl student in Vassar College, all my literary friends in the American universities were opposed to this outrageous theory of mine. They had to admit that the spoken tongue of the people was good enough for the popular novels, for that had been clearly demonstrated by the great novels of the sixteenth, seventeenth, and eighteenth centuries. But they all maintained that the vulgar language of the people, which had never been polished and refined by the great writers and poets of the nation, could not be used as the medium of poetry. I defended my position by pointing out that, throughout the history of Chinese poetry, all the best remembered verses of the great poets were written in the simplest language which, if not strictly the living tongue of the people, must be very close to the living speech of the time. In spite of the copious examples I cited to prove my thesis, my friends were not convinced, for it must be admitted the poets of the past never consciously wrote in the plain language of the people; they only slipped into it unwittingly and only on rare occasions of true poetic inspiration. The greatest bulk of Chinese poetry was composed in strictly conservative, highly polished, literary diction.

Being a pragmatist in philosophy, I proposed to my friends to experiment with the pei-hua in writing my own poetry. On July 26, 1916, I announced to all my friends in America that from now on I resolved to write no more poems in the classical language, and to begin my experiments in writing poetry in the so-called vulgar tongue of the people. Before a half-dozen poems were written, I had already found a title for my new volume of poetry: it was to be called "A Book of Experiments".

In the meantime, I began to study the history of our literature with a new interest and with a new methodology. I tried to study it from the evolutionary standpoint and, to my great surprise and unlimited joy, the historical development of Chinese literature presented to me a continuous though entirely unconscious movement of struggle against the despotic limitations of the classical tradition, a continuous tendency to produce a literature in the living language of the people. I found that the history of Chinese literature consisted of two parallel movements: there was the classical literature of the scholars, the men of letters, the poets of the imperial courts, and of the elite; but there was in every age an undercurrent of literary development among the common people which produced the folk songs of love and heroism, the songs of the dancer, the epic stories of the street reciter, the drama of the village theater, and, most important of all, the novels. I found that every new form, every innovation in literature, had come never from the imitative classical writers of the upper classes, but always from the unlettered class of the countryside, the village inn, and the market-place. I found that it was always these new forms and patterns of the common people that, from time to time, furnished the new blood and fresh vigor to the literature of the literati, and rescued it from the perpetual danger of fossilization. All the great periods of Chinese literature were those when the master minds of the age were attracted by these new literary forms of the people and produced their best works, not only in the new patterns, but in close imitation of the fresh and simple language of the people. And such great epochs died away only when those new forms from the people had again become fixed and fossilized through long periods of slavish imitation by the uncreative literati.

In short, I found the true history of Chinese literature to consist in a series of revolutions, the initiative always coming from the untutored but unfettered people, the influence and inspiration often being felt by the great masters in the upper classes, and the result always bringing about new epochs of literary development. It was the anonymous folk songs of antiquity that formed the bulk of the great *Book of Poetry* and created the first epoch of Chinese literature. It was again the anonymous folk songs of the people that gave the form and the inspiration in the developments of the new poetry in the Three Kingdoms and later in the T'ang Dynasty. It was the songs of the dancing and singing girls that began the new era of TV? or songs in the Sung Dynasty. It was the people that first produced the plays which led to the great dramas of the Mongol period and the Mings. It was the street reciters of epic stories that gave rise to the great novels some of which have been best sellers for three or four centuries. And all these new epochs have originated in new forms of literature produced by the common people, and in the living language of the people.

So my argument for a new national literature in the spoken language of the people was strengthened and supported by a wealth of undeniable facts of history. To recognize the pei-hua as the national medium of Chinese literature was merely to bring into logical and natural culmination a historical tendency which had been many times thwarted, diverted, and suppressed by the heavy weight of the prestige of the classical tradition.

This line of historical thinking was embodied in an article which I published on the first day of the year 1917 under the modest title, "Some Tentative Suggestions for the Reform of Chinese Literature." It appeared simultaneously in the Quarterly published by the Chinese students in America, and in a new liberal monthly called The Youth, edited by Mr. Ch'en Tu-shiu, one of the old members of the revolutionary movement, who years later became the founder of the Chinese Communist Party., To my great surprise, what had failed to convince my friends in the American universities was received with sympathetic response in China. Mr. Ch'en Tu-shiu followed my article with one of his own, under the very bold title "On a Revolution in Chinese Literature". In this article, he said:

I am willing to brave the enmity of all the pedantic scholars of the country, and hoist the great banner of the "Army of the Revolution in Literature" in support of my friend Hu Shih. On this banner shall be written in big characters the three great principles of the Army of Revolution: 1. To destroy the painted, powdered, and obsequious literature of the aristocratic few, and to create the plain, simple and expressive literature of the people; 2. To destroy the stereotyped and monotonous literature of classicism, and to create the fresh and sincere literature of realism; 3. To destroy the pedantic, unintelligible and obscurantist literature of the hermit and the recluse, and to create the plain-speaking and popular literature of a living society.

These articles were followed by my other essays, one "On the Historico-evolutionary Conception of Literature", and another on "A Constructive Revolution in Chinese Literature". They aroused a great deal of discussion. The revolution was in full swing when I returned to China in the summer of 1917.

What surprised me most was the weakness and utter poverty of the opposition. I had anticipated a formidable opposition and a long struggle, which, I was confident, would ultimately end in our success in about 20 years. But we met with no strong argument; my historical arguments were never answered by any defender of the cause of the classical literature. The leader of the opposition was Mr. Lin Shu, who, without knowing a word of any European language, had translated 150 or more English and European novels into the language of the classics. [1] But he could not put forth any argument. In one of his articles, he said: "I know the classical language must not be discarded; but I cannot tell why"!! These blind forces of reaction could only resort to the method of persecution by the government. They attacked the private life of my friend and colleague, Mr. Ch'en Tu-shiu, who was then Dean of the College of Letters in the National University of Peking; and the outside pressure was such that he had to resign from the University in 1919. But such persecutions gave us a great deal of free advertising, and the Peking University began to be looked upon by the youth of the whole nation as the center of a new enlightenment.

Then an unexpected event occurred which suddenly carried the literary movement to a rapid success. The Peace Conference in Paris had just decided to sacrifice China's claims and give to Japan the freedom to dispose of the former German possessions in the province of Shantung. When the news reached China, the students in Peking, under the leadership of the students of the Peking University, held a mass meeting of protest and, in their demonstration parade, broke into the house of a pro-Japanese minister, set fire to the house, and beat the Chinese minister to Tokyo almost to death. The

---

1 This was done by an assistant who verbally translated the original text into spoken Chinese which Mr. Lin re-translated into the classical language.

government arrested a number of the students, but public sentiment ran so high that the whole nation seemed on the side of the university students and against the notoriously pro-Japanese Government. The merchants in Shanghai and other cities closed their shops as a protest against the peace negotiations and against the government. The Chinese Delegation at the Paris Conference was warned by public bodies not to sign the treaty; and they obeyed. The government was forced by this strong demonstration of national sentiment to release the students and to dismiss from office three well-known pro-Japanese ministers. The struggle began on May 4, and lasted till the final surrender of the government in the first part of June. It has been called the "May 4 Movement."

In this political struggle, the Peking University suddenly rose to the position of national leadership in the eyes of the students. The literary and intellectual movements led by some of the professors and students of the university, which had for the last few years been slowly felt among the youths of nation, were now openly acknowledged by them as new and welcome forces for a national emancipation. During the years 1919—1920, there appeared about 400 small periodicals, almost all of them published by the students in the different localities—some printed from metal types, some in mimeographs, and others on lithographs—and all of them published in the spoken language of the people—the literary medium which the Peking University professors had advocated. All of a sudden, the revolution in literature had spread throughout the country, and the youths of the nation were finding in the new literary medium an effective means of expression. Everybody seemed to be rushing to express himself in this language which he could understand and in which he could make himself understood. In the course of a few years, the literary revolution had succeeded in giving to the people a national language, and had brought about a new age of literary expression.

The political parties soon saw the utility of this new linguistic instrument, and adopted it for their weeklies and monthlies. The publishing houses, which at first hesitated to accept books written in the vulgar language, soon found them to sell far better than those in the classical style, and became enthusiastic over the new movement. Many new small book companies sprang up and published nothing but books and periodicals written in the national language. By 1919 and 1920 the vulgar tongue of the people had assumed the more respectable name of the "National Language of China." And in 1920 the Ministry of Education—in a reactionary government—reluctantly proclaimed an order that, from the fall of the next year, the textbooks for the first two grades in the primary schools were to be written in the national language. In 1922 all the elementary and secondary textbooks were ordered to be rewritten in the national language.

Thus the problem of a new language for education, which had puzzled the last generation, was automatically solved by starting from a different angle of attack. The advocates of a revolution in literature had indirectly solved the problem of finding a suitable medium of education. For, as I have said before, no one wishes to learn a language which the men of letters are ashamed to use in producing their own poetry and prose. When I first returned to Peking in 1917, I tried to convince the leaders of an association for the unification of the national language that no language is fit for the schools which is not fit for the poets and prose writers; and that the language of the schools must of necessity be the language of literature. When these leaders raised the question of standardizing the national language, I told them that it was quite unnecessary. The poets, the novelists, the great prose masters, and the dramatists are the real standardizers of languages. In my article on "A Constructive Revolution in Chinese Literature", I pointed out that...when we have a literature written in a national language, then, but not until then, shall we have a national language of literary worth. Therefore, the first step is to produce in the national language as much good literature as possible. The day when novels, poems, dramas, and essays written in the national language are widely circulated in the country is the day when a truly worthy national language is finally established. Those of us who can write prose in the pei-hua at all have not learned it from textbooks or dictionaries, but have acquired its use through our early reading of the great novels written in it. Those great novels which we all loved in our boyhood days have been our most effective teachers in the use of the pei-hua; and the pei-hua used in the new poetry and prose of the future will be the standard national language of the China of the future.

In this prediction I was vindicated sooner than I had expected. The nation did not wait for the literature of the future to create a standard national language. It was already there, already standardized in its written form, in syntax, in diction, all by the few great novels which have gone to the heart and bosom of every man. When the call came for young writers to express themselves in a living tongue, they suddenly found, to their happy surprise, that they were already in possession of an effective literary medium which was so easy and so simple that they had acquired it without ever having been taught it and without even knowing it!

In order to understand the causes of such a remarkably rapid success in the literary revolution, in establishing the living national language in place of the classical language as the recognized medium of education and of literature, we must first analyze the qualifications which a national language ought to possess. The history of all the modern national languages of the European nations has revealed that a national language is always a dialect which, in the first place, must be the most widely spoken and most generally understood of all the dialects of the country; and which, second, must have produced a fairly large amount of literature so that its form is more or less standardized and its spread can be assisted by the popularity of the literary masterpieces. The Italian language began as the Tuscan dialect which was not only the most widely known but also the medium in which Dante and Boccaccio and other masters produced their new literature. Modern French began as the French of Paris which was fast becoming the official language of France. In the sixteenth century Francis I ordered all public documents to be written in the French of Paris, and it was in the same language that the poets known as the Pleiade consciously wrote their poetry, and Rabelais and Montaigne wrote their prose works. The same is true of the national languages of Germany and England. Modern English began as the Midland dialect which, being the language of London and the two universities, was the most widely understood dialect of the land, and which was the medium in which Wycliffe translated the Bible, Chaucer wrote his poetic tales, and the dramatists of the pre-Elizabethan and the Elizabethan eras produced their dramas. It will be easily seen that the national language of China possesses both of these qualifications. In the first place, the mandarin dialects which form the basis of the national language are undoubtedly the most widely spoken dialects of the country, being spoken from Harbin in the northeast to the provinces of Yunnan, Kweichow, and Szechuan in the southwest, covering more than 90 percent of the territory of China proper and Manchuria. The people from any part of this vast territory can travel to any other part without ever feeling the need of changing their dialect. There are, of course, local variations; but it is a real fact of national importance that students from Yunnan and Kweichow and Szechuan can travel thousands of miles to study in Peking and find, on arriving there, that their dialects are regarded as the most generally understood dialects of the country.

Second, the mandarin dialects have been the most popular vehicle for the literature of the people during the last 500 years of its continuous development. All the folk songs of these provinces are composed in these dialects. The popular novels were all written in them: the earlier novels were written in the popular language of the north and of the middle Yangtze Valley, some in the dialect of Shantung, and the more recent ones such as the famous *Dream of the Red Chamber* in the pure dialect of Peking. All these great novels have been most widely read by almost everybody who can read at all; even the literati who pretended to condemn them as vulgar and cheap know them well through reading them stealthily in their boyhood days. They have been the greatest standardizes and the most effective popularizers of the national language, not merely within the region of the mandarin dialects, but far into the heart of the regions where the old dialects still reign. I, for example, came from the mountains of southern Anhwei where the people speak some of the most difficult dialects, and yet I read and immensely enjoyed many of those novels long before I left my ancestral home. It was from these novels that I learned to write prose in the pei-hua when I was only 15 years old. The hundreds of young authors who have come into literary prominence in the last 15 years have mostly learned their art and form of writing through the same channel.

The question has often been asked. Why did it take so long for this living language of such wide currency and with such a rich output in literature to receive due recognition as the most fitting instrumentality for education and for literary composition? Why couldn't it replace the dead classical language long before the present revolution in Chinese literature? Why was the spoken language so long despised by the literary class?

The explanation is simple. The authority of the language of the classics was truly too great to be easily overcome in the days of the Empire. This authority became almost invincible when it was enforced by the power of a long united empire and reinforced by the universal system of state examinations under which the only channel of civil advancement for any man was through the mastery of the classical language and literature. The rise of the national languages in modern Europe was greatly facilitated by the absence of a united empire and of a universal system of classical examination.

Yet the two great churches in Rome and in East Europe—the shadowy counterparts of the Roman Empire—with their rigid requirements for advancement in clerical life, have been able to maintain the use of two dead classical languages throughout these many centuries. It is therefore no mere accident that the revolution in Chinese literature came ten years after the abolition of the literary examinations in 1905, and several years after the political revolution of 1911—1912.

Moreover, there was lacking in the historical development of the living literature in China the very important element of conscious and articulate movement without which the authority of the classical tradition could not be challenged. There were a number of writers who were attracted by the irresistible power and beauty of the literature of lowly and untutored peasants and dancing girls and street reciters, and who were tempted to produce their best works in the form and the language of the literature of the people. But they were so ashamed of what they had done that many of the earlier novelists published their works anonymously or under strange noms de plume. There was no clear and conscious recognition that the classical language was long dead and must be replaced by the living tongue of the people. Without such articulate challenges the living language and literature of the people never dared to hope that they might someday usurp the high position occupied by the classical literature.

The greatest contribution of the recent literary revolution was to supply this missing factor of conscious attack on the old tradition and of articulate advocacy of the new. The death knell of the classical language was sounded when it was historically established that it had died at least two thousand years ago. And the ascendancy of the language and literature of the people was practically assured when, through contact and comparison with the literature of the West, the value and beauty of the despised novels and dramas were warmly appreciated by the intellectuals of the nation. Once the table of values was turned upside down, once the vulgar language was consciously demonstrated to be the best qualified candidate for the honor of the national language of China, the success of the revolution was beyond doubt. The time had been ripe for the change. The common sense of the people, the songs and tales of numberless and nameless men and women, have been for centuries unconsciously but steadily preparing for this change. All unconscious processes of evolution are of necessity very slow and wasteful. As soon as these processes are made conscious and articulate, intelligent guidance and experimentation become possible, and the work of many centuries may be telescoped into the brief period of a few years.¹

[Further Reading]

1. (英)伯特兰·罗素著,杨汉麟译,教育与美好生活,河北:河北人民出版社,1999.
2. (美)约翰·杜威著,朱经农,潘梓年译,明日之学校,北京:商务印书馆,1993.
3. 陶行知,陶行知文集,江苏:江苏凤凰教育出版社,2008.

1　The story of the Literary Renaissance in China is vividly told in Dr. Tsi C. Wang's *The Youth Movement in China*, New York: New Republic Press, 1917.

7 Happiness

Passage 1 I Wandered Lonely as a Cloud   / 207
Passage 2 Don't Miss the Tide: Honorable Donald Johnston and His Dedication to
             the Sustainable International Development   / 210
Passage 3 The Treasure in the Forest   / 217
Passage 4 A Glimpse of 2020   / 226

7 Happiness

[本章导读]

人人都追求幸福，即便已经成为人们心目中的"幸运儿"，也仍然渴望掌握幸福的真谛。那么，如何才能获得幸福感呢？为了更为深入和全面地讨论这个意义重大、且又"仁者见仁，智者见智"的议题，本章分别从自然、理念、财富、时代四个角度，选取了四篇具有代表性的文章。

第一篇选自英国浪漫主义诗人威廉·华兹华斯（William Wordsworth）的代表作之一《我孤独地漫游，像一朵云》("I Wandered Lonely as a Cloud")。幸福是追求爱与美好，大自然的美好总会滋养我们的心灵，带来平和的心境。第二篇文章选自刘琛教授的《不要迷失大趋势：唐纳德·约翰逊爵士及其对国际可持续发展的贡献》("Don't Miss the Tide: Honorable Donald Johnston and His Dedication to the Sustainable International Development"）。约翰逊爵士一生秉持的多边主义可持续发展的理念、他对普通人的关注、他的视野与情怀，可以帮助年轻人理解理念和信仰如何影响人的认知和幸福感的获得。诺贝尔经济学奖得主保罗·萨缪尔森（Paul Samuelson）提出的幸福公式认为物质消费越大，幸福度越高，而欲望则与幸福成反比。第三篇是"科幻小说之父"赫伯特·乔治·韦尔斯（Herbert George Wells）的短篇小说《森林寻宝记》(*The Treasure in the Forest*）。小说讲述了两个英国人带着一张抢来的藏宝图，闯入森林深林寻找宝藏，最终被贪婪蒙蔽意识的故事。财富不一定会带来幸福，贪婪却必将导致毁灭。社会的迅速发展变化也影响着人们对幸福的解读。第四篇是哈佛大学经济学教授理查德·库珀（Richard Cooper）在 2004 年对未来世界做出的预测《2020 年一瞥》("A Glimpse of 2020"）。文中讨论了对世界未来发展至关重要的四个因素：人口增长、人均收入增长、计算与通信技术发展以及国际流动性增强、领导人更迭。这些因素正深刻地改变着世界，将全人类更紧密地联系在一起，成为"命运共同体"，而国际协作则是实现全人类福祉的有效途径。

幸福是人类永恒的追求，也是永恒的话题。对于幸福的解读的要诀也许就在伊壁鸠鲁（Epicurus）所说的"信仰和选择"，因为信仰决定行为。"我们不相信的，我们不会去做"（We do as we believe. If we do not believe it, we will not do it.）。"我们都希望收获快乐，但并不是所有的快乐都值得追求"（All pleasure is good because it is akin to us, while not all pleasure is worthy of choice.）。

7 Happiness

[Passage 1]

I Wandered Lonely as a Cloud[1]

I wandered lonely as a Cloud
That floats on high o'er Vales and Hills,
When all at once I saw a crowd,
A host of golden Daffodils;
Beside the Lake, beneath the trees,
Fluttering and dancing in the breeze.

Continuous as the stars that shine
And twinkle on the Milky Way,
They stretched in never-ending line
Along the margin of a bay:
Ten thousand saw I at a glance,
Tossing their heads in sprightly dance.

The waves beside them danced, but they
Out-did the sparkling waves in glee:
A Poet could not but be gay
In such a jocund company:
I gazed—and gazed—but little thought
What wealth the shew to me had brought:

What rhetorical device is used here?

Discuss the rhyme of this poem.

Why does the poet compare Daffodils to stars?

What rhetorical device is used here? Why?

What does it refer to?

---

1 Wordsworth, William, I Wandered Lonely as a Cloud, 1815, Poetry Foundation, https://www.poetryfoundation.org/poems/45521/i-wandered-lonely-as-a-cloud accessed November 1, 2021.

> 文化智慧阅读
>
> Explain the transition of the poet's mindset.
>
> What does it imply?

For **oft** when on my couch I lie

In **vacant** or in **pensive** mood,

They flash upon that **inward** eye

Which is the **bliss** of solitude,

And then my heart with pleasure fills,

And dances with the Daffodils.

I. Background Information

William Wordsworth (1770—1850) was the leading poet of the English Romantic Movement and Poet Laureate of the United Kingdom from 1843 until his death. He is remembered as a poet of spiritual and epistemological speculation, a poet concerned with the human relationship to nature and a fierce advocate of using the vocabulary and speech patterns of common people in poetry.

"I Wandered Lonely as a Cloud" (also commonly known as "Daffodils") is one of the most popular poems of Wordsworth. The poem was inspired by an event on April 15, 1802 in which Wordsworth and his sister Dorothy came across a "long belt" of daffodils while wandering in the forest. Written in 1804 (by Wordsworth's own account), it was first published in 1807 in *Poems*, in Two Volumes, and a revised version was published in 1815.

II. Notes

1. **O'er:** over

2. **Vale:** *n.* a valley

3. **Daffodil:** *n.* a tall yellow spring flower shaped like a trumpet. It is a national symbol of Wales

4. **Sprightly:** *adv.* lively; full of energy

5. **Jocund:** *adj.* cheerful and light-hearted

6. **Oft:** often

7. **Vacant:** *adj.* not thinking about anything in particular

8. **Pensive:** *adj.* thinking deeply about something

9. **Inward:** *adj.* existing within the mind

10. **Bliss:** *n.* extreme happiness

III. Reading Comprehension

Read Passage One, and choose the best answer to each question.

1. Which statement best identifies the theme of "I Wandered Lonely as a Cloud"?

(A) The beauty of nature brings people pleasure.

(B) Nature is the best inspiration for hopeful artists.

(C) Nature reflects the variety of emotions that humans feel.

(D) Humans rarely appreciate the beauty of nature that surrounds them.

2. Which lines could best support the theme?

(A) I wandered lonely as a cloud / That floats on high o'er vales and hills,

(B) A poet could not but be gay, / In such a jocund company:

(C) I gazed—and gazed—but little thought / What wealth the show to me had brought:

(D) In vacant or in pensive mood, / They flash upon that inward eye

3. How does the use of sound influence the mood in the poem?

(A) The poem uses free verse to create an unpredictable mood.

(B) The poem uses alliteration to emphasize the pleasures of nature.

(C) The poem uses repetition to show that nature is permanent.

(D) The poem uses a predictable rhyme scheme to create a cheerful mood.

IV. Questions for Further Thought

1. In the past, how has nature influenced your mood? Share the story.

2. How is the relationship between human beings and nature portrayed in Chinese poetry? Explain your answers with some examples.

文化智慧阅读

[Passage 2]

Don't Miss the Tide: Honorable Donald Johnston and His Dedication to the Sustainable International Development[1]

Nearly two years after the start of global disruptions due to COVID-19, in his New Year's Message 2022, UN Secretary-General António Guterres crystalized the essential challenge confronting the world already at a cross-roads is — "Test". "These are not just policy tests. These are <u>moral and real-life tests</u>" in pursuit of a new year of recovery.

In recently heated historical reviews on what the future holds fifty years after <u>President Nixon's historic visit to China in 1972</u>, "Questions" are basic to the outlooks.

When Tests, and Can we pass the tests have become a home to global concern, understanding global challenges through history, though in a different context, still and always, is a great inspiration. In doing so, the reflections upon honorable Donald Johnston and his extraordinary contributions to achieving the sustainable international development towards a better future globally may provide substantial referencing to our discussions at relevant points.

Johnston who left us on February 4, 2022 is a **trailblazer**. He held key cabinet positions under Prime Ministers Pierre Trudeau and John Turner from 1978-1988, and the first non-European to take office as the Secretary General of the OECD from 1996 to 2006 (two terms). Stepping into the international role from the domestic front, Johnston was able to understand the complexity of major issues concerning this globalizing world in an even-handed way, and **ignite** change for the world's greater good from a more complete perspective.

Under his **stewardship**, the recommendations constructive and practical for good

> Explain the "moral and real-life test" with examples.
>
> What do you know about the "visit"?
>
> Why is Johnston a "trailblazer"?

---

[1] Liu Chen, Don't Miss the Tide: Honourable Donald Johnston and His Dedication to the Sustainable International Development, *China Minutes*, March 7, 2022.

governance, and expansion of multilateral dialogue on matters of global concern in sustainable development, international cooperation, democracy, and education etc., had a key role either in helping governments manage risks, conduct reforms, and promote policy innovation (a prime example, he introduced Health as a work program to meet the challenges confronting healthcare), or in sparking OECD's potential to be a more efficient, effective, and responsible organization (he took the lead in a series of innovations important to OECD, such as the globally well-known the OECD Anti-Bribery Convention; the Ministerial Round Table on Sustainable Development, which is continuing to **grapple** with the international collective work on climate change; and in particular, OECD Programme for International Student Assessment). Looking back closely, the beneficiaries of which Johnston took care are the whole world.

Constructive, positive, and active attitude to innovation is the foundation of Johnston's understanding of sustainable international development. In face of unpredictable **trajectory** of globalization, he looked to see things differently and to embrace change positively. In his *Missing the Tide*, Johnston was from a historical angel meant to crystalize and share the invaluable international legacy in global governance, and international cooperation. What remains deeply meaningful to our world at the critical time is learning from the global governments, particularly in the 1990s, that why and how "there were a number of major challenges 25 years ago, but it seemed that leaders could turn them into wonderful opportunities for rapid and sustainable economic and social progress". Executing solutions together is the answer. He cited the collective efforts to establish World Trade Organization (WTO). This was not without challenge. In July 1997, the world faced the Asian financial crisis and with the increasing global interdependence of financial markets, the fear of a global crisis through **contagion** triggered various doubts and criticisms on the goal of WTO. However, the global governments then were confident of and committed to containment and resolution of that crisis augured well for the future. History tells the role of the courage and determination of this kind in sustainable international development. Evidently, WTO is seen as bringing economic growth and rising prosperity everywhere, but especially to the developing world because the new standards successfully enabled trade rather than aid to became the new mantra. Most importantly, the innovation in trade took a great number of people worldwide out of poverty and gave them the opportunity to play a

文化智慧阅读

Give some examples of the "walls" confronting globalization.

part in global economy.

Over the course of his lifetime, Johnston kept bashing into the walls against international cooperation and coordination. As Stephen Cutts elaborated in his Special to *Montreal Gazette*, "Johnston was conscious of the need for the OECD to remain relevant through both enlargement and its outreach program" despite the confrontations from member states objecting on the grounds that the major economies such as China were "insufficiently like-minded".

Delivering major benefits for all people beyond the economic work is at the heart of Johnston's concern. It provides another important dimension to identify the core message of his outlook of sustainable international development.

What is the influence of PISA on Chinese educators?

Johnston took care to energize youth to meet the demands of this ever-changing world. Keeping with the creation of the UN Millennium Development Goals, under his leadership, the world-famous OECD Programme for International Student Assessment (PISA) was launched in 2000. The goal of this policy is to support youth in learning for tomorrow's world. It is also a landmark international legacy far beyond education left by Johnston. One point critical to this: In China, the international comparative policy analyses of primary education have been observably expanded due to PISA. The best practices outside China from Finland, Japan, and Canada etc, for the first time caught attention of the Chinese educators when these countries ranked top on PISA.

What does "global citizenship" mean?

Johnston passionately advocated for support of youth global citizenship. He chaired for many years the McCall McBain Foundation (MMF) created by his friends John and Marcy McCall MacBain. Being extraordinary philanthropists, MMF committed 200 million for McCall MacBain graduate scholarships at McGill University. The scholarships focus on leadership potential. Importantly, his care is international. He was always glad to visit China, and share his insights with the Chinese students from middle schools to universities. In his very welcome lectures, he emphasized the significance to grow up to a truly global citizen and identified the path towards a person of this kind.

How could curiosity and cooperation help students? Compare with Salovey's speech, "A Culture of Curiosity" in Chapter 6.

He encouraged the Chinese students to be curious about different ideas and practices, and to exercise how to work together with the world as a team.

In her reflections upon WWII, Ruth Benedict, one of the most compelling intellectual figures in the twentieth-century American life wrote in her famous *The Chrysanthemum and the Sword*, "One of the handicaps of the twentieth century is that we still have the vaguest and most biased notions, not only of what makes Japan a nation of Japanese, but of what makes the U.S. a nation of Americans, France a nation of Frenchmen, and Russia a nation of Russians. Lacking <u>this knowledge,</u> each country misunderstands the other."

> **7 Happiness**
>
> Passage 2
>
> What does "this knowledge" refer to?

History repeats in this way. Looking at the fears hanging over the world right now, the questions that Johnston raised, and the answers that he tried to give are visionary.

The most important thing in his view of international sustainable development is <u>what makes good governance</u>. It is in the essence is humanity. As a footnote, President Nixon once illustrated China-U.S. relationship, "Today, China's economic power makes U.S. lectures about morality and human rights **imprudent**. Within a decade, it will make them irrelevant. Within two decades, it will make them laughable... unless we do more to improve living conditions in Detroit, Harlem, and South-Central Los Angeles."

> Identify some specific factors essential to good governance.

We are living in a globalizing world, like or dislike. "Globalization is changing the way the world looks, and the way we look at the world. By adopting a global outlook, we become more aware of our connections to people in other societies. We also become more conscious of that many problems the world faces at the start of the twenty-first century" stated by Anthony Giddens, an **eminent** British sociologist in his *Sociology* (4th Edition). In face of the various uncertainty, particularly, when misunderstanding, cynicism, and disengagement somehow outpace the efforts to correct them, Johnston's publications and associate practices for more than 60 years should be reread by China, and the world. In this sense, he is <u>forward-looking</u>.

> What makes Johnston a forward-looking leader?

Johnston's personality has a lot in common with that of all of talents around the world. They are the persons who you can glorify or vilify, but "the only thing you can't do is ignore them. Because they change things—they push the human race forward" (Steve Jobs).

As borders become **porous** to everything from infectious diseases to terrorism to cyber criminals, to climate change, the uncertainty, more urgent and more complicated, confronting the whole world has reached new serious and difficult milestone. It reminds me of Johnston's answer: "Moments of great difficulty are also moments of great opportunity, and what happens next is up to you."

I. Background Information

Miss the Tide: Global Governments in Retreat was published in 2017. It is the last book of Donald Johnston. In the book, Johnston discussed how the global optimism that characterized the 1990s evolved into pessimism and chaos.

The 1990s were a decade characterized by optimism about a great future that lay ahead for generations to follow. Major challenges were approached with a realization that the world leadership had the capacity not only to meet them, but to turn them into unprecedented opportunities for global social and economic progress.

Donald Johnston demonstrates that none of these opportunities achieved their objectives, and in some cases failed completely. Scrutinizing some of the most significant unfulfilled hopes, he looks at the failure of the West to engage effectively with a democratic Russia after the fall of the Berlin Wall, the European Union's fractious path to intending to become history's largest and most competitive economy, the expansion of the Marshall Plan concept to regions fractured by division and conflict, the diminishing prospect of global free trade and investment to stimulate economic growth and increase prosperity in the developing world, the absence of coordinated international actions to combat climate change, the pervasive corruption in corporate governance undermining healthy capitalism, and the growing threats to democracy.

Sifting through the economic, social, and environmental wreckage of the past twenty years, Johnston reflects on the failures and frustrations of international public policy. Can this rapid decline be arrested and reversed? In assessing the impotency of the international community to meet these challenges, *Missing the Tide* extracts some lessons to be learned and looks with cautious optimism to the future.

II. Notes

1. **Trailblazer:** *n.* a person who is the leader in a particular field, especially a person who does a particular thing before anyone else does

2. **Ignite:** *v.* to arouse

3. **Stewardship:** *n.* the act of taking care of or managing sth.

4. **Grapple:** *v.* to try hard to find a solution to a problem

5. **Trajectory:** *n.* a progression of development

6. **Contagion:** *n.* something bad that spreads quickly

7. **Imprudent:** *adj.* not wise or sensible
8. **Eminent:** *adj.* famous and respected, especially in a particular profession
9. **Porous:** *adj.* not retentive or secure

III. Discussion

Following is the text of UN Secretary-General António Guterres' video message to the high-level virtual meeting of the Group of Friends of the Global Development Initiative for Accelerated Implementation of the 2030 Agenda, held May 9, 2022. Read the message and discuss why we need to "give sustainable development goals 'a fighting chance'".

Time to Give Sustainable Development Goals "A Fighting Chance", Secretary-General Stresses in Message to Group of Friends Event on 2030 Agenda[1]

Excellencies, ladies and gentlemen,

We are fast approaching the mid-point of the time available to reach the Sustainable Development Goals. I will be blunt—progress is in peril. COVID-19, a fragile and uneven global economic recovery, climate change and conflicts are pushing our goals farther out of reach.

We see the results all around us. More poverty and hunger. More inequalities within and among countries. More denials of basic human rights—including for girls and women, who are still unjustly shut out of schools, the halls of power, and the boardrooms of business.

A scandalously unequal distribution of COVID-19 vaccines. Insufficient commitments to keep to our target of 1.5°C of global warming. Countries left unable to invest in development because of spiraling debt, inflation and a global financial system that is rigged against the poor. And a food, energy and financial crisis sparked by the war in Ukraine, which is weighing down progress for everyone.

We must do better. And we can. Your discussions through the Global Development Initiative can help move the needle on development progress across all countries. Through a reformed global financial system that improves access for developing countries so they can invest in their people, rather than servicing their debt.

---

1 António Guterre, Time to Give Sustainable Development Goals "A Fighting Chance", Secretary-General Stresses in Message to Group of Friends Event on 2030 Agenda, May 9, 2022, https://www.un.org/press/en/2022/sgsm21263.doc.htm accessed May 10, 2022.

Through climate commitments that match the scale of the crisis—and bold support for developing countries to leave fossil fuels behind and develop truly green and resilient economies.

Through supporting peace, advancing human rights and working for an end to all wars that scar our world and block progress for all. And through a renewed commitment to multilateralism and gathering in solidarity around shared solutions.

We can't lose more ground. It's time to rescue the SDGs [Sustainable Development Goals] and give sustainable development a fighting chance. For people. For planet. For our common future. Thank you.

IV. Questions for Further Thought

1. Discuss the core message of happiness manifested through "a Community of Shared Future for Mankind".

2. Discuss the relationships between happiness and sustainable development.

7 Happiness

Passage 3

[Passage 3]

The Treasure in the Forest[1]

The canoe was now approaching the land. The bay opened out, and a gap in the white surf of the reef marked where the little river ran out to the sea; the thicker and deeper green of the virgin forest showed its course down the distant hill slope. The forest here came close to the beach. Far beyond, dim and almost cloudlike in texture, rose the mountains, like suddenly frozen waves. The sea was still **save for** an almost imperceptible swell. The sky <u>blazed</u>.

Is the story set on a tropical island? How do you know?

The man with the carved paddle stopped. "It should be somewhere here," he said. He shipped the paddle and held his arms out straight before him.

The other man had been in the fore part of the canoe, closely **scrutinizing** the land. He had a sheet of yellow paper on his knee.

"Come and look at this, Evans," he said.

Both men spoke in low tones, and their lips were hard and dry.

The man called Evans came swaying along the canoe until he could look over his companion's shoulder.

How did the two men interpret the map?

The paper had the appearance of <u>a rough map</u>. By much folding it was creased and worn to the pitch of separation, <u>and the second man held the discolored fragments together where they had parted.</u> On it one could dimly make out, in almost obliterated pencil, the outline of the bay.

Why did the two tear the map apart?

"Here," said Evans, "is the reef, and here is the gap." He ran his thumb-nail over the chart.

"This curved and twisting line is the river—I could do with a drink now! —and this

---

1 Herbert G. Wells, *The Treasure in the Forest: Masterpiece Collection*, Createspace Independent Pub, 2014.

star is the place."

"You see this dotted line," said the man with the map; "it is a straight line, and runs from the opening of the reef to a clump of palm-trees. The star comes just where it cuts the river. We must mark the place as we go into the lagoon."

<!-- Why did Evans feel queer? -->

"It's queer," said Evans, after a pause, "what these little marks down here are for. It looks like the plan of a house or something; but what all these little dashes, pointing this way and that, may mean I can't get a notion. And what's the writing?"

"Chinese," said the man with the map.

"Of course! He was a Chinese," said Evans.

"They all were," said the man with the map.

They both sat for some minutes staring at the land, while the canoe drifted slowly. Then Evans looked towards the paddle.

"Your turn with the paddle now, Hooker," said he.

And his companion quietly folded up his map, put it in his pocket, passed Evans carefully, and began to paddle. His movements were languid, like those of a man whose strength was nearly exhausted.

<!-- Why didn't Evans feel happy? -->

Evans sat with his eyes half closed, watching the frothy breakwater of the coral creep nearer and nearer. The sky was like a furnace, for the sun was near the zenith. Though they were so near the Treasure he did not feel the exaltation he had anticipated. The intense excitement of the struggle for the plan, and the long night voyage from the mainland in the unprovisioned canoe had, to use his own expression, "taken it out of him." He tried to arouse himself by directing his mind to the ingots the Chinamen had spoken of, but it would not rest there; it came back headlong to the thought of sweet water rippling in the river, and to the almost unendurable dryness of his lips and throat. The rhythmic wash of the sea upon the reef was becoming audible now, and it had a pleasant sound in his ears; the water washed along the side of the canoe, and the paddle dripped between each stroke. Presently he began to doze.

...

<!-- Comment on Evans' dream. -->

He woke up. They were in the mouth of the lagoon.

"There are the three palm-trees. It must be in a line with that clump of bushes," said his companion. "Mark that. If we, go to those bushes and then strike into the bush in a straight line from here, we shall come to it when we come to the stream."

They could see now where the mouth of the stream opened out. At the sight of it Evans revived. "Hurry up, man," he said, "or by heaven I shall have to drink sea water!" He gnawed his hand and stared at the gleam of silver among the rocks and green tangle.

Presently he turned almost <u>fiercely</u> upon Hooker. "Give me the paddle," he said.

So they reached the river mouth. A little way up Hooker took some water in the hollow of his hand, tasted it, and spat it out. A little further he tried again. "This will do," he said, and they began drinking eagerly.

"Curse this!" said Evans suddenly. "It's too slow." And, leaning dangerously over the fore part of the canoe, he began to suck up the water with his lips.

Presently they made an end of drinking, and, running the canoe into a little creek, were about to land among the thick growth that overhung the water.

"We shall have to scramble through this to the beach to find our bushes and get the line to the place," said Evans.

"We had better paddle round," said Hooker.

So they pushed out again into the river and paddled back down it to the sea, and along the shore to the place where the clump of bushes grew. <u>Here they landed,</u> pulled the light canoe far up the beach, and then went up towards the edge of the jungle until they could see the opening of the reef and the bushes in a straight line. Evans had taken a native implement out of the canoe. It was L-shaped, and the transverse piece was armed with polished stone. Hooker carried the paddle. "It is straight now in this direction," said he; "we must push through this till we strike the stream. Then we must **prospect**."

They pushed through a close tangle of reeds, broad **fronds**, and young trees, and at first it was **toilsome** going, but very speedily the trees became larger and the ground beneath them opened out. The blaze of the sunlight was replaced by insensible degrees by cool shadow. The trees became at last vast pillars that rose up to a canopy of greenery far overhead. Dim white flowers hung from their stems, and ropy creepers swung from tree to tree. The shadow deepened. On the ground, blotched fungi and a red-brown **incrustation** became frequent.

Evans shivered. "It seems almost cold here after the blaze outside."

"I hope we are keeping to the straight," said Hooker.

Presently they saw, far ahead, a gap in the somber darkness where white shafts of hot

7 Happiness

Passage 3

Why did Evans change from "sleepy" to "fiercely"?

What did the two men see after landing?

sunlight smote into the forest. There also was brilliant green undergrowth and colored flowers. Then they heard the rush of water.

"Here is the river. We should be close to it now," said Hooker.

The vegetation was thick by the river bank. Great plants, as yet unnamed, grew among the roots of the big trees, and spread rosettes of huge green fans towards the strip of sky. Many flowers and a creeper with shiny foliage clung to the exposed stems. On the water of the broad, quiet pool which the treasure-seekers now overlooked there floated big oval leaves and a waxen, pinkish-white flower not unlike a water-lily. Further, as the river bent away from them, the water suddenly frothed and became noisy in a rapid.

"Well?" said Evans.

"We have swerved a little from the straight," said Hooker. "That was to be expected."

He turned and looked into the dim cool shadows of the silent forest behind them. "If we beat a little way up and down the stream we should come to something."

"You said—" began Evans.

"He said there was a heap of stones," said Hooker.

The two men looked at each other for a moment.

"Let us try a little down-stream first," said Evans.

They advanced slowly, looking curiously about them. Suddenly Evans stopped. "What the devil's that?" he said.

Hooker followed his finger. "Something blue," he said. It had come into view as they topped a gentle swell of the ground. Then he began to distinguish what it was.

He advanced suddenly with hasty steps, until the body that belonged to the limp hand and arm had become visible. His grip tightened on the implement he carried. The thing was the figure of a Chinaman lying on his face. The abandon of the pose was unmistakable.

The two men drew closer together, and stood staring silently at this **ominous** dead body. It lay in a clear space among the trees. Nearby was a spade after the Chinese pattern, and further off lay a scattered heap of stones, close to a freshly dug hole.

"Somebody has been here before," said Hooker, clearing his throat.

Then suddenly Evans began to swear and rave, and stamp upon the ground.

Hooker turned white but said nothing. He advanced towards the prostrate body. He saw the neck was puffed and purple, and the hands and ankles swollen. "Pah!" he said, and suddenly turned away and went towards the excavation. He gave a cry of surprise. He shouted to Evans, who was following him slowly.

"You fool! It's all right. It's here still." Then he turned again and looked at the dead Chinaman, and then again at the hole.

Evans hurried to the hole. Already half exposed by the ill-fated wretch beside them lay a number of dull yellow bars. He bent down in the hole, and, clearing off the soil with his bare hands, hastily pulled one of the heavy masses out. As he did so a little thorn pricked his hand. He pulled the delicate spike out with his fingers and lifted the ingot.

"Only gold or lead could weigh like this," he said **exultantly**.

Hooker was still looking at the dead Chinaman. He was puzzled.

…

Hooker looked into his face. "I'm going to bury that, anyhow, before I lend a hand with this stuff."

"Don't be a fool, Hooker," said Evans, "Let that mass of corruption **bide**."

Hooker hesitated, and then his eye went carefully over the brown soil about them. "It scares me somehow," he said.

"The thing is," said Evans, "what to do with these ingots. Shall we re-bury them over here, or take them across the strait in the canoe?"

Hooker thought. His puzzled gaze wandered among the tall tree-trunks, and up into the remote sunlit greenery overhead. He shivered again as his eye rested upon the blue figure of the Chinaman. He stared searchingly among the grey depths between the trees.

"What's come to you, Hooker?" said Evans. "Have you lost your wits?"

"Let's get the gold out of this place, anyhow," said Hooker.

He took the ends of the collar of the coat in his hands, and Evans took the opposite corners, and they lifted the mass. "Which way?" said Evans. "To the canoe?"

"It's queer," said Evans, when they had advanced only a few steps, "but my arms ache still with that paddling."

"Curse it!" he said. "But they ache! I must rest."

They let the coat down, Evans' face was white, and little drops of sweat stood out upon his forehead. "It's stuffy, somehow, in this forest."

7 Happiness

Passage 3

What might happen to Hooker if he buried the body first?

文化智慧阅读

Why was Evans so angry?

Then with an abrupt transition to unreasonable anger: "What is the good of waiting here all the day? Lend a hand, I say! You have done nothing but moon since we saw the dead Chinaman."

Hooker was looking steadfastly at his companion's face. He helped raise the coat bearing the ingots, and they went forward perhaps a hundred yards in silence. Evans began to breathe heavily. "Can't you speak?" he said.

"What's the matter with you?" said Hooker.

What was happening to Evans?

Evans stumbled, and then with a sudden curse flung the coat from him. He stood for a moment staring at Hooker, and then with a groan clutched at his own throat.

"Don't come near me," he said, and went and leant against a tree. Then in a steadier voice, "I'll be better in a minute."

Presently his grip upon the trunk loosened, and he slipped slowly down the stem of the tree until he was a crumpled heap at its foot. His hands were clenched **convulsively**. His face became distorted with pain. Hooker approached him.

"Don't touch me! Don't touch me!" said Evans in a stifled voice. "Put the gold back on the coat."

"Can't I do anything for you?" said Hooker.

"Put the gold back on the coat."

As Hooker handled the ingots he felt a little prick on the ball of his thumb. He looked at his hand and saw a slender thorn, perhaps two inches in length.

Evans gave an inarticulate cry and rolled over.

Hooker's jaw dropped. He stared at the thorn for a moment with **dilated** eyes. Then he looked at Evans, who was now crumpled together on the ground, his back bending and straightening spasmodically. Then he looked through the pillars of the trees and net-work of creeper stems, to where in the dim grey shadow the blue-clad body of the Chinaman was still indistinctly visible. He thought of the little dashes in the corner of the plan, and in a moment he understood.

What did Hooker understand?

What did Chang-hi's grin mean?

"God help me!" he said. For the thorns were similar to those the **Dyaks** poison and use in their blowing-tubes. He understood now what Chang-hi's assurance of the safety of his treasure meant. He understood that grin now.

"Evans!" he cried.

But Evans was silent and motionless, save for a horrible **spasmodic** twitching of his limbs. A profound silence brooded over the forest.

Then Hooker began to suck furiously at the little pink spot on the ball of his thumb—sucking for dear life. Presently he felt a strange aching pain in his arms and shoulders, and his fingers seemed difficult to bend. <u>Then he knew that sucking was no good.</u>

Abruptly he stopped, and sitting down by the pile of ingots, and resting his chin upon his hands and his elbows upon his knees, stared at the distorted but still quivering body of his companion. Chang-hi's grin came into his mind again. The dull pain spread towards his throat and grew slowly in intensity. Far above him a faint breeze stirred the greenery, and the white petals of some unknown flower came floating down through the gloom.

How did he know "sucking was no good"?

I. Background Information

Herbert George Wells (1866—1946) was an English novelist, teacher, historian and journalist. Prolific in many genres, he wrote dozens of novels, short stories, and works of social commentary, history, satire, biography and autobiography. Wells is now best remembered for his science fiction novels and is sometimes called "the father of science fiction". Some of his well-known works include *The Time Machine*, *The War of the Worlds*, *The Invisible Man*, and *The Island of Doctor Moreau*.

II. Notes

1. **Save for:** except
2. **Scrutinize:** *v.* to examine carefully
3. **Languid:** *adj.* moving slowly
4. **Furnace:** *n.* stove
5. **Zenith:** *n.* highest point
6. **Exaltation:** *n.* a state of elation or joy
7. **Ingot:** *n.* a solid piece of metal, especially gold or silver, usually shaped like a brick
8. **Chinamen:** this term is now considered outdated and offensive
9. **Lagoon:** *n.* an area of calm sea water separated from the ocean by a line of rock or sand
10. **Prospect:** *v.* to search an area for gold, minerals, oil, etc.
11. **Frond:** *n.* a long leaf of some plants or trees

12. **Toilsome:** *adj.* laborious

13. **Incrustation:** *n.* a hard outer covering or layer

14. **Ominous:** *adj.* suggesting that something bad is going to happen

15. **Exultantly:** *adv.* feel very happy and proud about something you have done

16. **Bide:** *v.* to remain or stay somewhere

17. **Convulsively:** *adv.* (of movements or actions) sudden and impossible to control

18. **Dilated:** *adj.* becoming wider or bigger

19. **Dyaks:** *n.* a member of a Malaysian people of the interior of Borneo: noted for their long houses

20. **Spasmodic:** *adj.* caused by muscles becoming tight in a way that cannot be controlled

III. Reading Comprehension

Read Passage Three, and choose the best answer to each question.

1. Which statement could best describe the theme?

(A) Treasure hunting is dangerous and should only remain in storybooks.

(B) Never underestimate the lengths one will take to protect something dear to them.

(C) Greed can overtake a person's perception and judgment.

(D) Theft will always be punished, one way or another.

2. How does Evans' dream best fit into the structural plot of the story?

(A) It recounts the story of how Evans and Hooker came to learn of the treasure.

(B) It foreshadows danger: they will be consumed by greed.

(C) It heightens the suspense, turning Evans' delusions of grandeur into actual hallucinations.

(D) It suggests that the treasure will be well-guarded, as if by a "devil."

3. What do the two men's reactions to the dead body show?

(A) These reactions show that Hooker is more aware of their situation; Evans only cares for the gold's status.

(B) These reactions show that the two men are more concerned with the treasure than potential danger.

(C) These reactions show that Evans cares more about money than his companion.

(D) These reactions show that Evans has a better focus on their goal than Hooker.

IV. Questions for Further Thought

1. Can money buy happiness? Illustrate your answers with evidence from your own experience, literature, art, or history.

2. How could greed cloud our judgment?

文化智慧阅读

[Passage 4]

A Glimpse of 2020[1]

>Why did Cooper choose 2020 as a case to forecast?

To help get our bearings in a complex and ever-changing world, it is useful to ask what the world will look like in a decade or two. Forecasting the future accurately is of course impossible. And of course we cannot forecast surprises, by definition. But by projecting known trends and tendencies, it is possible to say a remarkable amount about the broad outlines of the world one to two decades from now. In particular, we can identify with high confidence four factors, which we hardly notice from year to year, but which accumulate relentlessly over time, such that by 2020 they will have profoundly transformed the world as we now know it. The four factors are population growth, growth in per capita income, increasing international mobility among national firms and individuals, made possible and driven by both technological changes in transportation and communication, and the aging of existing political leaders (as well as everyone else).

For concreteness, I will focus below on the year 2020. The year should not be taken literally, but as the rough mid-point of one to two decades from now. That looks beyond the immediate issues of today, and allows the cumulation of small annual changes in the trends mentioned above. But it is also a comprehensible distance into the future, the same distance as the year 1988, which many adults can remember, is into the past.

A Celebration of the Past Half Century

But before turning to the future, I want to make some celebratory remarks about the past, the last half of the 20th century. Our daily newspaper and TV fare gives the

---

1 Richard N. Cooper, *A Glimpse of 2020*, 2004, https://scholar.harvard.edu/cooper/publications/glimpse-2020 accessed November 1, 2021.

impression that we **lurch** from one crisis to another, whether it be Kosovo or North Korea or Argentina or Iraq. From mid-1997 the world experienced a series of financial crises, from Thailand through Malaysia and Indonesia and Korea, then Russia and Brazil in 1998 and early 1999, Argentina in late 2001. Japan experienced its first serious post-1945 economic recessions.

It is therefore worthwhile from time to time to stand back from the immediate, pressing issues of the day to appraise how far the world has come since, say, 1950. The overall economic performance during the past half century has been nothing short of fantastic, in the literal sense: if someone had forecast in 1950 where the world economy actually was in 2000, he would have been dismissed by his contemporaries as living in a world of fantasy.

The immediate **antecedents** to 1950 were the Great Depression of the 1930s and the Second World War from 1939 (1937 in the Pacific) to 1945, followed by painful recovery in Europe, Russia, China, and Japan. Those disasters reflected in part a failure to construct a cooperative world following the First World War. The Anglo-American planners of the 1940s determined to do better. With help from representatives from other countries they created the United Nations, with its Security Council, plus a collection of economic institutions including the International Monetary Fund (IMF) and the World Bank, and laid the philosophical basis in the General Agreement on Tariffs and Trade (GATT) for what in 1995 became the World Trade Organization (WTO).

The basic philosophy underlying the United Nations is that threats to the peace anywhere in the world are of legitimate interest to all nations, and that collective action could be undertaken to preserve or restore peace. The basic philosophy of economic arrangements, against the background of the catastrophic Great Depression, was that national governments should take responsibility for stabilizing national economies and for ensuring high employment (something that was seen to be possible in light of the Keynesian revolution in economic thinking, with its emphasis on the potential of fiscal policy for economic stabilization); and that countries should avoid beggaring their neighbors through restrictions on international trade. Thus procedures were put in place, in the form of the IMF and the GATT, to eschew many forms of trade and payments restrictions, and to reduce over time the restrictions on imports that many

7 Happiness

Passage 4
Discuss the crises during this period.

What are the core values of the UN?

How did these procedures influence the world economy?

countries inherited from the 1930s.

Stabilization of national economies and liberalization of trade together have resulted in outstanding economic performance, both in the rich (mainly northwestern Europe and North America) countries and in the initially poor (developing) countries. World per capita income increased by 2.1 percent a year from 1950 to 2001, much higher than in any previous period, including the rapid industrializing period of the late 19th century (see Table 1). The average world citizen had an income nearly three times larger in 2000 than it was in 1950. What many forget—or never knew—is that several of today's rich countries were poor 50 years ago—Japan, Italy, Spain, to name three large ones. South Korea was considered economically hopeless. As these examples illustrate, economic development has occurred with economic growth, not only in these countries, but in many others as well.

Table 1
Growth in Per Capita Income (percent per annum)

1820—1870	0.6
1870—1913	1.3
1913—1929	1.0
1950—2001	2.1

Source: calculated from Maddison (2001) Maddison, Angus, 2001, The World Economy: A Millen

Summarize the other improvements in human well-being.

During this period other measures of human well-being also improved: the spread of **contagious** diseases was brought under better control; infant mortality dropped dramatically; longevity increased. Health and nutrition improved in most places. Smallpox, once the **scourge** of mankind, was banished entirely.

Partly for these reasons, world population grew during this period more rapidly than ever before, more than doubling in fifty years (2.5 to 6.1 billion). Prices also rose substantially, attributed by some to the uncritical adoption of Keynesian economic policies. In the United States the consumer price level was over six times higher in 2000 than it was in 1950 (4 percent a year, on average), and most other countries experienced even greater increases.

International trade outpaced the growth in economic output, growing more than 6 percent annually, partly a result of a cumulatively dramatic, but temporally gradual, drop in import protection over the period following eight rounds of multilateral tariff reductions. By 1995 tariffs on manufactured goods into the rich countries were only about ten percent of the levels they were in 1947, the year of the first multilateral round; the eighth was the Uruguay Round, concluded in 1994. A ninth round, the Doha round, was launched in 2002, and remains in its preliminary stages, **mired** in disagreement, as many earlier rounds were at a comparable stage.

International capital movements, **stifled** by the defaults of the 1930s and the disruptions of the Second World War, recovered more slowly, but by the 1990s extensive trans-border investment also occurred.

It is often pointed out <u>that this growth was very uneven, and that while many people are better off, many people are also poorer</u>. The first proposition is true, the second false, or at best deeply misleading, if "many" means a substantial portion of the world's population. The Indian economist Surjit Bhalla has calculated world poverty rates since 1950, using the World Bank's definition of poverty as US$1.00 a day in 1985, in purchasing power parity terms. He finds that the fraction of people in developing countries living below this poverty line fell from 63 percent in 1950 to 43 percent in 1980 and further to 13 percent in 2000. The absolute number of people living below poverty fell from 1223 million to 647 million, despite a more than doubling of the world's population. That much remains to be done should not lead us to ignore this great accomplishment.

The dominant economic characteristic of the late 20th century is that technical change, which has been occurring at a significant pace for two centuries, has been <u>institutionalized.</u> Processes and incentives have been established in the world's rich countries to ensure the search for new, useful ideas, even in the absence of a particular focused objective. This institutionalization ensures a constant flow of new practical ideas, many of which, once introduced, are irresistible. Consider how rapidly the fax machine spread; for those who have now become accustomed to it, life without fax is hard to imagine (although even the venerable fax is being replaced in many uses by email). But that is only one of thousands of new ideas, embodied in products and processes, which have been introduced over the past few decades.

These new technological ideas, combined with social order and the trained human beings who generate and apply them, <u>are the basis for modern economic prosperity.</u> Territory, resources, raw manpower, and military might play a much smaller role than

---

7 Happiness

Passage 4

Do you agree with the statement? Why or why not?

What does "technical change has been institutionalized" mean?

Why are they "the basis"?

they did in earlier, less successful eras.

The competitive system in which these new ideas are generated and introduced is one of controlled chaos: chaos because no one is in charge—tens of thousands of people are making decisions that will over time affect billions of people; controlled in the sense that they operate within a defined social, economic, and legal order, and the results of their collective behavior within that framework create a comprehensible if somewhat turbulent environment.

Forecasting the future accurately is impossible. It is possible, however, to identify some factors which we hardly notice from year to year, but which accumulate relentlessly over time, such that by the end of two decades will have profoundly transformed the world as we now know it. <u>We turn now to population growth, growth in per capita income, and improvements in computation and communication that will increase international mobility among national firms and individuals, reducing economic and ultimately cultural differences among different parts of the globe.</u>

> Comment on the forecast made in 2004.

Population Growth

Between 1960 and 2000 the world's population grew by 3.1 billion persons, or about 1.8 percent a year. Some slowdown in population growth occurred toward the end of this period, especially in China and in a number of middle-income countries, such as South Korea, as well as in the industrialized countries. But China was a major exception among low income countries. Population growth normally accelerates at first after a country begins to experience increases in per capita income, as longevity increases, as child-bearing ages are lengthened, and especially as infant mortality rates fall with better nutrition and medical care. A slowdown in population growth usually occurs only after per capita income reaches around US$1000.00, when modes of production change, parents realize that their children are likely to survive beyond infancy, and parents become better informed about family planning techniques. Outside China, there are still over one billion persons living in countries with average per capita incomes below US$1000.00, mostly in Africa and South Asia. Even if global population growth slows substantially, to 0.9 percent a year, the world population would still reach 7.5 billion by the year 2020, <u>an increase of 1.5 billion from 2000</u>.

> What does the "increase" imply?

More people mean more demand for energy—for warmth, food preparation, illumination, motive power, and production processes; more demand for food; more demand for fresh water; and more demand for housing and other forms of capital. It would take extraordinary efforts of a nature and magnitude not generally contemplated to alter this demographic projection significantly, since most of the future mothers have already been born, although more efforts now could have significant effects beyond 2020.

Almost all this population increase will be in relatively low income countries. And most of the growth will <u>occur in cities</u>. Indeed, during the next decade the world will switch from having a majority of rural dwellers to having a majority of urban dwellers, with implications for housing and other urban infrastructure, and with concentrations of people that make political action easier.

Demographic trends in Europe, Japan, and Russia, in contrast, suggest slow or even negative growth and a marked aging of those societies, with profound implications for the fiscal sustainability of the government entitlements that have been conferred on their publics. (<u>China too will age on the basis of its current population policies, but only later, after adding another 200 million people because of the large number of women still in child-bearing age, before declining after 2040.</u>) Before 2010 over 20 percent of the population will be 65 or older in Italy, Japan, and Germany, somewhat later in France and Britain. Indeed, thanks both to increased longevity and to declining natality in all the rich countries, the ratio of working age population to those over 65 will decline from 5.0 in 1990 to 3.5 by 2015. <u>Projections further out, to 2050</u>, on the basis of these trends suggest an absolute decline in the populations of Germany, Italy, and Spain. Japan's population is projected to drop to 100 million, 21 percent below the 127 million of 2000. Even greater percentage declines are projected for Russia and Ukraine. By this time also China and some other developing countries will be experiencing a decline in population. Peacetime declines in population are way outside our range of experience since the beginning of the industrial revolution around 1800; it is unclear how these societies will adjust to both the aging and to the decline in total population. Demand for schools and new housing will decline, and land will become more readily available; caring for the aged will become more demanding.

Like Europe and Japan, the United States and Canada have also experienced a decline in natural population growth, albeit more moderate, but over the years they have been far more receptive to immigration and thus can **replenish** their young adult population with willing immigrants from countries with more rapidly growing population.

Higher Per Capita Income

The second dominant feature of the world economy is the all-but-universal aspiration for higher standards of living in all but the richest parts of the world. In this respect the world has been westernized; it has absorbed both the notion and the expectation of material progress. So in future there will not only be more people, but more people wanting higher standards of living. And we now know how, in principal, to achieve higher standards of living: install a stable social system with incentives for effort and risk-taking, and engage with the world economy. Most of the world does not need to generate new technology or even savings to grow—increasingly those can be borrowed from the rest of the world. But it does require extensive investment in both physical and human capital; of the two, the latter is both more important and more difficult. Thus the state continues to play a key role in economic development, in providing for social order, proper incentives for effort, saving, and risk-taking, and widespread education. But it does not have to play the role of entrepreneur, investor, and manager as well. Indeed, in these roles, widely **espoused** in many countries in the 1960s, it is likely to inhibit development.

Economic growth everywhere implies economic and social change, and change almost invariably involves some losers even in an environment in which change is being generated by economic growth. Change involves stress and even **duress**. Established enterprises have extensive investment in existing ways of doing things—in their machines, their people, and their organizational hierarchy. It is much easier simply to carry on in established patterns than to change, and that is what most organizations, including business enterprises, prefer. Yet in western societies these business enterprises are, paradoxically, the principal instruments of economic change. They change because they feel compelled to do so by competition, by fear of losing their customers to other firms. The more far-sighted ones change on their own, to stay ahead of their actual or potential competitors. But for many firms and individuals change is disagreeable. Individuals can find that once-promising careers are now dead-ends, that once-learned skills are now obsolete. Some individuals adapt well, others do not. This is the essence of what Austrian-turned-American economist Joseph Schumpeter called creative destruction, and it is a process that, over time, has made the average individual in western countries unbelievably well off when viewed from the perspective of forebears only three or four generations earlier.

This lesson is being learned in former communist countries, where it runs against the strong apparent preference of many people for stability throughout one's life. It is also being learned in many developing countries, where it carries the possibility of social **upheaval**, since it is not possible to modernize economic activity and norms without also altering both norms and expectations in other areas as well, as Chinese leaders have discovered but to which they are only slowly becoming reconciled.

Can the earth feed an additional billion people? The answer is certainly affirmative. The scope for further extensive agriculture—adding cultivated land—is limited; but yields can continue to increase on existing cultivated land. Average yields are far below best practice, and best practice is continually improving, as we learn more about what nutrients plants need at each stage of their life cycle. **Irrigation** can be extended, where water is readily available. (Water scarcity in some regions of the world, however, will limit the scope for intensifying agriculture in those regions, such as the Middle East and northern China.) Moreover, growing knowledge about genetic engineering will permit more disease-resistant and insect-resistant plants, and even drought-resistant plants. The efficiency of livestock feeding can be further increased. While we are reaching the practical limits of harvesting native fish from the oceans, **aquaculture** can be extended to increase yields from the sea.

Historically, economic growth is associated with an enormous growth in demand for commercial primary energy. In the two strong decades following 1950 the demand for primary energy in the 24 now rich countries of the Organization for Economic Cooperation and Development (OECD) more than doubled; and in the two decades following 1965 the demand for primary energy in the developing countries **trebled**.

Modern economies are still based heavily on energy, even though the efficiency with which it is used is improving steadily and is vastly greater than it was 30 years ago, before the 1973 oil shock. Developing countries, in particular, rely increasingly on fossil fuels as they move from subsistence to manufacturing economies. Oil is still the unmatched fuel for transportation, and with modernization the demand for

---

7 Happiness

Passage 4

What does "this lesson" refer to?

How could the earth feed an additional billion people?

Explain the statement with examples.

Why are modern economies based heavily on energy?

transportation increases more than proportionately. (Synthetic oil can be made from coal and from natural gas, but it remains uncompetitive with petroleum in cost. Fuel cells may well supplant gasoline in the more distant future, but their impact will be modest in the next 15 years.)

Assuming a world growth rate of three percent over two decades (real gross world product would be 81 percent higher in 2020 than it was in 2000), the US Department of Energy projects the world demand for oil to grow by 33 million barrels a day (mbd) between 2001 and 2020, or by 43 percent. Of this increase in demand, less than 10 mbd are projected to take place in today's rich countries of Europe, Japan, and North America; the remaining 23 mbd increase will arise in today's relatively poor countries, over half in Asia (excluding Japan). China alone will import seven mbd in 2020, up from two mbd in 2001.

The world will not, perhaps surprisingly, have difficulty supplying this increase in demand for oil. Technological developments have greatly improved the prospects and reduced the costs of exploring for and developing new oil wells, both on land and under sea. But the most economical oil remains in the Persian Gulf region, and if the countries of that region are willing to undertake the necessary investments in exploration and development, this great increase in demand can be satisfied at only modest increases in price. (The DoE reference case projection assumes a price, in 2002 dollars, of $26 a barrel in 2020; other forecasters assume an even lower price.)

On these price and investment assumptions oil production outside of **OPEC** will grow modestly by 2020. Within OPEC, only Venezuela outside the Persian Gulf region can be expected to be a significant contributor, leaving most of the increase to come **incrementally** from the Persian Gulf countries. If these projections are realized, world oil production coming from the Persian Gulf will rise from 30 percent in 2001 to nearly 40 percent in 2020. Demand for oil tankers will also rise sharply.

We know from the experiences of 1973—1974 and 1979—1980 that a several-fold rise in oil prices, generated by an actual or an anticipated shortage of oil (world oil production did not fall in 1979, following the Iranian revolution and a decline in Iran's output, but anticipation of shortages led to extensive build-up of stocks), can play **havoc** with the macroeconomics of countries around the world, being largely responsible for the "**stagflation**" (deep recession combined with inflation) of the 1970s and the developing country debt crisis of the 1980s. So the damage from disruption in the flow of oil can be severe.

Higher growth will also affect the environment. The effect will be mainly unfavorable in low income countries, with their priority on raising incomes. It will be mainly favorable in higher income countries, as publics protest the foul air or water they must endure, and revenues are increasingly devoted to improving local environmental conditions. Greatly increased use of fossil fuels will of course increase emissions of carbon dioxide, thus contributing to future global climate change, but such change will be hardly noticeable during the next decade.

Continuing Advances in Information Technology

The third driving factor for the world economy will be the continuing revolution in computation and communication. Two decades from now the costs of computation and long-distance communication will once again have fallen by more than 90 percent, making them nearly "free" by today's standards. This will lead to much greater integration of the world economy, in the specific sense that business enterprises will increasingly take, and will be driven by competition to take, a more-than- regional or national perspective in framing their business decisions. This has been true of markets for produced output and sources of supply for a long time, and of sources of capital for the past two decades. But it will be increasingly so also for the location of production and the related issue of labor force. The secular decline in transportation costs, especially of air freight and bulk carriage, implies they are no longer a decisive factor for location of production of many goods. Not only Persian Gulf oil but also South African coal and Liberian iron ore can be moved long distances to market. Cheap long distance communication means that the "back room" activities of financial and other businesses can take place at great distance from headquarters, e.g.: in Ireland or India when the front office is in New York or San Francisco. Under these circumstances many industries in principle become footloose, able to locate at a variety of convenient places. They seek an inexpensive labor force able to meet the required skill qualifications, social stability, and a tax and regulatory environment favorable to low production costs. Offshore outsourcing, exaggerated recently in journalistic and political circles, will become more important over time, a natural outcome and benefit from advances in information technology and investment. These developments taken together imply that a country far out of line in one dimension that is not adequately compensated in some other dimension will lose those economic activities that do not require close proximity to markets.

Most importantly, information of all kinds will flow more cheaply and more quickly around the world than has ever been the case. This is true not only for scientific, financial, and political information, but also for technological, marketing, and cultural information. It will be ever more difficult for governments to insulate determined publics from obtaining information from abroad, even when the information is **detrimental** or even threatening to the governments in question.

The influence of higher mobility should not be exaggerated. The managers of many enterprises still have strong ties of loyalty to their home society and culture, they have useful but specialized knowledge about how best to operate in a familiar political environment, and they are subject to the **inertial** forces that attend most human action. Linguistic barriers remain. Recent research has shown that even so-called multinational firms undertake two-thirds of their investment in the home country. But the trend is clear: competitive pressures are eroding these factors, and more and more firms are moving some of their activities away from their historical bases. As always in economics, it is decisions at the margin, not the typical firm, that determine many outcomes.

Political Succession

One other factor can be predicted confidently over the passage of sufficient time: the death of today's political leaders. For many countries this will make little difference. Most democracies have well-established processes of succession and deeply rooted political traditions that result in smooth political transitions and substantial continuity in policy, especially foreign policy. Monarchies too have well-established patterns of succession, generally accepted by subject populations, whether by passage to the deceased monarch's eldest son (or, occasionally, to a daughter) or to a crown prince selected by members of the royal family. But personal dictatorships rarely have an accepted pattern of succession; death of the leader results in a power struggle among would-be successors, sometimes even to civil war.

Implications of the Identified Trends

What are the implications of these various developments? The first is that there will be many more "South Koreas" in the future, that is, developing economies that grow rapidly, democratize and gradually join the ranks of rich countries. The Asian financial crises will be seen by some countries from the perspective of 2020 as <u>adolescent growing pains</u>—unpleasant when it occurred, but making possible a stronger mature body. The growth of these countries will create some turbulence for others, since their exports will be concentrated in certain industries, thus posing adjustment problems for those industries in more mature economies; but by the same token their incomes, expenditures, and imports will also grow rapidly, creating market opportunities for industries in mature economies that are poised to take advantage of them. On balance, the development of such economies will also permit even higher living standards in the already rich countries. <u>Today's rich countries, however, will slowly decline in relative economics importance.</u> That is especially true of Japan, whose low growth, aging population combined with inhospitability to immigration assures a substantial decline in relative economic importance over the next few decades.

Second, however, countries whose leadership judges continued internal stability (at least of their leadership) to depend on aggressive activity toward their neighbors, to acquire resources, to protect ethnic minorities, or simply to keep neighboring countries or their own restless publics off guard. As national incomes rise, all governments will have greater scope for harvesting resources from their publics through taxation. Authoritarian governments can channel disproportionate amounts into military or other expenditures devoted to pursuing an aggressive foreign policy, and we can be reasonably confident that a number of countries will turn in that direction. Given the advance and spread of military technology, those adventures will be increasingly costly in human terms, and may threaten global peace. Other countries will therefore have to remain sufficiently armed to cope with these potentially aggressive countries, preferably to deter them from going too far in the first place.

<u>China</u> will experience the benefits of the "demographic dividend," when persons of working age are increasing more rapidly than dependents, in China's case children. If China achieves a plausible but still outstanding annual growth of seven percent (higher than the 6.6 percent assumed by the World Bank in its report on China in

文化智慧阅读

2020, to allow for some appreciation of the real exchange rate), China's Gross Domestic Product (GDP) would reach $4.2 trillion (in 2000 dollars) in 2020, or about 24 percent of US GDP in that year, and roughly equal to US GDP in 1972. It would be larger than Germany, but still significantly smaller than Japan. Chinese per capita income would increase by a factor of 3.4 from 2000, making Chinese much richer than now, but still poor by world standards.

What are the changes in China's population policies for now?

Under these circumstances, China's population will be vastly different from today, with greatly different attitudes, especially among the youth. The first individuals born under the one-child policy will be 40 years old in 2020, and everyone younger will have grown up in an environment of devoted parents, rapid economic growth, hope for the future, and awareness of both future economic and political possibilities.

The high GDP would put the Chinese government in a position, if it can tax effectively, to be a major player on the world scene, in **armaments**, trade, and foreign aid, just as the USA was in the mid-1970s. But the focus of a development-oriented China would be concentrated on continuing requirements for infrastructure—electric power; oil and gas; water for irrigation and for growing urban areas; roads, airports, and other transportation; urban housing; and heavy demands for higher quality education for everyone.

Explain the implication of "re-negotiation" for the world.

The aging in Europe will require a re-negotiation of the "social contract" that led to the creation of the modern welfare state in the 1950s and 1960s. Even though Europe is much richer today than it was then, it created entitlements for its citizens, especially for its older citizens, that will be fiscally insupportable under the expected demographic conditions noted above. Publicly provided pensions and health care are generous, and largely on a pay-as-you-go basis. Unfunded pension liabilities are high in all rich countries, ranging (in 1990) from 113 percent of GDP in the United States through 162 percent of GDP in Japan to an extraordinary 242 percent in Italy (Roseveare et al, 1996). Yet continental European countries are near to the practical limits on taxation, around fifty percent of GDP. With the expected increase in the ratio of aged to working age people, existing entitlements will be unsustainable without severely squeezing normal public expenditures, such as those on defense, education, and research. Taking away perceived rights is difficult in any country, especially democracies. Re-negotiating the terms of the social contract will be a major pre-occupation of European nations in the coming decades. The re-negotiation is likely to succeed—the alternatives are too unattractive—and the Netherlands is leading the way; but the process will be an agonizing one.

As incomes rise in developing countries, and as publics become better educated, they expect improvements in their well-being, and these days they expect governments to assure that. In rich countries, the initiatives for change will come from business firms, and increasingly also from non-governmental organizations. In developing countries, much investment will be needed in public infrastructure (roads, water and sewage, etc.) and in improved housing—all intensive in the use of capital. If governments fail to provide adequately for the required physical infrastructure, and for social infrastructure such as an ordered society and improved education, people will become restless. They will engage in politically disruptive activities, or they will migrate.

We are likely to see the reassertion of religious, ethnic, and tribal differences as some states fail to live up to expectations in delivering economic development or public services, as external influences grow, and in some cases as governments are increasingly recognized as predatory. Again, increased migration is likely to eventuate as a consequence of population pressures, state failures, and information from outside the country.

What are the implications of increased interdependence for government economic policy? Individual countries cannot impose stiff regulations and expect to retain the economic activities that are especially hard hit, unless for one reason or another the activities are immobile, or unless the firms in question see an offsetting benefit to themselves flowing from the stiff regulations. Over time, the economic activity will shift to lower cost locations. With increasingly mobile production, there will be growing conflict between each nation's exercise of its sovereign rights of regulation and its ability to retain the heavily regulated activity.

An analogous problem applies to taxation, especially taxation of corporate income or of interest, dividends, and capital gains on financial investments. Through their pricing on intra-corporate transactions, corporations can shift profits from regions with high corporate profit tax rates to those with low ones, thereby reducing or at least deferring their total taxes. With the internationalization of two-way communication and of securities trading, individuals can hold their financial investments in many parts of the world, in many names, and thereby avoid national taxation. Indeed, many countries today do not even attempt to levy taxes on the overseas financial earnings of their residents.

The same factors that increase the international mobility of legitimate businesses also increase the international mobility of non-profit non-governmental organizations (NGOs), of illegitimate business, and of political organizations relying on terrorist actions to gain publicity for their causes. Organized crime will increasingly operate across national boundaries to **confound** national police authorities. Some NGOs, as well as official international bodies, will be relied upon to perform locally some of the 20th century functions of government, such as distributing food in times of harvest failure or even providing police protection of sorts. Such activities may be highly regarded by the local populace, but of course they bring with them information and ideas from abroad as well as goods and services, and their very presence underlines the ineffectiveness of the host government.

Implications for governments

High mobility of business enterprise reduces the effectiveness of traditional nation-based regulation, taxation, and law enforcement. But of course governments are not **oblivious** to this trend. They attempt to cope with the increased mobility in a variety of ways: import prohibitions, extra-territorial reach, de-regulation. But they also increasingly recognize the need to cooperate with other like-minded governments, and even sometimes those that are not so like-minded. Cooperation is especially evident in the area of financial regulation, where traditionally domestic agencies, such as the Securities and Exchange Commission, increasingly collaborate with their counterparts to preserve the effectiveness of their (now collective) actions. Tax and law enforcement authorities, such as the Federal Bureau of Investigation (FBI), are also moving toward greater exchange of information. So increased mobility of enterprises, and of organized crime, will also lead to new patterns of cooperation among national authorities, at least at the technical level, and at least among like-minded governments such as those in the G-7. By 2020 these practices in all likelihood will have become habitual.

Where national governments have manifestly "failed," or where they abuse their citizens grossly, or where they provide sanctuary or even encouragement to international terrorism or organized crime, there is likely to be increased external interference in their so-called internal affairs. Such a development raises a whole host of practical and legal questions which the international community is only beginning to recognize, and which it is reluctant to face squarely since the principal **interlocutors** in such a discussion are the representatives of states. But as it occurs, as it must, the role of the United Nations and other international organizations will increase, and these developments will mark the beginning of the end of the **Westphalian state system**.

I. Background Information

In the 1970s, Richard N. Cooper developed the "locomotive theory" of international fiscal coordination, in which three nations (Japan, Germany, and the US) would "pull" the global economy to safety following a recession in the mid-1970s. The idea was put to the test at the 1978 Bonn Summit of G-7 Leaders attended by Carter, who had appointed Cooper to the State Department post the year before. At the gathering, the nations agreed on a joint statement of commitments regarding economic policy—the first successful agreement of its kind and a model for future such accords. The establishment and continuation of the G-7, and later G-8 and G-20 meetings of world leaders to focus on joint economic policy, years after Cooper's work, are examples of his influence both as a researcher and policy expert.

Most economists live in a world of theory, using careful calculations to predict the future. But Richard N. Cooper believed theory couldn't tell the whole story when it came to solving real-world problems, particularly when they involve the whole world—which he amply demonstrated after a global recession in the 1970s. He brought realism, institutional understanding, and historical experience to economics, not just mathematical technique.

II. Notes

1. **Lurch:** *v.* to make a sudden, unsteady movement forward or sideways
2. **Antecedent:** *n.* a thing or an event that exists or comes before another
3. **Contagious:** *adj.* disease spreads by people touching each other
4. **Scourge:** *n.* something that causes a lot of trouble or suffering
5. **Mired:** *adj.* involved in a difficult situation
6. **Stifle:** *v.* to prevent or constrain

7. **Replenish:** *v.* to fill up again

8. **Espouse:** *v.* to support or adopt

9. **Duress:** *n.* threats or force

10. **Upheaval:** *n.* a big change that causes a lot of confusion, worry and problems

11. **Irrigation:** *n.* watering of lands

12. **Aquaculture:** *n.* the growing of plants in water for food

13. **Treble:** *v.* to become three times

14. **OPEC:** Organization of Petroleum Exporting Countries (an organization of countries that produce and sell oil)

15. **Incrementally:** *adv.* increased regularly

16. **Havoc:** *n.* great disorder and confusion

17. **Stagflation:** *n.* an economic situation where there is high inflation (prices rising continuously) but no increase in the jobs that are available or in business activity

18. **Detrimental:** *adj.* harmful

19. **Inertial:** *adj.* lacking energy

20. **Armament:** *n.* the process of increasing the amount of weapons

21. **Confound:** *v.* to confuse and surprise

22. **Oblivious:** *adj.* not aware of sth.

23. **Interlocutor:** *n.* a person who takes part in dialogue or a conversation

24. **Westphalian state system:** a term used in international relations, supposedly arising from the Treaties of Westphalia in 1648. It is generally held to mean a system of states or international society comprising sovereign state entities possessing the monopoly of force within their mutually recognized territories. Relations between states are conducted by means of formal diplomatic ties between heads of state and governments, and international law consists of treaties made (and broken) by those sovereign entities. The Westphalian system reached its peak in the 19th and 20th centuries, but it has faced recent challenges from advocates of humanitarian intervention.

III. Writing

Read the following excerpts from news reports, and write an approximately 300-word essay comparing them with the predictions made in Passage Four.

Xi declares "complete victory" in eradicating absolute poverty in China[1]

BEIJING, Feb. 25 (Xinhua) Chinese President Xi Jinping announced on Thursday that China has secured a "complete victory" in its fight against poverty.

—Over the past eight years, the final 98.99 million impoverished rural residents living under the current poverty line have all been lifted out of poverty.

—Combined with poverty-reduction results since the late 1970s, China is responsible for over 70 percent of the global reduction in poverty over the period.

—Xi said the country has blazed a poverty reduction trail and formed an anti-poverty theory with Chinese characteristics.

—Xi demanded efforts to consolidate poverty alleviation achievements and initiate a dovetailing drive of "rural vitalization."

China Unveils Details of Three-child Policy, Support Measures[2]

BEIJING, July 20 (Xinhua) — China on Tuesday released a decision allowing a couple to have three children and rolling out a slew of support measures, ranging from tax breaks to more nurseries and flexible work leave to encourage births.

—By 2025, China will basically establish a policy system that actively supports births with better services and lower costs in childbearing, care and education.

—The country will scrap fines for couples who violate the family planning law to have more children than they are allowed.

—To legitimize the three-child policy, China will revise the law on population and family planning.

—A key task in implementing the three-child policy is to improve support measures and relieve families of their worries to unleash the childbirth potential, official said.

IV. Questions for Further Thought

1. List the most important changes that happened in your family in the past decade (2010s—2020s).

2. Which changes bring you a sense of happiness? And which not?

---

1 Xinhua, Xi Declares "Complete Victory" in Eradicating Absolute Poverty in China, *XINHUANET*, February 25, 2021, http://www.xinhuanet.com/english/2021-02/26/c_139767705.htm, accessed May 18, 2022.
2 Xinhua, China Unveils Details of Three-child Policy, Support Measures, *XINHUANET*, July 21, 2021, http://www.xinhuanet.com/english/2021-07/21/c_1310073319.htm, accessed May 18, 2022.

[Mini-task for Chapter 7]

Debating

Organize a debate about "Money is important for happiness." Express your views either for or against this statement.

[Further Reading]

1. Tal Ben-Shahar, McGraw-Hill Professional, *Happier: Learn the Secrets to Daily Joy and Lasting Fulfillment*, New York: McGraw-Hill Companies, 2007.

2. Lisa Swerling, Ralph Lazar, *Happiness is...: 500 Things to be Happy About*, San Francisco: Chronicle Books, 2014.

3. (美)亨利·史密斯·威廉姆斯著，佘卓桓译，幸福的科学，北京：中国人民大学出版社，2016.

4. 刘琛，改革开放以来中国形象的国际传播：从多元文化主义到软实力理论的中国反思与实践，北京：北京大学出版社，2020.

5. 孙英，幸福论，北京：人民出版社，2004.